Praise for *Shine*

"An important book for the complex and transformative times we are living and leading in. Carley Hauck charts a pathway forward of the essential, game-changing inner skills leaders and employees need to create a workplace and world that serves everyone. By embracing all parts of ourselves—the dark and the light—and leaning into learning new skills, *Shine* teaches that we can bring our best and whole self to work and to our changing world."

—CHIP CONLEY, American hotelier, hospitality entrepreneur, speaker, and author of *Wisdom at Work*

"*Shine* is the book for you if you want to awaken the next level of leadership and business in yourself, at work, and be a force for good in the world. Carley Hauck illuminates a pathway for anyone with the call to lead with research, tools, practices, and compelling stories that will truly inspire you. You will never see leadership the same way."

—SHERYL O'LOUGHLIN, CEO of REBBL, cofounder of Plum Organics, and former CEO of Clif Bar & Company

"*Shine* is a dynamic, practical, and visionary book at the cutting edge of a new wave of thought leadership centered on sustainability and self-awareness. Carley Hauck introduces innovative exercises that will help leaders with diverse lifestyles hone a solid foundation of resilience and tenacity, proving that the most effective leadership development begins within. The seamless blend between real-world stories and data-driven studies illustrates how the modern-day paradigms of power and business require a new standard of leadership, one that Carley is well equipped to usher in. More than an insightful toolkit for anyone looking to thrive in pressurized corporate environments, *Shine* is an emotional detox for the soul."

—JENNIFER BROWN, diversity and inclusion consultant and author of *How to Be an Inclusive Leader*

"*Shine* is an important book that highlights the essential leadership skills for today's world. Carley guides you through the important inner game one must cultivate to lead consciously at work and in life. The practices, research, and authentic stories will inspire you to create a new kind of workplace and world that prioritizes people and the environment."

—MIKE ROBBINS, author
of *We're All in This Together*

"In this illuminating and kind book, Carley Hauck provides a field guide, brimming with wisdom and practice, to 21ˢᵗ-century leadership. *Shine* is such a timely and deeply needed book, one urgently requiring attention during our complex times. This wonderful book will give you hope, courage, and a sense of wonder at what we might become."

—DACHER KELTNER, PhD, director
of the Greater Good Science Center
and author of *The Power Paradox*

"An important contribution by Carley Hauck to help businesses and individuals live in authenticity and wholeness. *Shine* exudes an honest and earnest care, and blends science, personal story, interviews, and optimism in a mix that will help any who crosses its path."

—FRED LUSKIN, PhD, director of the
Stanford University Forgiveness Projects
and author of *Forgive for Good*

"Carley Hauck gives us a playbook to build our self-awareness, strengthen our resilience, and live and lead with our lights on. The world needs all of us to *Shine* a little brighter right now."

—SCOTT SHUTE, head of mindfulness
and compassion programs, LinkedIn

"Carley Hauck offers us a valuable platform from which to both know one's own self better, and then to bring that more aware self to the role of leadership by tuning in to what matters most. *Shine* will help us all realize exactly what we need to do first, next, and always to create a better workplace and world."

—SCOTT KRIENS, cofounder of
1440 Multiversity, former CEO
of Juniper Networks

"Carley Hauck has been teaching others how to use their gifts to make this a better world for a long time now. In *Shine*, she's finally put her experience into a wonderful, engaging book that can show us how to bring out the best in ourselves to support the flourishing of our workplaces and planet."

—JAMES BARAZ, author of *Awakening Joy* and *Awakening Joy for Kids*, cofounder of Spirit Rock Meditation Center

"Carley Hauck has done the unimaginable. She has woven the practical and the spiritual, the mindful and the heartfelt, the individualistic and the relational, in the perfect sacred balance. With her tools and insights, we are finally ready to co-create the kind of conscious capitalism that is utterly essential for humanity going forward. Without this, we are lost. *Shine* lights the way home."

—JEFF BROWN, author of *Grounded Spirituality* and *An Uncommon Bond*

shine

shine

IGNITE YOUR INNER GAME
TO LEAD CONSCIOUSLY
AT WORK AND IN THE WORLD

CARLEY HAUCK

sounds true
BOULDER, COLORADO

Sounds True
Boulder, CO 80306
© 2021 Carley Hauck
Foreword © Lynne Twist
Sounds True is a trademark of Sounds True, Inc.

Published 2021

Book design by Kate Kaminski, Happenstance Type-O-Rama

 The wood used to produce this book is from Forest Stewardship Council (FSC) certified forests, recycled materials, or controlled wood.

Printed in the United States of America

Library of Congress Cataloging-in-Publication Data

Names: Hauck, Carley, author.
Title: Shine: Ignite Your Inner Game to Lead Consciously at Work and in
    the World / Carley Hauck.
Description: Boulder, CO : Sounds True, 2021. | Includes bibliographical
    references.
Identifiers: LCCN 2019022896 (print) | LCCN 2019022897 (ebook) | ISBN
    9781683642671 (hardcover) | ISBN 9781683643234 (ebook)
Subjects: LCSH: Leadership—Moral and ethical aspects. | Mindfulness
    (Psychology) | Values. | Social responsibility of business.
Classification: LCC HD57.7 .H3887 2021 (print) | LCC HD57.7 (ebook) | DDC
    658.4/092—dc23
LC record available at https://lccn.loc.gov/2019022896
LC ebook record available at https://lccn.loc.gov/2019022897

10 9 8 7 6 5 4 3 2 1

To all those who feel called to lead and be
part of the new paradigm of leadership
to change the world for the greatest good.
You inspire me, and I am rooting for you.

Contents

Contents

Foreword

In your hands, you hold a book that can change your life. It is filled with inspiration, stories, and practical wisdom to ignite your leadership and wake you up to your soul's purpose. My friend and colleague Carley Hauck has been inspiring leaders, organizations, and students at Stanford University and other business schools with skills to inspire the mind and open the heart to what really matters.

Our capitalist economy has produced great wealth at enormous costs. The underlying corporate behavior is a predominant cause of global challenges such as climate change, social injustice, and increasing worldwide economic disparity. Our current economy is linear—it has a beginning and an end. Companies dig up materials, turn those materials into a product, and then ship that product to an end user, who eventually tosses it in the trash. But that system has to change. According to one of Google's sustainability projects, "In 2017, global demand for resources was roughly 1.7 times what the Earth can support in one year, which means the linear economy model will soon slam into the edge of its physical limits."[1] What we need now is a regenerative model in which we design products, materials, and supply chains with cycles that are reusable and safe for human health and the environment.

Companies, and the men and women who lead them, have enormous power in shaping the world we all live in. There are more than 7.5 billion people on this planet, and that number is growing. Pollution does not see color, age, gender, or race. We need to creatively come together to ensure that there are enough resources for everyone to thrive.

Business is the largest institution we have, and the responsibility and opportunity that come with it are amazing, especially for leaders and entrepreneurs. We have been in a trance, focused too much on external worth and not enough on developing our self-worth and conscious inner game.

Our inner game directs our outer game, Carley reminds us. How developed is your inner game?

Leaders and businesses should shift to a new paradigm where businesses compete not just for customers but for how they can do best for the world. When you listen to what you most care about and align those values with how you lead yourself, your colleagues, and your business, you will triple the bottom line for people, planet, and profit. When you lead from your heart, all actions align with that clear vision, purpose, and mission.

What can we do individually and collectively to begin to retire these unwholesome thoughts and structures in our world?

The first thing we need to do is wake up and expand what is possible. We should stay committed to practices that ignite us so we can be the light and shine the light for others as well. It's about having the kind of developed and conscious inner game Carley talks about in this book.

In these pages, Carley lays out the path for a better workplace and world using practical exercises, modern scientific research, and the inspiring stories of nine conscious leaders who embody these ways of living, being, and leading at work and in the world. You will learn how to develop your leadership with dignity, humility, compassion, and strength. Read these words slowly. Savor them and practice the exercises in this book. Use them to lead with love and to transform your life and the world.

May it be so.

Lynne Twist

Spring 2020

Introduction

Conscious leadership is not something we typically learn in business school, but today leaders of every generation are being invited into a new era of leadership. Conscious leadership embodies a new mindset, a new operating model of "wholeness" that is connected to the core parts of ourselves, and to what I describe as our *inner game*. Conscious leaders have a strong sense of purpose; they know leadership is about serving and following a calling to positively transform the workplace and the world. They want to reconnect to their inner nature and create and lead soulful organizations that enhance all of life. The inner qualities that enable that kind of leadership, the ways in which real-world leaders bring them to the workplace, and how you too can bring your inner game forward are the subjects of this book.

On Tuesday, January 15, 2018, chief executives of the world's largest public companies received a letter from the CEO of BlackRock, one of the world's most influential investment firms, informing them that their companies would need to do more than make a profit if they wanted to receive BlackRock's financial support. "Society is demanding that companies, both public and private, serve a social purpose," Laurence D. Fink wrote. "To prosper over time, every company must not only deliver financial performance but also show how it makes a positive contribution to society."[1]

Fink's letter highlighted what many of us in the "conscious business" world have known for a long time: that companies, and the men and women who lead them, have enormous power to shape the world. It is up to business leaders, Fink cautioned, to ensure that there are enough resources available for everyone to thrive.

In order to keep up with the rising complexity of our world, a new way of leading and operating is essential. Yet in 2018, when the company Deloitte surveyed more than 14,000 CEOs across twenty-three industries, it found a clear complexity gap in leadership consciousness: leaders didn't feel they had the skills to address the multiple complexities we all face.[2] Working professionals today are dealing with challenges we have not witnessed before, including:

- Disruptive innovations

- More diverse ages in the workforce than ever before, with younger populations desiring a new, more remote, and flexible way of working

- Market volatility

- A worldwide pandemic

- High levels of stress, burnout, and depression

- Systemic issues related to climate change, resource scarcity, and the disruption of ecosystems

For the last decade, I have worked with conscious leaders as a learning architect, leadership development professional, and executive coach. I have observed certain inner qualities that conscious leaders possess and will support this new era of leadership in meeting these complexities. A conscious inner game is the capacity for *self-awareness, emotional intelligence, resilience, love, authenticity*, and *well-being*. To help encourage and foster these characteristics I developed the Shine Leadership System, a program of experiential practices and skills. I have used this system at companies like LinkedIn, Bank of the West, Pixar, Genentech, Intel, Clif Bar & Company, and high-growth startups. I have found that leaders who possess these qualities create caring, innovative, and collaborative workplaces.

This book will teach you how to lead by helping you grow a strong, conscious inner game that will become the core of your leadership: the internal qualities, beliefs, and values that determine how you show up and navigate life and the workplace. The inner game is your internal operating system—a set of skills that steadies you and strengthens your mind, body, and heart. A strong inner game supports the flow and release of your emotions and keeps you open, curious, and resilient. And these qualities determine how you lead.

Once you've cultivated and enhanced your inner game, you'll be able to more effectively withstand the storms and challenges of life, solve pressing challenges at work and in the world, and truly shine in your leadership role. Most businesses focus on the outer game or leadership competencies, but to become a strong, conscious leader, you must first develop your inner game skills and add these essential elements to your leadership toolbox—and your life toolbox, too.

Your inner game directs your outer game—how others experience you on the outside, in life and the workplace. Your inner game informs how you communicate, make decisions, and guide and motivate your team, and ultimately, how you align your values in leadership and business. Technology can solve an infinite number of business challenges, but the human element in the workplace can never be replaced by artificial intelligence. Business is fundamentally about relationships and human decision-making, and that's why when we evolve and grow our inner game to positively influence our outer game, we can solve big challenges together—flourishing at work, creating belonging, healing the planet, and repairing the world.

My Leadership Journey

I believe that leaders have vast power to influence businesses and the world as a whole in positive ways. My own journey toward conscious leadership began when, as a child, I watched my father bring work stress home, and home stress to work. We bring our whole selves with us wherever we go, and the way my dad related to stress and life in his leadership role as an attorney was not the way I wanted to navigate my world. I wanted to find a more graceful, resilient, and joyful way to live and lead. And that is exactly what led me to develop the tools and inner-game leadership skills I teach and that are included in this book.

I took the next step of my journey at age nineteen when I read His Holiness the Dalai Lama's book *The Art of Happiness*. I was hooked by its straightforward and clear message of living a life of ease, happiness, and resilience. Because of the book, I began a meditation practice, and over the twenty-plus years since, I have discovered many new gems by sitting and quieting my mind, turning toward and finding refuge in my body, and opening my heart.

I created a curriculum based on these practices while attending graduate school, then moved to San Francisco, where I taught two different courses infused with meditation and embodiment practices at the Jewish Community Center of San Francisco. A few months later, a human resource professional at the law firm Littler Mendelson contacted me to ask if I could come in and teach the lawyers how to increase their resilience to stress. After thinking about it for a moment, I said, "Yes, I can." And that was the turning point, the moment when I stepped into my larger purpose of supporting leaders in accessing their greatest gifts and purpose.

My work with leaders, businesses, students, and faculty at Stanford University and University of California, Berkeley's Haas School of Business is informed by my love of research and human-centered design. I think of the role I play with companies as *healing business*. To do this, I design leadership and development programs for workplaces and foster cultural learning and leadership transformation through initiatives that enhance psychological safety, trust, and caring, and belonging in these settings. The interaction of the mind, body, and heart, and bringing one's wholeness to work and life have always been areas of fascination for me, in both research and implementation.

I'm also interested in the intersection of disease, stress, healing, and organizational health, and my education and career choices have reflected that. I studied health psychology and organizational psychology in graduate school and have always loved research and being part of research studies. Between undergrad and graduate school, I was selected as a National Science Foundation fellow and conducted three months of research in a neuroscience lab at Kent State University, assessing the effects of post-traumatic stress disorder (PTSD) on the body's physiology, particularly the effects of stress hormones. Later, while studying health psychology in graduate school, I developed a ten-week program that integrated meditation, exercise, and socio-emotional learning for cancer patients. I continued to work with cancer patients at California Pacific Medical Center's Institute for Health & Healing, in the fields of integrative medicine and counseling, and teaching courses to help people train their minds, open their hearts, nourish their bodies, and lead more resilient, healthy, and courageous lives.

While I was working with leaders and companies through my business, Leading from Wholeness, I pursued my love of research and became a lead consultant/facilitator on two six-year studies with the University of California, San Francisco's Osher Center for Integrative Medicine, funded by the National Institutes of Health. These studies observed the long-term benefits of mindfulness and other practices to support resilience to stress, reduction of the stress hormone cortisol, weight loss, emotional regulation, well-being, and the prevention of type 2 diabetes. This study confirmed that much of the curriculum I'd been teaching had solid scientific evidence to back it up.

During this time of research and applying these concepts of meditation and healing in the workplace, I also dove more deeply into the study of Buddhism and integrated its wise teachings into my personal and professional life.

Then, in 2013, my life changed in the most amazing way. A friend and colleague, Fred Luskin, called me. He explained that Stanford University was looking for new adjunct faculty and was interested in bringing some new electives into its course curriculum. He had shared my teachings and curriculum with the staff.

"What do you think about teaching at Stanford?" he asked me.

"Fred, you had me at hello," I said.

I've been happily teaching at Stanford ever since, covering a variety of topics related to mindfulness, resilience, healthy conflict, forgiveness, and embodied leadership. After I began teaching at Stanford, Fred and I collaborated and spoke on the subjects of forgiveness, happiness, and emotional intelligence, both at Stanford and at other professional organizations.

I also teach on the subjects of leadership at University of California, Berkeley's Haas School of Business and at other business schools around the country and the world.

I share the highlights of my journey to offer a broad explanation of how I arrived at the tools and techniques you will learn in this book. While the path has not been a straight line, everything I've learned in and out of the lab, has reinforced my belief that there are numerous sources we can draw upon to develop our best selves.

I have found through my teaching, coaching, and serving leaders that when an individual leader is off balance and not leading from a whole and healed place, it will impact the ability of the entire workplace to perform, care for one another, collaborate, and innovate. That means the product or service this business puts out into the world will have a less-than-positive impact. So, the more we can heal and transform on the inside, as individuals (the inner game), the more connected, resilient, innovative, and caring our workplaces will be (the outer game). And because *the workplace and our natural world are connected*, business can be a platform for positive change that prioritizes the well-being of people and the planet first. That connection is the primary motivation in my work and was the impetus for this book.

Healing the Workplace and the World

I first heard internal whispers of protecting people and the planet when I was a young child walking along the beach in St. Augustine, Florida, my family's summer vacation spot. There, I found lots of trash and plastic and, inevitably, plastic bags that I filled with litter. I brought these stuffed bags back to the condo my family rented.

I remember my mom looking at me with a bewildered expression and saying, "Carley, what am I supposed to do with these bags of trash?"

"Mom, the trash isn't supposed to be in the ocean or on the beach," I said. "A sea turtle is going to think it's a jellyfish and eat it."

This desire to be a good steward of the Earth didn't stop there. Five years ago, I was playing with my then four-year-old nephew Cooper, who like me has a strong love of the ocean and marine life.

He looked up at me and said, "Auntie Carley, can we save the oceans together?"

I was moved by his invitation and felt responsible for making sure Cooper and all future generations can enjoy a world where healthy coral reefs and marine life still thrive. With a trembling in my heart, I said, "*Yes* sweetheart, we can." At four years old, he was already connected to the world he was inheriting and had asked me to take a stand with him.

You, my friend, *are* the Earth. The Earth is mostly water and so is your body; you are around 60 percent water. We are living systems, our workplaces are living systems, and the planet is a living system. If any of these systems is unhealthy or imbalanced, it affects the whole. You can't flourish at work or at home if there is no clean air, water, or soil, right?

We will continue to explore this interconnection throughout the book, focusing on how realigning and upgrading your inner game will positively impact the possibilities of business and the health of the planet. In other words, the inner transformation will create the collective outer transformation. I wrote this book because I want to live in a world with conscious, resilient, caring, and courageous leaders who speak up and align their actions around what matters. We desperately need leaders who are self-aware enough to lead from their hearts and prioritize people and the planet. I am taking a stand to inspire leaders and businesses to do the right thing: to be a platform for positive change and to create new systems and ways of doing business to cultivate a flourishing Mother Earth and a world that works for everyone.

Remeasuring Success

This evolution in leadership is vital because the way we've been leading and doing business is no longer sustainable or smart. The evidence of this is loud and clear. A report issued in October 2018 by the Intergovernmental Panel on Climate Change, a group of scientists convened by the United Nations (UN) to guide world leaders, states that the emissions path we are currently on is likely to take us to 1.5 degrees Celsius of warming by 2040.[3] This means that, as temperatures rise, many of the biggest cities in the Middle East and South Asia will become lethally hot in the summer. We will experience more dramatic food shortages, wildfires, and a mass die-off of coral reefs.

The UN advises that to prevent this, we must reduce 2010's greenhouse gas emissions by 45 percent by 2030.[4] As I write, that date is only ten years away. Businesses must be prepared for the adverse impact and damage of climate change, such as mega-fires, mega-storms, and increased heat.

The emergency of climate change is the most important issue of our lifetime. It also offers the biggest business opportunity of the twenty-first century: that of harnessing greater efficiencies from the world's natural resources, business models, and supply chains. Leaders and businesses must transcend their commercial and self-interests and factor climate sustainability into their growth operations. The inspiring leaders I will introduce you to in this book do this well.

In 2016, 70 percent of CEOs believed the UN's Sustainable Development Goals would create a clear framework to structure sustainability efforts, and in 2019, 48 percent of CEOs implemented sustainability into their operations.[5] Since we created the climate crisis, we can uncreate it. But to shift the tide, we must awaken to a new paradigm in leadership. And when you bring a strong inner game forward in your own workplace and in your life as a whole, you can be part of that.

Leading the Way

The next population of leaders and workers, Millennials and Generation Z, are a force to be reckoned with, and they are already leading the way in conscious leadership and business. Generation Z alone makes up 25 percent of the population, a larger cohort than Baby Boomers or Millennials. They are predicted to account for 40 percent of all consumers by the time this book is published.[6] Millennial and Generation Z employees and leaders want to know they're making a difference, and they choose employers who expect them to step up to this commitment.[7]

In a 2016 workplace study, 64 percent of Millennials considered a company's social and environmental commitments when deciding where to work; 64 percent wouldn't take a job with a company that didn't have strong corporate social responsibility; and 83 percent said they would be more loyal to a company if they had opportunities to make a positive impact on social and environmental issues.[8] Additionally, the Deloitte Global Millennial Survey 2020 explores the views of more than 27,500 Millennials and Generation Zs, both before and after the start of the COVID-19 pandemic, to understand their perspectives on business, government, climate, and the pandemic, among other issues. The survey reveals that despite the individual challenges and personal sources of anxiety that Millennials and Generation Zs are facing, they have remained focused on larger societal issues, both before and after the onset of the pandemic. If anything, the pandemic has reinforced their desire to help drive positive change in their communities and around the world. And they continue to push for a world in which businesses and governments mirror that same commitment to society, putting people ahead of profits and prioritizing environmental sustainability.[9]

This population of workers and our next generation of leaders value prioritizing people and planet over profit. They want opportunities to learn and grow, work flexible hours, enjoy a work-life balance, and be members of work cultures that encourage diversity, inclusion, and belonging.[10] They are demanding changes in the way business is done, and to keep this rising talent, businesses must nurture these desires.

The good news is that companies that have dedicated themselves to helping the world flourish also do best by the measures that ultimately count—a triple bottom line of people, planet, and profit. When we lead from our hearts, all actions align with that clear vision, purpose, and mission. Companies guided by leaders who are aligned with an altruistic mission and purpose financially outperform the market average by 42 percent![11] How does the leadership achieve these goals and values? By cultivating a vital culture of trust, loyalty, and commitment, and by leading with a strong, conscious inner game.

Learning from Others

In these pages, I will introduce you to inspiring thought leaders who have been touched by a deep calling as a result of loss and difficulty. They made changes, took risks, and committed to learning, growing, and healing. And because they did, they've flourished individually, and their businesses are creating a positive, sustainable impact in the world. I've learned their "recipes" for resilience and have seen the ways in which they acted with courage, made tough decisions, and led from vulnerability.

I know from personal and professional experience that leadership and entrepreneurship can be both difficult and inspiring. In this book, I will share with you the science and data behind the workplace leadership trainings and interventions I've conducted with the Shine Leadership System over the last decade. I have used this system with thousands of team members and emerging, middle, and C-suite (executive) leaders from a variety of industries including finance, health, technology, and startups. That's how I developed the wonderful practices I include in this book, practices that will help you grow your leadership game.

The book also draws upon the latest research on leadership, emotional intelligence, psychological safety, neuroscience, vulnerability, resilience, climate science, sustainable finance, systems theory, corporate social responsibility, and diversity, inclusion, and belonging. All of these topics and values are essential to becoming a conscious leader in business. I also interviewed many incredible experts and business leaders in these fields and share what I have learned from them.

An Armchair Tour of *Shine*

Here is the adventure that awaits you:

Shine is divided into two parts. In part I, Awaken Your Inner Game, we will explore in depth the six elements of a strong inner game, with one chapter devoted to each.

Chapter 1 is about *self-awareness,* the foundational inner game that supports you in understanding your strengths, blind spots, motivations, and behaviors, and how these impact others. In chapter 2 you'll develop *emotional intelligence,* learning how to navigate feelings of anger, sadness, and fear with confidence so you can bring your outer game of empathy and attunement into the workplace and beyond. Here, we integrate mind and emotions. The focus of chapter 3 is *resilience*, and it's all about adapting to the constant state of change in business and the world. In this chapter, we add the body to the mind-plus-emotions equation.

In chapter 4, the subject is *love*, and you'll learn to lead with love, creating caring and collaborative workplaces; here, we add the dimension of the heart. Chapter 5 delves into the topic of *well-being* and discusses how to prioritize your inner well-being so you can work smarter, not harder, and prevent burnout. All aspects of you come into play here. Finally, in chapter 6, you learn to cultivate the inner game of *authenticity*, which means embracing all your parts, including the darker aspects of yourself, so you can grow and evolve into your best self. When you bring authenticity to your leadership, you encourage vulnerability, forgiveness, trust, and belonging to your team, which enables it to shine its ultimate positive potential.

You will emerge from part I having integrated all aspects of yourself so you can bring forth your power, brilliance, and whole self to work and the world. And along the way, you will draw inspiration from the stories of men and women who have been down all of these roads before and are leading brilliantly and with great success.

Part II, Lead with Your Light On, at Work and Beyond, moves your inner game into the outer world. Chapter 7 teaches you how to have what I call *brave exchanges*—truthful, constructive discussions that strengthen teams and improve results, no matter what changes and challenges your business is facing. In chapter 8, you'll learn a whole new way to measure the success of your business: by how it makes a positive and sustainable impact in the world. Here, you'll get reacquainted with the leaders you've been meeting as you journeyed through the book and learn what this looks like in practice. The last chapter in part II contains a vision of how we can all commit to waking up the world and transforming our organizations into instruments of healing for workplaces around the globe and for our precious planet.

Each chapter concludes with a list of affirmations related to that chapter's topic. Each affirmation is a powerful ingredient in the "recipe" to help you embody the chapter's principles and shine.

How to Use This Book

The tools and skills we will explore here together will engage your whole self. Sprinkled throughout the book you will find a variety of exercises to help you build your inner and outer game. Many of these are simple, and some can be done at your desk, while others will provide a short and well-deserved break from your work routine. Many of these practices include journaling, so I recommend you dedicate a notebook or journal to your travels through this book.

When you cultivate your inner game, you will transform your leadership and way of living and leading on the outside. For example, as you cultivate the inner game of love, people will perceive you and the way you lead yourself and others as open, friendly, authentic, forgiving, generous, and compassionate. In other words, *your inner light will shine* in how you speak, the way you move, and the energy you emit when you walk into a room.

The best way to use this book is to focus on one or two exercises per chapter that resonate with you. Daily practice and embodiment are key. Try each of them for a month and let yourself soak up these new ways of being, one at a time, allowing for integration, before you try the next exercise. This is the key to creating habits that last. Developing as a leader is about having the courage to change as well as embracing continuous personal and professional learning and growth.

As you read the book and awaken your inner game, remember that this complex system and structure aligns with the larger living system: your body. Your mind, emotions, heart, and body are all parts of the system, and when they are returned to health and then integrated, you will return to wholeness. This optimizing process—and the reasons why it is so vital for leaders—will be demonstrated through this book.

This Book Is for You

This book is for anyone who feels the call to lead. It isn't just for people who are presently leaders in their workplace. Leadership is broader than that and is not defined by a title. This book will speak to you if you feel the call to *be* the change that the world needs now. This book is for you, if you:

- feel frustrated about the world's state of affairs and wish to uplevel and learn management and leadership tools from role models

- want to learn how to be a conscious leader as you develop leadership skills in your workplace or plan to apply for a leadership position

- feel burned out and need a reset

- want to lead from a place of inspiration, joy, and purpose

- are a CEO who feels your higher purpose is greater than making money, and you want to elevate humanity and the world through how you lead, manage others, and conduct business

- are an entrepreneur who appreciates lifelong learning and personal growth

- believe that by improving your self-management skills on the inside, you will become a better leader and manager on the outside

- are an entrepreneur looking to create a business model and culture that puts people and planet first

- want to grow into a leadership or management role

I believe the tools you learn here will support you in cultivating a strong, brilliant inner game that will help you influence and inspire greater collaboration and belonging at work and in the world. Bringing your whole and best self to work will encourage your team and workplace to flourish. Your awareness of the challenges facing our world as a whole can inspire other minds and hearts to wake up, and together we can heal the divisions of our world and create a sustainable planet and ecosystem that thrives. We need each other's support for a collective response to today's complexities. And that starts with knowing ourselves and growing the qualities inside that allow us to *shine* from the inside out. *To be the light.*

PART I

AWAKEN YOUR INNER GAME

Are you ready to shine? In part I you'll learn how to develop all the key qualities that conscious leadership entails. Here, you'll find information, stories, and practices on the six elements of a strong inner game: self-awareness, emotional intelligence, resilience, love, well-being, and authenticity. Let's dig in!

Cultivating Self-Awareness
Taking the First Step Toward Conscious Leadership

> The solutions to our current problems cannot be solved from the level of consciousness that created them. They can only be solved from a higher order of consciousness, one that is more complex than the complexity we face.
>
> —ALBERT EINSTEIN

Do you want to learn how to be a more conscious leader? Are you eager to develop the kind of leadership skills that can elevate humanity? Do you appreciate lifelong learning and personal growth? Do you want to lead at work from a place of inspiration, joy, and meaning? Conscious leaders are moved by a higher sense of purpose than simply pursuing the bottom line; they know that leadership is about serving and following a call to transform the workplace—and the world.

A conscious leader:

- Believes in lifelong learning and development
- Leads with integrity, personal responsibility, and humility
- Honors the humanity of all their employees and clients

- Is committed to the higher good of the workplace and the world

- Cultivates the ability to respond rather than react to ups and downs

- Takes ownership for their mistakes and then forgives, repairs, and seeks resolution

- Creates psychological safety by leading with vulnerability and authenticity

- Deeply values cultures that encourage diversity, inclusion, and belonging

Cultivating the inner game skills I highlighted in the introduction will enhance your development as a leader and support the new paradigm of conscious business. When your inner game remains strong amidst the waves, you will rise and flourish as a leader and in life.

The inner game is your *internal operating system*—a set of skills that steadies you and strengthens your mind, body, and heart. It supports the easy flow and release of your emotions and keeps you open, curious, and resilient. Your inner game comprises the core of your leadership—the internal qualities that determine how you show up and navigate life and the workplace.

Here in the first chapter of part I, you'll delve into the first quality of a strong inner game: self-awareness. Self-awareness is recognizing your thoughts, feelings, and physical sensations as they arise and pass in each moment. It is pausing to turn within and reflect on your experiences and motives, and the consequences of your actions. As you cultivate self-awareness, you will quickly find that others will perceive you as confident, present, capable—even visionary. When you walk into a room, your inner light will shine through your words, actions, and the dynamic energy you emit.

Self-awareness is the first step of the journey toward effective leadership because when you see yourself and your patterns clearly, you are able to make appropriate decisions and necessary changes that wouldn't have occurred to you otherwise. Think about it: you can't change what you can't see.

Another key advantage of developing self-awareness is that when you understand yourself, you have greater awareness of how others view you too, and you can better navigate your interactions.

Awakening to Your Purpose

What really matters in the small amount of time we live on the planet?

—SCOTT KRIENS, cofounder of 1440 Multiversity

Scott Kriens is the cofounder of 1440 Multiversity, a center for personal and professional development located in California's Santa Cruz Mountains. At 1440 Multiversity, people receive support and guidance on aligning their lives and their work with their heart's calling. Scott believes that self-awareness is the first step in leading effectively and authentically. "If we don't know who we are and what matters to us inside," he told me, "we can't align with depth in how we live and work."

These days, Scott meditates daily, but he spent forty-five years working from the outside in, ignoring who he was on the inside. What changed for him? In 2004, when his father passed away, Scott became painfully aware of the fragility and preciousness of life, sparking changes both personal and professional, and moving him to create 1440 Multiversity.

Inner Game Practice
KNOWING THE SELF

And this brings you to your first exercise. To cultivate a greater level of self-awareness, locate your journal. Then ask yourself these questions:

- What are my motivations at work and beyond?

- What are my desires?

- What do I value?

- What are my joys?

- What are my fears?

- What are my strengths?

- What are my weaknesses?

Yes, they're big questions, but they hold the keys to self-knowledge and self-management. As you write down your answers, pay special attention to any that get your heart pounding. Then take a few minutes to contemplate what you learned from this deep dive into self-awareness.

From Contemplation to Action

Next, look at your answers with an eye toward developing conscious leadership qualities. Identify one quality you intend to explore and ultimately master. Perhaps it's one that's connected to a weakness you wrote down. Or maybe it's something you know is a strength that you think you could enhance or expand.

Have you identified a work behavior you want to change? Think about feedback you've received from colleagues: Has anyone pointed out an element of your leadership style that challenges your team? What obstacles keep you from performing your best work every day? For example, do you identify and blame other people and situations—elements outside of yourself—for diluting your effectiveness or derailing your success? Ponder these questions and write down what you discover, understanding that naming your obstacles is the first step toward transcending them.

Now you can create an *intention* to help you transform a flaw or weakness into a strength. If you have developed a reputation as an unsympathetic, cold, or impatient boss, for example, you can write, "I want to become more compassionate when . . ." or "I will show more empathy when . . ."

When we name an aspect of ourselves with humility and then write it down or say it out loud, we reinforce its importance, develop more clarity around it, and hold ourselves accountable to change. You may notice that the simple act of writing down your intention helps you be more present and listen to others with more care and focus.

Here are the next steps to help bring your new intention forward:

- Declare it and share it. Share your intention, aloud or in writing, with three people who can hold you accountable and witness your commitment.

- Create a mindful affirmation to remind you of your intention and greater commitment, and then align your actions around your intention. If you want to be a better listener, for example, remind yourself of this desire multiple times a day. You could say something like, "I am listening without an agenda. I am present right here and now."

- Don't be attached to the outcome but be fully committed to the process. You don't have control over what happens in life, but if you show up fully in your commitment, you will gain clarity and move closer to achieving what you desire.

Leaders Are Learners

Your willingness to embrace continuous personal growth and self-improvement, combined with your courage to change, will help you develop as a renewed and more effective leader. As the authors of an article in *Harvard Business Review* concluded, "Leaders who are *in learning mode* develop stronger leadership skills than their peers."[1]

Now let's keep the momentum going; it's time for another exercise. This next one is something I developed to help people more deeply set an intention while also allowing them to remain open to new solutions.

Think back to a time when a viable solution or a pearl of wisdom popped into your mind. This probably happened when you were distracted by another task and had let go of trying so hard to solve the problem—that's how creative juices flow. Letting go is what the following practice is all about, thereby making space for new ideas to form.

Inner Game Practice
OPEN AWARENESS

1. Find a comfortable place where you won't be disturbed for ten minutes. If you can, do this exercise outdoors or looking through a window at a natural environment.

2. Set an intention for your practice, whether it's the one you named earlier or the intention of simply creating space for new ideas to flow.

3. Bring your attention inward, either by closing your eyes or shifting your gaze down toward the floor or the ground. Choose where you will focus your attention: on the rhythm of your breath, on physical sensations, or on sounds. Allow yourself to bring your full attention there. Notice the inflow and outflow of breath, and slow your breathing. Keep your eyes closed or your gaze downward for two to three minutes. Now open your eyes and let your gaze rest gently on one spot in front of you. Notice what moves or changes.

4. When a thought, a sound, or a physical discomfort distracts you, simply name it "thought," "sound," or "sensation" to detach it from any greater meaning. This labeling technique brings your attention away from wandering thoughts and back to your present experience.

5. After a few minutes, shift your attention back inside yourself and become aware of your breath, physical sensations, or sound. These are the three anchors that can help you focus and concentrate. Notice where your feet are touching the floor, your posture, and the temperature of the air on your skin. If you feel drawn to sound, allow your mind to linger there. Return your attention to your breath, body, or sound.

6. For ten or more minutes, alternate your attention from closed eyes or downward gaze with an inward focus to open eyes with an outward focus.

When you finish this meditation, write about your experience. Did your intention shift as a result? Did you brainstorm any fresh ideas?

Mindfulness: Presence of Mind

Powerful leaders display presence of mind. They are a force of stability and wisdom in the face of ordinary little blips as well as extraordinary problems that threaten to pull a company or organization down. Meditations such as the exercise you just practiced help you pause and ignite your focus, listen deeply, adapt more easily, and concentrate on and prioritize the tasks that matter most. They train your mind to be in the here and now, and as we just explored, allow your best ideas to arise. Meditation is not about not thinking or achieving the absence of thoughts; it's about pausing without judgment to be with whatever is happening at the moment. This is not always easy, as you will discover when you practice—you may not like staying with the present moment if you're feeling boredom, agitation, sadness, anger, doubt, or restlessness.

There is a lot of evidence of the value of this practice. According to the American Mindfulness Research Association, more than seven hundred scientifically based journal articles on the benefits of mindfulness were published between 1980 to 2019.[2] This vast body of research shows that a regular meditation practice helps increase emotional intelligence, compassion, attunement, a growth mindset, resilience and creativity, and it develops stronger decision-making skills—all essential qualities of conscious leaders.

In the workplace, one of the most important qualities of conscious leadership is the ability to be with what is and then respond to what is needed. We don't have control of the past or the future. What we can control is how we arrive in the present, how we bring our presence of body and mind to the moment at hand. With this kind of self-awareness, instead of growing anxious or assigning blame, we can assess whatever situation may present itself with clarity and search for solutions.

It's the Journey, Not the Destination

This is an endless journey, and we are all in it together.

—DAVID YEUNG, founder and CEO of Green
Monday, Green Common, and OmniFoods

David Yeung is the founder and CEO of Green Monday (a spin-off of Meatless Monday, the popular US-based movement) and a chain of vegan grocery stores in Hong Kong and Singapore called Green Common. While in his early twenties, David saw the link between what he was eating and how it was harming animals and the planet and decided to shift to a plant-based diet, which led him to start his sustainable food businesses. He models his values and leads from the inside out, within his company and in the world.

David grows his self-awareness muscle by meditating fifteen to thirty minutes, or up to an hour if he has time, most days. He practices mindfulness every day through mindful listening, speaking, eating, and walking. David believes mindfulness is an essential tool for leaders who are constantly drawn in multiple directions and must find ways to remain centered. To David, leadership is about forming alliances and making progress. Every day, he asks himself, *Am I making progress?*

For my part, I practice a sitting meditation every morning for fifteen to thirty minutes, and sometimes, if I need it, I meditate twice a day. This has been a core practice of my life for the last twenty years, and I feel an imbalance if I miss even one day. But even ten to fifteen minutes, three to four days per week, is an effective dose for training the mind and cultivating greater focus and presence.

My daily sitting meditation practice varies, but when I want more focus and concentration, it is often similar to the Inner Game Practice: Open Awareness exercise on page 22, only simpler and more direct. Instead of shifting my attention from closed eyes to open eyes, as you do in step 6 of the exercise, I keep my eyes closed and focus on being fully in the moment, first noticing the sensation of my feet touching the floor and my body making contact with the chair. I breathe deeply on the inhale, visualizing the air rising up from the bottom of my feet to the top of my head. I sit up taller, bringing my shoulders back and leaning back in my chair. I say silently, "I am here" over and over again, and when my mind wanders, I bring my attention back to my breath or simply ask, "What am I aware of now?" (I also label my thoughts "thoughts," as in step 4 of the exercise.)

When I finish my practice, I give myself a few minutes to slowly reconnect with the world before I jump back into my next task.

If you find you are feeling particularly restless, try a walking meditation instead of a sitting meditation. Walking meditation is wonderful to practice when you're outside where you can breathe in the fresh air. You can put one foot slowly and mindfully in front of the other, feeling the ground under your soles and heels. Take one step at a time, being aware of the lifting, carrying, and placing of each foot, until you cover a ten- to fifteen-foot radius. Notice the sounds, sensations, and aromas of the outdoors, and your own thoughts and feelings.

Give this practice a try and then write down what you learned about your thought patterns and yourself. Meditation is a powerful tool for self-awareness and can help you feel grounded and calm.

Beginner's Mind

Learning to meditate is one of the best investments I've made in life.

—MARC BENIOFF, cofounder and CEO of Salesforce

Marc Benioff is the cofounder and CEO of Salesforce, a technology and customer success platform. Marc learned about meditation from Thich Nhat Hanh, a Vietnamese Buddhist monk who was nominated for the Nobel Peace Prize by Martin Luther King Jr. for his work in seeking an end to the Vietnam War. I'll let Marc speak for himself on how he sees the value of meditation.

I am hardly the first business executive who's gone on a quest or spiritual exploration and come back from such a journey as an evangelist of meditation and mindfulness. From the outside, this might seem like a frivolous self-indulgence or some flash-in-the-pan Silicon Valley fad, but I can tell you with utmost certainty this practice hasn't just made me a happier more productive human being, it supports me to think deeply and has been an essential business strategy. If you charted all the periods of growth at Salesforce that have resulted from some major course correction I pursued, you would find that those moments were nearly always preceded by a period of time when I made a point to unplug and reconnect with myself and have a beginner's mind.

The Power of Uni-Tasking

You may believe that doing several things at once helps you get more done and is basically a job requirement. But as it turns out, your productivity goes down by as much as 40 percent when you multitask.[3] The human brain simply isn't capable of doing more than one thing at a time well, and cultivating mindful self-awareness can help you understand where to place your focus and how to best channel your capabilities.

Outer Game Practice
UNI-TASKING IN SIX STEPS

This is your first outer game practice, as it includes taking external action.

- Identify a single task that has priority. Close your email, turn off your phone ringer, and identify the time span during which you will focus on this task, and then attend to *only* that task until you complete it. When you're writing an email or a report, simply write with the total focus of your whole being. When you're reading something important, simply read. When you run an errand, just do that, and when you return home, tackle the next task with the same focus and concentration. Try this for a day or even for the next hour or two. You'll find that your mind stays relaxed and fresh, and you have more energy to accomplish the next item on your list.

- Write your daily to-do list in your journal, but not before you ask yourself: *What can I realistically accomplish in the day?* I like to focus on no more than five tasks at the top of the list. If yours is much longer than that, edit your list so you can successfully achieve your priorities.

- When interruptions arise, as they will, take a deep breath and note the irritation you may feel—labeling it "frustration" or whatever word feels right—and then allow yourself to let that feeling go. Stay mindful during the interruption and create a boundary. You might say something like this to the person who interrupted you: "I look forward to talking with you more, but I need to get back to work now." When you can refocus, take another deep breath and then dive back into your task.

- Take intentional breaks to refresh and clear your mind. Researchers of attention and productivity recommend that people take several breaks during their workday to increase productivity and focus. The perfect length for focus is fifty-two minutes, followed by a seventeen-minute break.[4] Get up from your desk, stretch and shake your limbs, take a walk, and gauge your energy. Do you feel depleted or steady? Do you have the energy you need to meet your tasks in an efficient and creative way? Ask yourself: *What do I desire? What would give me more ease and balance?* And write what you discover about yourself in your journal. The answers will help you reset and begin again.

- Do a mini-meditation during an intentional break. Step away from your device or computer and roll your shoulders in circles up and back three times. Move your body in whatever way it's yearning to move. I like to sway back and forth, bend forward, or stretch my arms overhead. Take a few deep breaths, inhaling through your nose and exhaling through your mouth. Make some noise to release tension; sigh or say, "Hah!" Bring your attention inward if you like, or you can simply look at an object or the view before you with a soft gaze. Let everything go and allow your mind and body to slow down. Integrating an affirmation in this practice will help you keep your mind and body in peaceful sync. You can try the ones I chant: "Right here. Right now," or "All I have is within me; all I need flows to me." Or create your own.

- Practice self-care and self-kindness. Remember, you can accomplish only so much in one day.

Most people feel the pressure to do more and to do it faster, but speed and juggling tasks invariably cause problems. One recent study showed that people who were distracted by incoming email and phone calls saw a ten-point decrease in their IQ![5] What's the impact of a ten-point drop? It has the same effect as losing a night of sleep and has more than twice the impact of smoking marijuana. It has been found that it takes twenty minutes to regain the same concentration and focus after you have been interrupted. In fact, multitasking can actually damage your brain. Multitaskers who use many media devices at the same time and switch their attention back and forth are found to have less brain density in the anterior cingulate cortex, a region responsible for empathy as well as cognitive and emotional control.[6] Technically, multitasking is "switch tasking," or rapidly shifting from one thing to another, which involves interrupting ourselves unproductively and ultimately losing time.[7]

The rapid switching from one thing to another is such an ingrained habit that many of us feel unfamiliar with the idea and practice of unitasking. Your next exercise will reverse the damage of multitasking and bring your attention to just one thing.

Wake-Up Call

I believe that when you care about people more than the bottom line, everyone can flourish.

—LINDA LOCKWOOD, former chief of staff/senior vice president of human resources at Bank of the West

Linda Lockwood, senior vice president of human resources at Bank of the West (recently retired), worked in the banking industry for thirty years. When she received a breast cancer diagnosis, she reached out to me to help her navigate the difficult months of treatment and healing and develop a stronger inner foundation. Prior to her health scare, she had worked ten- to twelve-hour days and commuted long hours. She didn't eat a nutritious diet, nor did she have a regular exercise routine or a lot of time for play or rest.

Linda discovered the gem inherent in her "wake-up call" and nourished her heart and soul with a weekly yoga practice. The *asanas* supported her deep dive into self-awareness—not only awareness of her physical body, but also of her emotions and motivations.

> She shifted her mindset and changed patterns that weren't helping her, or her workplace, to thrive. She has now settled into a conscious vision of how to live her life with more well-being and lead in the world.

Turn Knowledge into Practice

Now that you have taken some time to explore the inner game of self-awareness, what actions and practices are you willing to commit to in order to further develop this quality? I encourage you to write down your chosen "practice of the day" or of the week in the form of one affirmation or intention that you will note in a journal and/or on two sticky notes. Place one sticky note on your bathroom mirror and one on your computer monitor as a reminder.

Consider intentions like these:

- Today I am conscious, clear, and resilient.

- I lead with my heart and spread compassion to those I meet.

- I turn fear into curiosity.

- I commit to being kind to myself.

- I speak my truth with empathy, clarity, and inclusiveness.

In addition to your planned meditation practice, look for opportunities during the day to incorporate mini-meditations, sitting meditation, walking meditation, or the Inner Game Practice: Open Awareness exercise. Notice when you are overwhelmed by multitasking and decide to engage in uni-task practices.

Self-Awareness Recipe

Following are the ingredients for your first conscious leadership recipe, the recipe to create self-awareness. Affirmations support us by empowering our minds to perform positive, forward-thinking actions in the world. I invite you to try those that resonate in the list below, and/or create your own. Bring these affirmations into your day as gentle reminders of your intention to thrive and lead from a conscious, clear, and courageous place.

- I cultivate self-awareness.

- I am present and focused.

- I understand my motivations and desires.

- I lead with authenticity.

Learning What Our Feelings Can Teach Us
Becoming More Emotionally Intelligent

> Part of the purpose of becoming more emotionally
> intelligent is developing the capacity to have your feelings,
> without becoming unglued. We want to have them, listen
> to them, and then find calm.
>
> —ADRIAN JAMES, cofounder and president
> of Omada Health

We are emotional creatures, and as much as we sometimes wish we could leave our emotional thoughts and feelings at home, it is not possible. If you are like most humans in the workplace, you've likely cried in a bathroom stall or lost your temper with a teammate. Finding ways to consciously embrace your emotions as part of being human will serve you in developing empathy and compassion, and in understanding the wisdom underneath your feelings. And when you can turn toward your feelings with kind awareness, you will be able to connect with others more authentically and navigate the moods of your team members with greater confidence. Using the practices in this chapter you'll learn to befriend your feelings (even the most difficult ones), tend to them, and increase your resilience and empathy.

What Are Emotions?

Emotions are responses to stimuli, internal or external. These responses are a combination of thoughts, sensations, and actions. Psychologist Robert Plutchik has identified eight main emotions: anger, anticipation, joy, trust, fear, surprise, sadness, and disgust.[1] Emotions often happen without us being aware of them, especially if we are out of touch with, or incongruent with, our inner emotional life. But what we feel and how we process and respond to these feelings underlies our emotional states. (To familiarize yourself with a full range of emotional states, please see appendix A on page 261.)

Our perception of events colors and causes our emotional response, and the nervous system works in tandem with the brain to take over our emotional experience, even if we don't want it to. We alternate between peaceful, present, and connected (the *parasympathetic* nervous system: rest and digest) and stressed, distracted, and disconnected (the *sympathetic* nervous system: fight, flight, or freeze).

Emotional intelligence is one of the most important skills leaders can cultivate. The term was coined in 1990 by Peter Salovey and John D. Mayer, who described it as a form of social intelligence that involves the ability to monitor your emotions and discriminate among them, and to use this information to guide your thinking and actions.[2]

There are four aspects of emotional intelligence:

- self-awareness
- self-management
- social awareness
- relationship mastery

Self-awareness and self-management are the inner game components of emotional intelligence, and when you cultivate these inner skills, they expand outward into greater social awareness and relationship mastery. Emotionally intelligent leaders speak up with grace and strength amid unsettling experiences such as reorganization, challenging team dynamics, and conflict. Emotional intelligence supports better decision-making, open and honest communication, creativity, innovation, and trusting relationships.

Because emotional intelligence requires being in tune with yourself, the self-awareness you developed in the first chapter provides a strong foundation for developing the other three aspects of emotional intelligence. When you learn to self-regulate your emotions, the cornerstone of self-management, you will lead more effectively and create a safer, more supportive workplace.

Begin to cultivate the inner game of emotional intelligence by asking yourself how comfortable you are with your emotions. Try this quick self-assessment consisting of four statements. Consider how true they are for you and score your answers on a scale of 1 (strongly disagree) to 10 (strongly agree).

1. When I experience difficult emotions, I easily come back into balance.

2. When I am feeling strong emotions, I find it hard to think about anything else.

3. If I am annoyed or angry at work, I am able to navigate and express my feelings and needs.

4. I feel uncomfortable expressing sadness, fear, and/or anger at work.

As you are self-reporting, it is important not to judge your answers. Rather, keep a mindset that asks, *What did I learn?*

If you scored between 1 and 3 on questions 1 and 3, your emotional resilience might be on the lower side. If you scored between 7 and 10 on questions 1 and 3, you are able to bounce back easily from strong emotions and you have a higher resilience. Similarly, if you scored between 1 and 3 on questions 2 and 4, you have high emotional resilience. If you scored between 7 and 10 on questions 2 and 4, your emotional awareness is in a lower range, and these are areas to improve and grow.

Write down any epiphanies in your journal.

Inner Game Practice
NEST

Most of us were trained to be afraid of our feelings. In our culture, we go to great lengths to numb, hide from, and protect ourselves from our emotions through over-eating, alcohol abuse, overachieving, workaholism, technology addiction, sex, shopping, and other distractions. Inner game practices that develop emotional intelligence can help us sit with and move through our feelings, no matter how scary they seem at first. When we face our emotions, we can live with authenticity—with our inner and outer selves more fully congruent.

I developed this practice I call NEST after a challenging breakup. I wanted a tool to help me to stay calm during heated arguments as well as when triggers arose. I have since practiced NEST in my relationships with friends, family, and colleagues, and it is a core practice in the Shine Leadership System communication modules. My students tell me it is a powerful tool for navigating the workplace. This exercise brings awareness to our emotions and supports self-management during times of challenge.

Whenever big feelings rise, try these four steps to bring yourself into full awareness of these emotions and then harness the wisdom within them. The acronym NEST will help you remember the sequence of steps:

1. **Number.** Identify a number on a scale from 1 to 10 that captures how triggered you are feeling, with 1 being

I feel calm and 10 being *I am about to lose it.* A score over 5 means you are feeling activated and likely not leading from your heart. Identifying your number gives you direction on when to pause and when to act.

2. **Emotion.** Identify your emotions. It's likely the emotion will be one of the *big three*: anger, fear, or sadness, which we'll explore later in the chapter. Allow every emotion to *be.* All feelings are welcome. There is no need to push anger, fear, or sadness away. When you name your emotions, you can accept, let go, and make peace with them. You can control your reactions rather than letting the emotions control you.

3. **Sensation.** What bodily sensations are you feeling? Bring a sense of curiosity and kindness to your experience. Examine how much space this physical sensation takes up in your body. Is it a little bit, a medium amount, or a large quantity? Ask yourself, *If this space were to make a sound, what sound might it make? A growl, a sigh, an oooh?* The more you can stay in your body rather than diving into a mental story, the more quickly the emotion will pass through you.

4. **Thought.** Examine the thought you are thinking at this moment. Is this lifting you up or bringing you down? Every feeling has an underlying need. Ask yourself, *What do I need that would best support me?*

Return to NEST any time you're feeling overwhelmed. Just as a bird's nest holds fragile eggs, this practice can help you hold (and release) your most vulnerable feelings.

The Emotional Benefits of Mindfulness

As you learned in chapter 1, mindfulness is the key to self-awareness. It's also an essential aspect of self-management. MRI scans have shown that after subjects complete an eight-week course on mindfulness practice, the brain's "fight or flight" center, the amygdala, appears to shrink.[3] How does this work? The simple exercise of returning your attention to one thing over and over again in a meditation practice begins to change the structure of your brain, *particularly in the areas that manage emotions* (fear, sadness, anger) such as the amygdala. The cerebral cortex is the oldest part of the brain and is associated with functions such as awareness, concentration, attunement, and decision-making, and the nature of the connection between the cerebral cortex and the amygdala changes following a regular routine of meditation. Neuroscientist Dan Siegel, author of *Mindsight: The New Science of Personal Transformation*, points to research that shows that by meditating, we can increase the areas of the brain that control stressful emotions and decrease the size of the areas that generate them.

Thus, the practice of meditation not only enhances our self-awareness, but also helps us become aware of our emotions and regulate them. Many professionals in the area of neuroscience and emotional intelligence use a shorthand to describe identifying and regulating emotion: "You have to name it to tame it." The more technical term is *affect labeling*. When we identify and acknowledge our feelings, we can *be* with them, and then they pass. Many of us worry that if we acknowledge heavy feelings, they will burden us all day. But this is not true; the lifespan of most emotions is only ninety seconds, as Jill Bolte Taylor shares in her book *My Stroke of Insight: A Brain Scientist's Personal Journey*.[4] (Though the emotional lifespan of grief, loss, and/or trauma will likely be longer.) When we are mindful of our emotions, we can discern the deeper desires or needs beneath them.

In the next few sections, we'll focus on three of the eight main emotions that my coaching and teaching have shown me are the most challenging to navigate in the context of work: anger, fear, and sadness. Here, you'll explore how to mindfully navigate and harness these three emotions so you can lead with clarity and authenticity.

Lean into Fear

Fear and anger are two of our most common feelings. When we perceive something as threatening or stressful, our sympathetic nervous system is activated and as a result our heart rate and blood pressure increase (fight/flight/freeze). Fear is usually the first emotion we perceive, consciously or unconsciously, when stress, uncertainty, or challenge is present. Anger often follows as the secondary emotion. In other words, we feel fear first and then anger comes in to protect us.

Fear often arises when we don't feel safe. As humans evolved, we constantly scanned for potential dangers in our surroundings in order to survive. In the emerging field of neuroscience, this tendency to be on the lookout for what might harm us is called the *negativity bias*.[5] (70 to 80 percent of our thoughts are negative!) While this way of thinking helped our species evolve, it doesn't support living and leading from a place of love and compassion in the workplace. It is helpful to remember that since you know that most of your thoughts are negative, you have the option to begin to reframe a given situation to see the good in others and to see a given interaction as one you can navigate. (We will delve into this more in the next chapter as we develop a growth mindset.)

To make friends with fear, turn toward your feelings and the physical sensations in your body with attention, understanding, and care. In my experience, it is uncertainty about the unknown that often drives the feeling of fear. We don't have much control over what happens in our lives but we *can* choose how to respond.

Remember: every feeling has an associated need beneath it. That means we can ask our feelings questions in order to understand the wisdom they hold. For instance, what might you say to *welcome* fear, to acknowledge it and let it be there? There are a couple of questions I often ask: "How will you help me grow?" and "What is the worst thing that could happen?" By asking questions like these, you loosen fear's grip and turn the emotion into curiosity. When you feel your fear and allow it to be, you can move toward the other side of fear—toward courage, a vital quality for mission-driven leaders.

Inner Game Practice

MAKING FRIENDS WITH FEAR

This is a short sitting meditation that focuses on how fear lives in your body. If you notice fear inside you, find a quiet place where you can sit and be present to it.

- Identify where your fear resides inside your body. What physical sensations are you aware of?

- Then give fear the persona of a small child and get to know it. How old is this part of you? What does this child part of you need in order to feel safe and protected? Speak to him or her with kindness and compassion. Ask, "What do you want me to know?"

- Take your time listening for the answers, and when you feel ready, repeat this affirmation: "I am safe, and I am here for you."

- After you return to the present moment, write in your journal about what you experienced and discovered. Is there anything else your inner child wants to illuminate?

A version of this meditation is available on my website.[6]

Soothing Fear

My infant niece, Marley, is usually a calm baby, but when she is upset, I find that rocking, swaying, and singing calm her down. And guess what I've realized: *my own* fear responds like Marley's. When I move my body and imagine rocking and cradling myself, I am soothed and the fear dissipates. I invite you to try it—it really works! Another way I can calm down and transform fear is by imagining lovingly sharing a pot of lavender tea with my emotions. Imagery is a powerful tool for making peace with fear.

Do either of these methods speak to you? If not, what action, image, or metaphor might feel regenerative and nourishing when you are experiencing fear and help you make friends with it? Use your method to explore what your fear wants to tell you. Notice how you feel in your body once you've befriended this part of yourself.

The Power in Anger

Anger can be used for good, but if wielded without awareness, it can be destructive. Over the course of your life, you may have developed habitual reactions to anger that are now etched into your brain, and once you are in a reaction rut like that, it becomes more difficult to change your response.

Jason, a leader I have supported through coaching, helps save companies from decline and bankruptcy. When he first started making decisions in this role, he listened to both his intellect and his emotions—until his communication challenges at home impacted his approach on the job. His wife wasn't comfortable speaking about emotions, and every time he expressed something difficult, she shut down (her flight response). Over time, Jason ignored more and more feelings, and his anger and resentment grew. Eventually his anger erupted, and he had increasing outbursts at home *and* at work. This pattern ended their marriage.

Then, Jason and I worked together to cultivate his inner game of emotional intelligence. He used the NEST exercise on page 36 to feel and identify the anger in his body and to understand the need beneath his anger. He came to understand that the anger in his relationship revealed his need for respect and connection, and he learned to welcome anger instead of stuffing it down until he erupted. This enabled him to find ways to release and transform anger with understanding, empathy, and compassion.

When anger arises, it often points to a violation of your boundaries and signals a need to protect yourself and reassert that boundary. I know this dynamic well. For many years, I stuffed anger and wouldn't allow myself to feel it when it came up. I was good friends with fear and sadness, but as a teenager, I got into trouble when I expressed anger or tried to assert an opinion that differed from my dad's. We can handle anger in a variety of ways: erupt with rage, skillfully express it, or suppress it. When I was younger, I didn't want to make waves with my parents or my schoolmates who showed hostility, so I shut down my voice and repressed my anger.

But the inability to be with anger doesn't make it go away. It just seeps out in unhealthy ways. One common way it does this is through saying yes to a request when you really want to say no. When you don't let yourself feel anger, which supports healthy boundaries, it can create a pattern of saying yes a lot and overcommitting your time and energy—a prescription for resentment and more anger.

Embodiment practices can help you create a healthy relationship with anger. Anger lives in different parts of the body. I find anger often lives in the belly and can be released through a variety of physical means. Yelling (in a safe setting). Kickboxing. Jumping up and down. Saying "Ha!" repeatedly. Whacking a pillow on your bed or stomping your feet into the ground. The more you can do to emotionally release physical sensations in your body, the more joy and safety you will feel inside yourself.

Give yourself full permission to feel the physical sensations of anger in your body. When you can feel it, you can notice your boundaries and speak your truth more easily and confidently. You can see anger and all its flavors, from impatience to rage, as a powerful ally that you can use for good. With awareness and compassion, you can use the feeling of anger to stand up against injustice, to speak up bravely when you have an important contribution to make in a meeting but are being talked over, and to create healthy boundaries at work.

Anger and Vulnerability

A beautiful quality of anger is that it supports you in being vulnerable and authentic. If you can't express your anger, you can't open your heart because you have too much armor protecting your vulnerability. But the more you turn toward your anger, the more comfortable you will feel to embody and express vulnerability.

It's time we encourage healthy anger. There is needless, reactive conflict and there is healthy, necessary conflict. Anger supports healthy, appropriate boundaries, and honoring these offers the divine possibility of collaboration and resolution.

You can use your meditation practice to help you *stay* with the physical sensations in your body as they arise and *be* with the feelings instead of stuffing them or erupting. Next time you meditate and experience anger, note where this emotion lives in your body. What can you do to harness its fire? One of the wisest of Buddhist teachers, Thich Nhat Hanh, said, "Hold on to your anger and use it as compost for your garden."[7] If we use it responsibly, anger can be a powerful ally for compassionate change.

Inner Game Practice
THANKING YOUR ANGER

When anger arises, here are two important questions to ask:

- What needs to be protected?
- What needs to be restored?

Explore these questions in your journal and write down your discoveries.

Anger is here to protect you, and when you give it room to do its job, there is no reason to be afraid of it. Instead, you can explore these questions and learn what anger has to teach you. Once you have this insight, you can say, "Thank you, anger, for protecting me." This will help you express anger skillfully and assert healthy boundaries at work.

In your journal, write "Thank you, anger, for _____." How does it feel to show gratitude for this emotion?

Emotions and Gender

A few years ago, when I was facilitating a course on emotional intelligence in the workplace, some female students shared that they were prone to bursts of sadness to the point of tears at the office. One student, Tina, described herself as an emotional person, an aspect of herself that she fully accepts outside of work. But when she has strong feelings on the job, she told us she tends to feel anxious and ashamed and quickly stifles those feelings.

In an article titled "Crying at Work, A Woman's Burden," Kimberly Elsbach explains that the reason women are more likely to cry in the workplace than men is "because women aren't socialized like men, they carry an extra burden of emotional labor." Elsbach's research shows that both frustration and stress can cause people to cry at work, but criticism is the biggest driver of tears. Concerning women leaders, she concludes, "If you cry in response to criticism, it can be seen as a sign of lacking toughness and hardiness and an inability to make good decisions, which negatively impacts women in leadership positions." People who teared up during a meeting or a performance review were evaluated negatively, even with contempt. So, it stands to reason that most participants studied didn't want to cry at work, and did anything to keep from doing it, including pinching their flesh.[8]

Elsbach found a few differences between men and women in regard to crying at work. Men were uniformly perceived more positively than women. The "baseline" view of women is "women are emotional and lack control."

Crying confirms that stereotype. Men, meanwhile, are thought to be strong and unemotional. When they cry, people think, *Something horrible must have happened* or *Somebody made them cry*. Men were assessed more positively if they expressed sadness: *It made me feel closer to him* or *It humanized him*.

With greater awareness of our feelings and our gender norms and biases, we can learn to embrace everyone's feelings regardless of race, color, conforming or nonconforming gender, or status.

What We Feel, We Heal

Most leaders in many workplaces right now identify as white, cis-gendered, heterosexual men. In his book *Men's Work: How to Stop the Violence That Tears Our Lives Apart*, Paul Kivel describes what he calls "the man box," the dominant and acceptable behaviors that define what it means to be a man, and explains the *enforcement* of this narrowly defined set of traditional rules. A man must be strong, able bodied, and stoic; must suppress emotions other than anger and excitement; and must not express vulnerability. He has to be the major breadwinner of the family, follow a heterosexual lifestyle, be sexually aggressive, and take an interest in playing or at least watching sports.

What I want to emphasize for our purposes here, as we explore emotional intelligence, is that the current cultural norm for men is to *not* express emotion. And when men don't feel they can express the full range of their emotions at work, they either don't bring their whole and best selves to work and/or they exhibit aggressive behavior.

There are a couple of examples of this that you're probably familiar with if you've been in the working world for any length of time. The first is men speaking over women, people of color, nonbinary genders, LGBTQIA+ people, or others who are different from themselves. The other is "mansplaining," that is, explaining what a woman has said—as though she can't competently speak for herself—or commenting on or explaining something to a woman in a condescending, overconfident, and often inaccurate or oversimplified manner. Both of these behaviors can be viewed as hurtful and can erode trust and psychological safety over time. We will go into this topic more deeply in chapters 6 and 7.

Destructive dynamics like these are why making the conscious effort to cultivate emotional intelligence is so important. The take-home here is that when men and women can embrace all of their emotions, they don't have to engage in these behaviors. They can become stronger, more inclusive leaders and advocates, with a mission that supports all people and groups to join together as allies. The practices in this chapter are designed to facilitate this shift.

Inner Game Practice
SOOTHING SADNESS

How can you express sadness at work without internalizing embarrassment, shame, or the fear that you'll lose status? You can begin by *listening* to your sadness. Let its wisdom steer you in the right direction. Sadness often arises when you are feeling loss, disappointment, or a need for balance in your busy life. To take the latter point, a normal day could include a work commute, responsibilities at work, family life, and self-care. If one task strays off schedule, this can throw your whole day—and your emotions—off balance, and suddenly you're feeling teary. Sadness asks that you slow down and feel. It allows you to "let in and let go" of things, people, and narratives so you can release into and surrender to what is. When sadness presents itself, I invite you to be with it. If you do, you'll come back into balance more quickly.

Here's a practice that lets you be with your sadness by making it the focus of a sitting meditation.

- After you've centered yourself and checked in to see where in your body you feel that sadness, imagine a wise and loving figure cradling you in their lap. You are enveloped in their loving arms. As the being strokes your head, saying, "It's okay, I am here," you can feel its presence and support, and the gratitude that accompanies this comfort.

- Now you can prepare to return to your day. Feel your mind, heart, and body realigned. Feel centered and strong. Open your eyes and transition into your day slowly. You might notice that after a bout of sadness or tears, it's difficult to jump headlong into the next task. This is the wisdom of your body whispering to you—it needs time to come back into balance. That's why when sadness comes up during coaching sessions in the workplace, I invite my clients to take a stroll, do some gentle stretching, or practice some other form of movement before they go back to their desks.

Another technique is to invite strength and grace into your mind with a supportive affirmation: "I know this is difficult *and* you will be okay. You've got this." Gentle stretching, walking, and/or deep breaths can help move sadness through your body too. To deepen this practice, you can check out my *Soothe with Sadness* meditation audio.[9]

Inner Game Practice

SURRENDERING TO SADNESS

After you have felt and released this emotion from the body in the exercise above, another practice is to ask the following questions of sadness:

- What needs releasing?

- What needs allowing and kindness?

Explore these questions in your journal and write down your discoveries.

The benefits of allowing yourself to feel the emotion that is arising include accessing your intuition, making more effective decisions, tuning into the feelings of your employees, and acting from a place of empathy and compassion.

Breathe Deep

Losing it is normal, but it wastes so much time as a leader. Your friends, family, and coworkers know you are human and you are a good person, but if you become unglued at work in a leadership role, it often affects so many other people.

—ADRIAN JAMES, cofounder and president of Omada Health

Adrian James, cofounder and president of Omada Health, has identified three emotions that trigger his reactive response: pride, guilt, and insecurity. When he feels one of these three things, he knows it's not a good time for him to write an email or conduct a challenging conversation. He has learned it's better to pause, get out of his head, and be in his body, and that doing so supports him in being more calm, resilient, and focused. Adrian stays tuned-in to his inner game skill of emotional intelligence through deep breathing. He then asks himself, *What am I noticing? What am I feeling? What do I need?*

When Adrian's two-year-old son, Adam, is upset, Adrian takes deep breaths with him. He notices that regardless of whether or not Adam calms down, the practice is so effective that Adrian himself calms down right away. Breathing allows him to be with the discomfort without reacting.

Surfing the Waves

Your emotional abilities—the ways in which you perceive, use, understand, and manage emotions—contribute to how you function socially: how you surf the waves of emotion you and others you interact with experience during the day. Imagine that one of your colleagues walks into a weekly meeting and is passive, nonresponsive, and a bit aloof. If you mine these nonverbal cues, you might interpret that he needs gentleness, care, and compassion that day. This is an emotionally intelligent response. However, if you overlook the meaning of his mood, you might jump on him and blurt, "Hey, Steve, I needed that email response yesterday! What is going on with you?" And that approach might not be good for business—or for Steve.

When you are mindful of your feelings, your reaction to them changes. You don't need to rush to put out the fire, and you can be mindful of others' feelings too. You discover the need that the feeling is trying to communicate. Also, when you are mindful of your feelings, your own breathing becomes lighter and calmer, and as a result, you see the bigger picture and can understand and collaborate with your fellow employees better.

How to Become a More Empathic Leader

From the beginning of this chapter we have been developing greater awareness of and capacity to manage our own emotions. This leads to more
social awareness and thus empathy, an important quality of conscious,
emotionally intelligent leaders. Empathy can be defined as the ability to
understand another person's experience, perspective, and feelings. A study
by the Center for Creative Leadership found that managers who show
higher levels of empathy toward their team are viewed more positively
overall on their performance of decision-making, coaching, engaging, and
planning/organizing.[10]

Developing greater capacity for empathy becomes even more important as more and more teams are distributed around the world and working
remotely. Although phone and video conferencing are wonderful tools,
when team members are not physically present with one another it can be
easier to miss what others are actually experiencing. The key is to be mindful of this and learn the nonverbal cues to watch for so we can put ourselves
into another person's shoes. You can also use the Outer Game Practice:
Zoom In/Zoom Out on page 158 in chapter 6 to assess the emotional state
of each team member at the beginning of a meeting.

Psychologists Daniel Goleman and Paul Ekman identified three different kinds of empathy:[11]

- **Cognitive empathy.** The ability to put yourself in someone else's
  place and understand their perspective. This quality enables leaders
  to assess what others are feeling. It is also a natural outgrowth of
  self-awareness. The executive circuits in the brain that allow you to
  notice your thoughts and monitor your feelings give you the ability
  to transfer these skills from yourself to another. One way to grow your
  cognitive empathy is to ask, *What would happen if I put myself in this
  person's shoes?* or *What might I have done if I had this experience?*

- **Emotional empathy.** The ability to feel what someone else feels.
  Another name for this is *emotional contagion*. This is what happens
  when you are interacting with a distraught colleague and begin
  to feel down and distraught too. It is important that you connect

with what people are feeling, but you don't want to be rocked by their feeling state. One way to grow your emotional empathy is to allow your positive or negative feelings to surface while listening to a coworker's emotional experience. Ask yourself, *When have I experienced a similar story? How did I feel when this happened to me?* Here is an important distinction: cognitive empathy is *empathy by thought* and emotional empathy is *empathy by feelings*.

- **Compassionate empathy.** The ability to move into action with empathic concern. This is what many coworkers typically react to in the workplace. For example, when a team member reports that he or she doesn't have the complete information to finish a deliverable, a leader might jump in and/or assign someone to help with one of the related tasks. A question that can help you build compassionate empathy is *What supportive action would I want or need if I were in this person's shoes?*

We all want to be seen, felt, and heard. Developing empathy supports appropriate boundaries while allowing you to be with and to acknowledge another's range of experiences. Empathy says, "I am here with you and I know this struggle and have lived this experience."

Inner Game Practice
DEVELOPING EMPATHY

Bring to mind a colleague at work who is experiencing difficulty. Ask yourself the following questions to help develop your empathy:

- What would I do?

- How would I feel in a similar situation?

- What would I want or expect from my manager?
- What would I not want?

Note your answers.

Empathy in Action

When Linda Lockwood, whom you met in chapter 1, is in a meeting and a colleague has dug in their heels (and the meeting progress is stuck), she uses reflective listening (paraphrasing what she hears), offers empathy, and follows up with action. For example, "Okay, I got it. I hear how important it is to you that we address security and risk. This makes complete sense. I am on top of it. Who specifically should I address?" The simple tactic of reflecting and acknowledging a person's experience, wants, and needs can be a bridge to a powerful connection, no matter the other person's rank in relation to yours. When you integrate your self-awareness and emotional intelligence skills, you can lead with greater empathy. This will foster a culture of trust, create deeper connections, and support your organization in meeting its business goals, leading to more resilient team members and an agile, flourishing workplace.

As we near the end of this chapter, I encourage you to identify the aspects of emotional intelligence you want to develop to achieve greater empathy and relationship mastery. When you commit to practicing the exercises in this chapter, you will learn to navigate feelings with greater consciousness and have better capacity to influence all the relationships in your work and home life. Cultivate your inner game of emotional intelligence and you will develop the outer game skills to respond rather than react to emotions. Treating your coworkers with empathy supports good rapport and teamwork. Ask yourself, *What am I feeling?* and *What am I wanting?* to gain greater access to your feelings during the workday.

Emotional Intelligence Recipe

And now, your emotional intelligence ingredients list:

- I welcome all of my feelings with compassion and grace.

- I express fear, sadness, and anger with skill and strength.

- I cultivate empathy toward everyone at work and in the world.

- I am becoming more emotionally intelligent.

3

Flourishing in Uncertain Times
Meeting the Waves with
Resilience and Grace

I want to be the calm in the storm and model to others
how to refocus when things have gone awry and come back
to the conversation and agenda that really matters.

—AARON TARTAKOVSKY, cofounder and
CEO of Epic CleanTec

The World Health Organization has labeled stress a "global health epidemic." In 2018, Gallup's Global Emotions Report collected data from 154,000 adults in 145 countries and found we had reached the highest level of unhappiness ever measured.[1] Collectively, people worldwide are struggling with stress and fear, and the world is in more pain today than we have ever seen it.

The root of our stress and unhappiness is clear; it's caused by the way we are working and our disconnection from nature, from ourselves, and from each other. When we perceive this intensity of stress individually, there is no possibility of coming together to solve the massive problems that confront us collectively. This is why we need to cultivate strong inner resources so we can rise to meet the challenges and complexities in the outer world with resilience.

Have you ever gone through a difficulty in your life that you didn't think you could survive at the time, but then did? This is resilience, and the inner game skills you developed in the first two chapters—self-awareness and emotional intelligence—are key building blocks for increasing such resilience within yourself. How do we define resilience?

> Resilience is the process of adapting well in the face of adversity, trauma, tragedy, threats, or significant sources of stress—such as family and relationship problems, serious health problems, or workplace and financial stressors.

Stressful life events, trauma, and chronic adversity can have substantial impacts on brain function and structure and can result in the development of PTSD, depression, and other psychiatric disorders. Fortunately, most individuals do not develop such illnesses after they experience stressful life events and are thus thought to be resilient, people who can "bounce back" by relying on internal and external resources of support.[2]

In this chapter, we'll take a look at how to train your brain for the inner skill of resilience. This will show up in your outer game as:

- A desire to learn
- Persistence in the face of setbacks
- Seeing your effort as a path to mastery
- Learning from criticism
- Showing empathy
- Shifting the mood of your team
- Finding inspiration in others' success

Cultivating a Growth Mindset

In her book *Mindset: The New Psychology of Success*, Carol Dweck, a Stanford University colleague, explains that our mindset exists on a continuum—from "fixed" to "mixed" to "growth." Our bodies are always evolving, and so are our minds. People with a fixed mindset believe that they possess only certain basic abilities, intelligence, and talents—and that's it. Their goal is to look smart and never fail.[3] A person with a fixed mindset who is going through a re-organization and layoffs in the workplace might say, "Why can't we keep doing things like we used to? It seemed to work well enough. Why all the changes?"

Those who have a growth mindset, on the other hand, understand that they can learn new skills and advance with new experiences and can grow and develop as people. They are up for the challenges ahead and, more importantly, are part of innovative solutions. A person with a growth mindset might say, "How does this difficulty, obstacle, or change feel to me?" versus "Why is this happening to me?" There is a feeling of empowerment when we can see all experiences as an opportunity for learning and growth. When we ask ourselves the second question, "Why is this happening to me?" we may see and experience ourselves as stuck and take on a mindset of power-lessness and/or victimhood. With self-awareness, we have choice over what kind of a mindset we want to cultivate and choose—fixed or growth?

With a growth mindset, our focus is on improving ourselves—that's the desire-to-learn piece of resilience—while with a fixed mindset, our only aim is to try not to fail. The fact is that every leader and entrepreneur takes daily risks, and when we take risks, we will fail. Therefore, every effective leader has learned to *fail fast*. Failing is part of what strong leaders sign up for. We fall and then we dust ourselves off and get back up. No business venture is successful upon first creation; look to Steve Jobs' beginnings to discover the many trials and errors that resulted in founding Apple. The silver lining of failing is learning how to stand up again with strength and grace; that's what a strong inner game of resilience teaches you. And your mindset is a major factor in this—it has a huge impact on how you lead, communicate, solve problems, and collaborate with others.

Resilience to Stress

Our stress response evolved to save us from attack or danger, like an encounter with a saber-toothed tiger, or a natural disaster like a flood or fire. Such experiences, hopefully, were rare, but in our modern-day, plugged-in culture, our nervous systems and stress responses are constantly triggered. New research finds that people use their smartphones for an average of five hours a day and check them eighty-five times in a day.[4] This means we're constantly being stimulated and reacting. Our nervous system is always "on," releasing more cortisol—the stress hormone—into our bloodstream. Cortisol causes our pupils to dilate (so we can see more clearly) and our heart rate and blood pressure (to increase to divert blood to our larger muscles). While these processes are useful in the short run, such continual stress doesn't support anyone in terms of long-term health, focus, or effective leadership.

Elissa Epel is one of the premier researchers on how thought patterns and stress wear down telomeres, the "caps" on DNA that protect cells from illness and aging. When Elissa and I observed the long-term benefits of meditation on stress during a six-year research study at University of California, San Francisco's Osher Center for Integrative Medicine, she concluded, "Our cells are listening to our thoughts."

This is why cultivating a growth mindset is so important if we want to develop resilience to stress. And one way to cultivate resilience is to examine the stories we tell ourselves about perceived stressors, threats, or change. Then, we can greet the challenge by feeling the emotions that arise and engaging in creative and adaptive thinking. This is resilience.

My Resilience Story

In November 2018, the Camp Fire in Northern California and the Woolsey Fire in Southern California raged for close to a month. Where I lived, the atmosphere was so thick with pollution and smoke that I couldn't see the sun. For weeks I was steeped in the toxic fumes of "very unhealthy" air quality, and I struggled to focus and function. Many people lost their homes in those fires, some their lives, and the whole town of Paradise, California, literally went up in smoke. I felt distress and grief for those who had suffered, and my own feelings of fear and uncertainty were high, as were those of most Californians. On top of that, two days before the fire began, I received the news that my largest corporate contract would be paused in the New Year due to budget cuts, and I didn't have a backup client to replace the income I'd been receiving from the contract. This was a terrible blow in itself, which was then exacerbated by the fires and smoke.

Can you imagine trying to work when you can't breathe the air? I was feeling shaky at best; my financial foundation, the state where I lived, and even the things I took for granted like clean air were severely challenged. Then, I took a pre-planned work trip to Omaha, Nebraska and Phoenix, Arizona to teach the skills of resilient leadership. I knew I was fortunate to be able to leave the fire zone for perspective, space, and clean air, but I had no idea when I left how deadly the fires would become. I was teaching the tools and skills you'll be learning in this chapter and, as is often the case, I was given more challenges to prove I knew my material. It was almost as if the universe was saying, "So you think you're an expert in resilience? *Prove it.*"

I remember asking myself, *Carley, what can you **control**? Can you see these setbacks as a **challenge** and an opportunity for learning and growth? How can you **trust** that this is for you and is serving your greatest good? What can you **commit** to in order to get through this with grace and strength?* My answers were simple. I can control what I am doing in each moment and put one foot in front of the other. I will use my mindfulness practice to stay with *what is.*

I tried to stay in the present and reframed the dire situation with some inner dialogue: *You can get through this. This will pass.*

If I were in the direct path of the fire, the question I'd likely ask myself would be simple: *First and foremost, how do I find safety?* My hope is that I'd remember to stay present and to use my inner game skills to face the moment. These mega-fires are likely the new norm in California, caused by increasing temperatures due to the climate crisis. So here, as in many other regions of the world grappling with climate change, growing internal resilience is vital to becoming climate resilient.

Inner Game Practice

JOURNALING FOR RESILIENCE

When you find yourself in a challenging situation, ask yourself these questions and write your responses in your journal:

- What can I control?

- Can I see this as a challenge and an opportunity for learning and growth?

- Can I trust and surrender to what is?

- How can I commit to moving forward?

You can also journal about how you've demonstrated resilience in the past to remind yourself that you're more resilient than you may know. In what ways have you shown resilience? How can you learn from your past actions?

Meet Your Inner Critic

Befriending your inner critic is key for becoming a resilient leader. Nearly everyone recognizes their inner critic: that judgmental inner voice that points out your flaws, keeps track of whether you are making progress, and reinforces your sense of unworthiness. That tough critic reminds you, *Whatever you do is never enough.*

It is important to notice what keeps you in a fixed place versus a growth place. Being unaware of your inner critic's triggers might bring you into a fixed place—perhaps the challenge feels too difficult to face. But if you have developed the inner game of self-awareness, you will be conscious of your triggers. That will give you the opportunity to embrace a growth mindset, and you *will* move forward.

Like most leaders, you have set a high bar for success. You climbed the ladder in your organization because you stood out, took the initiative, and inspired others to follow you.[5] The negative, and likely unsustainable, aspects of this part of you are that you push yourself hard and have high expectations. Perhaps you beat yourself up for not being good enough, and it's likely that you extend this to your colleagues, your direct reports, and your personal relationships.

Even the most accomplished leaders have inner critics of varying intensities and tendencies. The inner critic operates out of fear and is motivated to keep us safe from harm—but left unchecked, it can impact our self-confidence and self-esteem.

Below are the four main types of critics I have identified in myself and my leadership clients. You might resonate with more than one, but after you read their descriptions, you may want to explore the inner critic you relate to the most.

1. The Impostor

Many men and women in leadership positions believe they are not intelligent, capable, or creative enough for the task, despite evidence to the contrary. This form of inner criticism is so widespread that there's even a term for it: *Impostor Syndrome.* I have supported many Silicon Valley company leaders and taught MBA students at University of California, Berkeley's Haas School of Business who told me flat-out, "I have Impostor Syndrome."

No matter how many times they've proven themselves capable, they're sure someone is going to find out they don't know what they're doing. A 2011 study published in the *International Journal of Behavioral Science* found that an estimated 70 percent of people experience Impostor Syndrome at one point in their lives.[6] What does the impostor sound like?

"I don't have what it takes." "I don't belong here." "I have to compete rather than collaborate if I want to get ahead." A famous self-identified imposter was Maya Angelou. Even after writing eleven acclaimed books and succeeding as a thought leader, she still couldn't escape the nagging doubt that she didn't deserve her accomplishments. Albert Einstein felt the same way.

2. The Perfectionist

The perfectionist wants you to do the absolute best that can be done. This is positive, unless doing your best becomes "I am not enough" or "I am not doing enough." The perfectionist, or taskmaster, might say, "I am worthy because I am working eight- to twelve-hour days," or "I must finish this project today, even if I have to stay at my desk all night," or "I'm the only one who can do it right." The perfectionist is highly focused on achievement and external success and is prone to workaholism.

3. The Boss

The boss needs to control the team and the situation. If you're the boss type, you desire certainty, and if you lack control, anxiety and/or anger arises. You believe asking for help is too vulnerable and a sign you're losing control, so you always take the lead and believe that only you can accomplish the task. Your controlling behavior and struggle to delegate can lead to burnout.

4. The Pleaser

The pleaser wants to be liked and loved and often says yes rather than no out of fear of being rejected. The pleaser's yes, when offered regardless of feelings and needs, is a recipe for resentment. The pleaser values harmony and aims to avoid conflict.

Shifting from Inner Critic to Inner Wisdom

Your inner critic isn't trying to hurt you. Its goal is to protect you, and it has undoubtedly employed brilliant strategies to keep you safe and help you thrive. Your inner critic helps you avoid losing status, influence, love, power, or safety, but it can derail your confidence or clarity unless you see it for what it is: fear.

The good news is that you can train your mind to look for the good in yourself and others and embrace your strengths and weaknesses. The more you can see and embrace the voice of your inner critic, the more power you have in responding to it. When we learn how to be more accepting of the inner voice we create inner belonging, and inner belonging lays the groundwork for a culture of belonging in the workplace and the world.

I invite you to get to know your inner critic and befriend these voices. Once you listen and really hear them, you will choose to lead from a more perceptive place—your inner wisdom.

Inner Game Practice
BEFRIENDING YOUR INNER CRITIC

With this practice, I'm asking you to document the voices of your inner critic in your journal for one week. Give these voices names. Then notice whether your energy increases or you feel depleted, anxious, or insecure. Let your inner critic speak on the page. What does it want to tell you?

You can label your inner critic when it arises, or you can prompt yourself throughout the day to acknowledge what part of you is leading. For example, if you have a tendency to be the pleaser or the perfectionist, you can ask, *Am I being pleasing or controlling?* If you recognize which inner critic is leading, you can lean back and choose to do the opposite. For example, if the pleaser is running the show and your focus is on the person you want to please, you can change that tune by noticing what *you* are feeling and need-ing and express that. If the inner controller is leading, acknowledge that this is the part of you that feels scared, and then choose to soften, relax, and calm yourself down, and/or ask for what you want. If you just name it aloud (regardless of whether or not you receive what you want), you can tame it.

The inner critic deeply wants to be seen and heard, so if we acknowledge its voices and their underlying needs, inner wisdom can lead the way. Labeling these voices and experiences gives you the opportunity to make different choices.

Another technique you can try is to assign a differ-ent voice to your inner wisdom. One of my coaching clients, Elizabeth, named her loudest inner critic The Perfectionist. To counterbalance this nagging voice, she brought in the compassionate voice of Mr. Rogers, saying, "Elizabeth, you are doing enough, and you are loveable."

The voice of an inner critic says, *I am not enough as I am. I have to compete. I don't belong here.* While the inner-wisdom voice affirms, *I am complete. I am capable. I belong.* This exercise shows you how to shift from critical to wise.

What does your inner wisdom want to tell you? Let it speak to you as you write in your journal.

Inner Game Practice
BE MINDFULLY INCREDIBLE IN FIVE EASY STEPS

When I was teaching at Pixar, I created a meditation program for employees called Be Mindfully Incredible. I love the movie *The Incredibles*, and it was a fun and resonant way to sync the title of the class with Pixar's culture. The point of this Be Mindfully Incredible exercise is to talk back to your inner critic and remind yourself you are awesome!

1. Label the thoughts that your inner critic is chattering in your mind. This is a moment of mindfulness. What voice or part is leading the way? If you are lost in a negative thought, acknowledge it by labeling your experience, and then let it go.

2. Swat it away. I sometimes think of negative thoughts as bothersome flies in the air. They buzz around you for a while, and then you think they're gone but they come back. Give the "flies" a good swat and say, "Not now. Stop!" Then tell yourself, *Be here.*

3. Sing a happy song. Sometimes when I am in a negative state of mind, I sing an upbeat, empowering, positive tune, like "Let Love Rule" by Lenny Kravitz.

4. Use a positive antidote. If you notice you are feeding a certain thought, like *How did I get on this team?*

Everyone is so much smarter than me, change your tune and feed yourself an opposite thought. For example: *I have many gifts and talents, and I know I am a valuable member of this team.*

5. Integrate a positive thought with an empowering movement. Your mind and body are connected, and the latter is both a pathway for transformation and a tool for reminding you what your purpose is. If you say, "I move through challenges and thrive afterward," bring this into a movement. Your body will make a new memory and pattern.

It can be helpful to write down these new affirmations and experiences so you can refer back to them when you need a dose of inner wisdom.

Resilience Using the Elements: Earth, Air, Fire, and Water

Stress, difficult feelings, and trauma live in our physical bodies, and it's impossible to be resilient if you hold tightly to these states. One way to release stress and ignite and shift negativity is by moving your body. You can use the elements of nature to guide you in moving and discharging emotions. Different feelings call for different kinds of movement and sound. I encourage you to experiment with these elemental practices and discover which ones work best for you. This is another way to upgrade and deepen your inner game.

Earth

This one is about grounding. One day I got stuck in horrible Los Angeles traffic on my way to the airport after teaching a leadership team building off-site. I felt stressed all the way to the airport and arrived at the gate with barely five minutes to spare. Fear coursed through my body. I had two options: get on the flight and sit with fear for the duration of my trip or pause to shake it off. I found an uncrowded spot in the terminal and spent thirty seconds shaking my arms and legs, releasing the fear on each exhale, patting my arms and legs with love and kindness, and brushing fear off my legs and arms with my hands. I felt so much better. I happily walked to my gate, stayed calm on my flight, and arrived safely home.

After you allow yourself to feel the bodily sensations of fear, anger, and sadness, it's empowering to shake off those emotions. You can do this anywhere, but being outdoors is ideal because you receive nature's healing benefits too. Ground your difficult feelings into the earth by shaking, breathing, and appreciating the elements of nature. Complete the practice by honoring the Earth and what she gives to you, and then place both hands on the earth and say, "Thank you, Mother Earth, for holding this for me."

If we honor and respect the Earth, she will honor and give abundantly.

Air

Sounding is another way of saying "making noise." Sounding helps you discharge emotions from your physical body and acknowledge what you are feeling. It could be a deep breath and then an exhale with the sound "Haaa," or a soothing sound like "Vooo." Sounding "Vooo" when you want to soothe fear or sadness can feel like a gust of wind passing through your body and blowing the feelings out. The sound "Haaa" is helpful when you feel angry. You can first use the "breath of fire" exercise below and then exhale out what you don't need with a "Haaa." I realize making noises at work might not be cool, so take it outside or to a private space indoors. You can practice at home, too.

Fire

This breath-of-fire exercise releases tension from the body. I bring this powerful kundalini breathing technique into my morning meditation practice. I also practice it during the day—especially when I need a burst of energy or want to move out of anger or other difficult emotions.

Start with a short period of thirty seconds and increase the pace of your breathing. Then, increase the duration to one minute or more.

1. Sit up tall with your shoulders back and your chin resting in a comfortable position.

2. Breathe in and out through your nose quickly. As you breathe, pull in your abdomen during the exhale, and press it out during the inhale. Imagine your stomach filling up with air as you inhale and allow your stomach to flatten as you exhale.

3. If you like steps 1 and 2, try this modification. Put your hands in front of an area of your body where you feel an intensity of energy, and then breathe out the sound "Haaa." For example, if I notice I haven't been speaking my truth, I will practice breath of fire for ten to fifteen seconds, then place my hands near my throat chakra and exhale out "Haaa." As I make this sound out loud, I also move my hands in a sharp jab away from my throat. This helps me clear the energy that is keeping my speech quiet and contracted. You can go through all seven chakras—from your crown to your root—cleansing and clearing energy with the breath-of-fire practice and then the sounding of "Haaa." I invite you to experiment with the variation that works best for you.

When you're done, pause and take a few deep breaths and feel the energizing benefits of the practice.

Water

Water is about movement. Over the years, I have discovered that physical release through dance, yoga, hiking, or walking is healing and beneficial. You can take short walking breaks, do yoga, or dance for ten to fifteen minutes throughout the day to move energy. As you dance, imagine you are moving emotions through your body like a river.

Experiment with each of these elements and rotate between earth (shaking), air (breathing and sounding), fire (breath of fire), and water (dance, walking, or yoga). Identify which practices work best for you and how they make you feel, then create a routine around them.

Everything Is Energy

Energy is the new currency.

—ARVIND GOEL, vice president of business transformation at
Bank of the West

Arvind Goel is a leader at Bank of the West. One way he shifts the mood from tense to relaxed is by staying transparent with what is surfacing in the moment and naming it. He intentionally radiates pleasant and playful energy, then brings the focus back to business and the matter at hand.

Shifting the Mood of the Team

You have the power to build your team's resilience by shifting your energy and the energy of your team. Imagine you are at a team meeting, either in person or remote, and you know that the assembled group is highly competent and efficient, but you sense disconnection. As you listen to the discussion, you hear a few people present the *only* solution to a problem; their oppositional stance is firm, and each member of the group struggles to be "right." Imagine how challenging it will be to work as a team under these circumstances.

How can you shift the mood from fixed and stubborn to open and collaborative? By naming what you are observing yourself, aloud, and *challenging the story*.

What story is each individual team member carrying? For example: "This process is not going to get us anywhere. I know the way forward. Why won't anyone listen?" What feeling is each individual team member holding? They're likely feeling fear, frustration, or anger. Perhaps they worry that their coworkers will deem them impostors, and they will lose status or power. What is their need? To retain their status while finding effective and creative solutions.

When you notice your team is irritated or tense, step back and get curious. Ask yourself if you were the one who brought forth the negative energy that contributed to this mood. Is wisdom emerging that you can't yet see? You can set the tone of the room (or virtual room) with the powerful currency of your energetic vibration through the way you speak and your nonverbal cues, and by asking questions to gauge how everyone is feeling. To shift the energy of the group, start by downregulating—breathing deeply in and out of your belly, which slows down your nervous system and your speech.

Once you have assessed the mood, story, feelings, and needs beneath the group's tension, try naming them with the team. You could say something like, "Hey everyone, we have a big project ahead of us and there's a lot of pressure to do it well. We all have expertise, but it seems we aren't collaborating to find solutions. I know that's what we all want. Could we spend a few minutes talking openly about our feelings, hopes, and shared agreements for this project, and what might be getting in the way of our success?"

This process invites authenticity. When we listen with empathy, name the feelings transparently, and seek to understand each other, we create psychological safety, which is defined as "being able to show and employ one's self without fear of negative consequences of self-image, status, or career."[7] When psychological safety is established, there is a shared belief that interpersonal risk-taking can be done safely.

When safety is present, the story and feelings of the team will shift. You can establish trust and reset, moving from "stuck-ness" to resilient action. At the end of the meeting, outline the cues you used so the team can use them later to build resilience in their collaboration.

Resilience Recipe

- I lean into discomfort and lead courageously.
- I focus on solutions more than problems.
- I tame the critical voice and heed the voice of wisdom.
- I am resilient.

Leading with Love
Showing Appreciation, Care, and Compassion

By drinking in positive energy, I am getting the energy I
need to fuel me.

—SHERYL O'LOUGHLIN, former CEO of Clif Bar &
Company and REBBL, and cofounder of the Women
on Boards Project and the J.E.D.I. Collaborative

Imagine a typical Monday. You got a decent night's sleep, went to the gym
before work, and brown-bagged your healthy lunch. You're feeling great,
and ready to meet the workday. You drop off your things at your desk and
walk into your first morning meeting. As soon as you open the door, you
sense the tension in the room; your team members are not engaging with
each other. You say, "Good morning," but almost no one greets you. This
is your moment of choice: Do you jump into this bath of negativity or do
you keep yourself open?

Our natural instinct is to lead from love, but in our go-full-steam-ahead
culture, love can sometimes get left behind, especially at the office. This
chapter will support you in cultivating the inner game of leading from your
heart, not your head.

I've learned a lot from listening to Bob Chapman, CEO of Barry-Wehmiller. He has acquired 101 businesses and since 1987 has experienced 18 percent compound revenue growth and 14 percent compound share price growth.[1] How does he achieve these incredible numbers? When he acquires a new company, he leads from love. First, he doesn't fire a soul. Instead, Bob helps struggling employees and cultures by saying, "You are safe here. We're going to train you on leadership and culture, and we're going to be patient." He leads with compassion, from employee relations all the way to his overall corporate strategy. For instance, when he acquires a business, he doesn't expect returns in the first quarter or even the first year.

The idea is simple: create a workplace culture that truly values and cares for employees, and the rest of the transformation, including profitability, will take care of itself. The inner game of leading from love increases your outer game qualities and skills, such as forgiveness, empathy, taking responsibility for your actions, and making amends—for instance, apologizing when you hurt someone's feelings.

Lead with Love

Do you ever notice yourself on a negative train of thought, one where you keep repeating the same negative sentence over and over again?

- I don't like _____ about my job.
- I don't like _____ about my coworker, my romantic partner, or _____.
- My life just isn't what I want it to be.

As you keep riding this train, you'll notice your body tensing up and your overall enjoyment of the day declining. Research shows that this kind of obsessive thinking and rumination is associated with binge eating, anxiety, depression, a lack of self-esteem, and greater irritability and restlessness.[2]

But this is really no surprise. Remember, the mind has a strong tendency to look for the negative—recall the inner critic in the last chapter. When we befriend that critic and gain greater awareness of both our positive and negative thoughts, we can stop unconsciously scanning our environment for threats and instead assume positive intent, which provides the opportunity for the heart to open naturally. This kind of openheartedness is what I mean by love in the Shine Leadership System, and it's a far more wonderful and satisfying place to operate from than the scarcity-based energy of fear.

One of the practices I recommend is to cultivate this form of love, is a meditation known as *lovingkindness*. This practice resonates with me because it nurtures loving enthusiasm, which is the foundation of leading from love. Lovingkindness consists of well-wishing, for oneself or for others. It has been one of my core practices for the last fifteen years, and I integrate it into my daily sitting meditation practice and into regular thoughts and phrases throughout the day. It can transform the way you lead and how you interact with others, and it is essential in helping you love yourself so you can lead with love in the world.

Research psychologist Barbara Fredrickson and her colleagues have discovered that practicing seven weeks of lovingkindness meditation increases the qualities of love, joy, contentment, gratitude, pride, hope, interest, amusement, and awe.[3] In her research, she found that these positive emotions resulted in improvements in a wide range of personal resources, such as mindfulness, awareness of the purpose of life, social support, and decreased symptoms of illness. And this, in turn, predicted increased life satisfaction and reduced depressive symptoms.

Other research has found that regularly practicing lovingkindness meditation activates and strengthens areas of the brain that are responsible for empathy and emotional intelligence. And if that isn't enough to persuade you of its benefits, a recent review of mindfulness-based interventions (MBIs) concludes that lovingkindness meditation may be the most effective practice for increasing compassion.[4]

Practicing seven weeks of lovingkindness meditation also boosts the connection and activity between the prefrontal cortex's executive centers and the brain's circuitry for joy and happiness. The stronger the connection, the more altruistic a person becomes and the more likely they are to actually step in and help when there is a need.

Research also shows that speaking to yourself like a good friend for seven days straight lowers depression levels for three months thereafter and raises happiness levels for six months.[5]

I wouldn't mind a spoonful of that medicine every day, would you?

Lovingkindness meditation is typically practiced by reciting a sequence of affirmations repeatedly. As we've seen before in this book, the mind is continually busy, so when we give it the instruction to think loving and kind thoughts toward ourselves or others by repeating affirmations, it can steady the mind, calm the nervous system, and allow the heart to be more open and accepting of ourselves and others. The repetition itself can also be a very powerful concentration practice.

When we use our mind to make it easier for the brain to lead from the heart through well-wishing, our natural response in the face of difficulty or suffering is compassion. While it's certainly possible to be compassionate without building a foundation of lovingkindness, it tends to be far more challenging. That's why I really encourage you to add this practice to your toolbox and integrate these kinds of statements into your daily life. I have seen lovingkindness enhance people's ability to lead from love in ways that are absolutely transformative.

Lovingkindness: Be the Love

Love is the greatest universal energy we can tap into, and it is so much more powerful than fear. But how do we build our love muscle so we can have plenty in reserve when we need it most? I cultivated this next exercise to help me lead from love. It's a practical lovingkindness meditation that I have enjoyed leading for employees at some of the largest, most innovative companies in the Bay Area.

When I offered an off-site training at Genentech, I brought the inner game practice of leading from love into a one-day training for the senior leaders of an engineering team. Three weeks later, when I was following up on the effects of the training with one of attendees, a woman said, "Carley, I wanted to tell you how impactful the training has been for us. In just three weeks there is a palpable difference in the level of kindness and compassion we show one another. I feel deeply grateful."

Let this meditation practice help you find more opportunities to lead from love.

Inner Game Practice
LOVINGKINDNESS—BE THE LOVE

Find a quiet, comfortable place to sit. Sit up tall, but in a relaxed and comfortable posture. Close your eyes and bring to mind someone for whom you already have a lot of love and affection. Notice how they appear to you. You can silently say their name, and when you feel ready, send this person lovingkindness by repeating one or two of the following phrases that resonate with you.

- May you be safe and protected.

- May you be healthy in mind and body.

- May you be happy.

- May you feel all the love in your life.

- May you love and accept yourself as you are.

- May you share your love well.

Notice what it feels like in your body as you offer these phrases and imagine how the person you envision will respond to your well-wishes. Take as much time as you need with this until you feel ready to move on.

Now focus this practice on yourself. Start by bringing to mind the person for whom you just offered lovingkindness, or think of someone else. Then, repeat one or two of the phrases above, only this time, imagine the other person is offering them to you. Allow yourself to fully receive these blessings.

How do you feel about receiving love and kindness from this person? Keep coming back to the phrases and repeat them until you start to feel more comfortable with receiving lovingkindness. If you add an image of yourself being and feeling happy, that feeling of happiness can help deepen the impact of the phrases.

When you feel ready, bring your awareness back to your breath, open your eyes, and slowly transition back into your day.

Offering yourself lovingkindness is the first and most important step toward cultivating your inner game of love. I can't overemphasize the importance of starting this practice *now*. If you are looking for the negative in yourself, the energy you emit looks for what is wrong or lacking in the other. This leads to scarcity thinking and creates a wound of "not-enoughness." The wound of not-enoughness has harmful consequences individually, collectively, and environmentally, as we will see and address in subsequent chapters. If you take away only one gem from this book, my strong recommendation is this inner game practice: be the love.

Lovingkindness Detox

You can think of lovingkindness as a detox for negative thoughts, which means at first you might predominantly see and feel the negative. It's like drinking a really healthy, green lovingkindness juice when your body is used to super-sugary mocha lattes. At first, your body will bring up all the goop that needs to be cleansed, but if you keep drinking the lovingkindness juice, you will feel more energized and healthier, and it will have a lasting effect. After you've practiced for a while, you'll begin to feel what I like to call the "lovingkindness glow." It's a lot like the glow you feel after a cleanse or a really great kale salad, and it's a wonderful way to shine.

Chief Love Officer

When Sheryl O'Loughlin was the CEO of REBBL (an acronym for Roots, Extracts, Berries, Bark, and Leaves), a company that makes high-quality herbal elixirs, she called herself the "chief love officer." Sheryl feels deep devotion to the missions of the products and companies she has been instrumental in supporting—such as Clif Bar & Company, Plum Organics, and REBBL.

She stays connected to her love of product, people, and the planet with a daily gratitude practice. She feels incredibly grateful for the love of her friends and family, and for her morning run in nature. Sheryl told me that she feels fueled by love, and that it works this way: the more she takes in the good and receives love, the more she is able to love in return. Sheryl believes connection to love creates the greatest power of all.

At REBBL, her love spread into the company's cause—to be a sustainable beverage company that stands for a world without human trafficking and creates mutually beneficial relationships with the farmers who grow the ingredients that go into the product.

Wired for Compassion, Wired for Care

We learned in the last two chapters that when we perceive stress or danger, we have a tendency to move into fight, flight, or freeze mode to survive the stressor. But Shelley Taylor, a psychology professor at the University of California, Los Angeles, looked through dozens of studies conducted over the last thirty years—ranging from rats to monkeys to people in diverse cultures—and found that we cultivate a "tend and befriend" attitude toward challenge, danger, or perceived stress, and this supports us in our prioritization of the "we," not the "me."[6]

My friend and colleague Dacher Keltner, professor of psychology at University of California, Berkeley, and founding director of the Greater Good Science Center, has studied and written about compassion and many other contemplative practices in-depth. He tells me humans are profoundly caregiving by design.

There is a strong evolutionary argument for this thesis, from Charles Darwin to the most recent research. Compassion is our defining instinct, and with good reason: our offspring are among the most vulnerable mammals on Earth. This means that as we evolved, we needed to organize our communities to care for others, in particular vulnerable beings. In short, we've evolved into compassionate beings; we are wired to care.

When Love Meets Suffering

Now let's tease apart lovingkindness and compassion. Lovingkindness is a well-wishing for oneself or for another. Compassion is an interpersonal process that involves the ability to notice, feel, or perceive another person's pain and to be with that person's suffering or take action to alleviate it. When lovingkindness is present, compassion naturally arises because we care about the suffering of the person we are wishing well. Both qualities recognize that we are not alone; we are all in this together.

Too often, our drive and passion for purpose, service, and accomplishment lead to burnout and a lack of compassionate self-care. For the first five years of my own entrepreneurial journey I worked ten- to twelve-hour days Monday through Friday and then over every weekend while building my business and living in the fast lane. I always chose work and being of service. I was motivated by purpose and felt the financial pressure of living in the expensive Bay Area without any venture capital or a business partner to cushion the path forward.

I loved my work, but after a while it was the only thing I gave my attention to, and things felt very off balance. I will share more about how I turned this around in the next chapter as we explore well-being and self-care routines. But the first step in creating a more joyful and balanced relationship with my work was to acknowledge that I was depleted, my relationships were suffering, and I deserved care. Compassion is one of the biggest catalysts for change, and compassion starts with you. After all, how can you have compassion for others if you don't offer it to yourself?

One way to practice self-compassion on a daily basis is simply to notice when you are not being kind or compassionate with yourself and to label that. For instance, you might be unconsciously repeating harsh or judgmental questions such as *How am I screwing up?* or *Is what I've done enough?*

When you see this, simply label your experience and answer it: *Oh, isn't that interesting* or Other good answers to that voice are *I am doing enough* and *I am being the best that I can.* Then, you can identify which of the four critics from chapter 3 may be present. With this new awareness, you can see how you are tilting toward the negative and replace that thought with one of the self-compassionate statements in the practice exercise that follows.

Inner Game Practice
SELF-COMPASSION EXERCISE

Recall a time in the last few days when you experienced difficulty of some kind. Then, begin the practice by breathing in and out through your heart and slowing down the rhythm of your breath. Invite compassion toward yourself with these simple phrases. If you find it challenging to offer yourself compassion, imagine someone else who feels love for you saying the words:

- This is a hard moment right now.

- May I find ease in this struggle.

- May I find peace and healing.

- May I be kind to myself.

Repeated neural activity—that is, thinking the same thoughts again and again—builds new neural structures, which is why affirmations are so effective.

Another way to bring this practice into your daily life is to begin your day with a phrase such as, *How can I be kind to myself today?*

When you talk to yourself in this gentle and nurturing way, everything feels so much better. When your thoughts are kind, your actions tend to be kinder too. Find the voice and language that feel best for you and notice whether your actions are more caring in response.

The Enemies of Self-Compassion

I often hear from people that a self-compassion practice is difficult, especially at first. People tell me, "Self-compassion feels so indulgent" or "I'm uncomfortable being so nice to myself." So, let's name some of self-compassion's enemies and take a close look at them so this practice of self-compassion can become natural and easy for you.

Self-Pity

One of the main enemies of self-compassion is self-pity. Self-pity tends to exaggerate the extent of your personal suffering—as if you are the only one in the world who is struggling. It can also move you into feelings of victimhood and isolation. Self-pity might sound like this: "I am the only person who knows what it feels like to be passed over for a promotion or transferred to a team in another office."

Self-compassion, on the other hand, allows you to see the commonality of your experience rather than making you feel isolated and disconnected. It might sound like this: "This is a hard moment, and I know I am not the only one experiencing this. Other leaders were moved around and reshuffled too. I am going to be nice to myself during this time, ask for the support I need, and bounce back."

Self-Indulgence

Some people tell me they're reluctant to be self-compassionate because they're afraid they'll wind up letting themselves get away with anything. But self-compassion is not the same as self-indulgence. Self-indulgence might sound like this: "I had a really long week at work and I am going to reward myself by doing nothing all night. I'm going to eat as much ice cream as I want and binge on that new Netflix show." Sometimes you might really need this kind of time to decompress, but when a moment like this arises, you can ask yourself, *What choice supports me in feeling empowered, healthy, and compassionate?*

Compassionate acts toward yourself lead to feeling happy and healthy in the long term. Giving yourself over to pleasure in the form of drugs, overeating, or being a couch potato may feel good in the moment but will ultimately harm you. Healthy activities like eating mindfully, meditation, and finding enjoyable ways to keep your body active and moving will give you the long-term health and happiness you are looking for. We'll look at health and well-being practices in the next chapter.

Self-Criticism

Self-criticism, which we have explored in earlier chapters, is the third enemy of self-compassion. For many of us, it's our default mode—until we learn to be aware of our negative thoughts and cultivate greater self-compassion.

In a discussion of self-compassion, there's another angle of self-criticism to consider. Self-critical thoughts tap into our reptilian brain. When we're being critical of ourselves, we release the stress hormone cortisol that prepares us for fight or flight. So, we can actually think of self-criticism as an assault upon ourselves and an attack on what we perceive as our problem—not exactly a compassionate act. Cortisol has also been shown to increase the amount of belly fat the body stores, particularly in women. And self-criticism keeps us from seeing outside of ourselves to the bigger picture and the connectedness we have with others.

An Exercise in Self-Compassion

Earlier this year, I facilitated an annual leadership team building off-site with a CEO and twelve senior leaders for an organization that is spread out across the US. The CEO had reached out to me because she was seeing the dangerous signs of burnout in herself and the team. The objectives for this training were to increase trust among the team members, develop greater internal and thus external resilience, and, most importantly, create new agreements and accountability for better work-life flourishing and teamwork.

To achieve these outcomes, I introduced the practice of self-compassion as a central pillar to foster greater care among the team and to increase resilience. I'd like to share with you one of the exercises they engaged in.

I asked the leaders to listen to two pairs of statements and then share their experience of what it was like to hear it.

Statement 1. "I can't believe you are so late to this meeting! What were you thinking? Now we are going to look incompetent to the client and our customers."

Here are some of the responses I heard: "I feel angry." "I feel ashamed." "I feel guilty." "I feel stressed." "I feel afraid." "My body feels tense." "I want to leave (flight)." "I want to fight." These feelings are all signs that the nervous system is feeling threatened by criticism.

I then asked them to do some deep breathing and invited them to shake their bodies and release their earlier feelings before I offered up the second statement:

Statement 2. "Thanks for being so prepared and present in the meeting today. I really appreciate all your contributions, attention, and effort with this project. I think our client walked away feeling satisfied with our solutions to their problem."

I immediately saw people relax and smile, and I heard responses like "I felt seen." "I felt acknowledged." "I felt encouraged." "I felt inspired." "I felt relaxed."

Then I asked, "Which statement inspires you to follow and collaborate with me?" Everyone chose statement 2. Then I asked them which way of speaking would likely encourage more teamwork and buy-in. Again, they all agreed on statement 2.

We may think we need to whip ourselves into shape, pull all-nighters, and push until we drop, but this kind of behavior often creates burnout and even disease. Kristin Neff, a psychologist and expert on self-compassion, has conducted a lot of research on the topic and has discovered that when we focus on negative or critical thoughts, our nervous system responds as if we are in danger.[7] We move from a calm and open place to a fearful and contracted place where we don't feel safe and our focus shifts to survival. And when we're in a survival mindset, it is impossible to see the bigger picture, find creative solutions to problems, or create inclusive and safe workplaces.

Compassion amid Negativity

We all experience a variety of difficulties at work, some of which may be the result of a downsizing that triggers suffering—and not only among those who are laid off. Research shows that downsizing also unsettles and distresses the remaining employees, who are concerned about their colleagues' loss and their own job security.[8]

We are all emotionally connected. The scientific literature has identified that both positive and negative emotions can actually spread among people.[9] This phenomenon is called *emotional contagion.* As a working professional or leader in today's increasingly collaborative, team-oriented business environment, you have likely experienced this. For instance, when someone excitedly tells you with a big smile that she just got promoted, you'll smile back. If, on the other hand, your friend tells you his father passed away last week, you will probably feel sad—whether you knew your friend's father or not—because your friend is so sad.

Emotional contagion is a form of social influence that can occur between two people, but it also can happen in larger groups. Think of the collective rage that spreads among a group of workers when confronted with superiors who argue that financial cuts are a necessary measure to make the organization healthy again.

Research has found that you can use your awareness of emotional contagion (also called *mood contagion*) to create more positive team dynamics—dynamics that increase performance and decrease turnover—by consciously managing your own emotions and the emotions you want to spread.[10]

I am often asked by leaders and other professionals, "How do I shield myself from negative energy at work?" The key is to approach each interaction with colleagues and team members mindfully, by taking deep breaths, taking a compassionate stance concerning the difficulties of another, and holding compassionate boundaries for yourself so you aren't rocked by what the other person is going through.

How to Say No with Heart

I was presenting to a hundred employees on the topic of increasing resilience to stress, and during the seminar, I asked the employees what was causing stress in their lives. One of them, a woman named Cheryl, said, "My boss stresses me out." When I inquired further, she told the group that a few times a day, her boss would text her with an alarming tone, such as "Get in my office now!" Cheryl said that when she received these texts, she would immediately freeze up and wouldn't know what to do or say for several minutes. She didn't feel safe addressing her boss when he was furious and she wanted to avoid conflict, so she did nothing.

This became a habitual pattern between the two of them; after each text, Cheryl automatically shut down and waited until she felt ready to respond. This led to more aggressive outbursts from her boss and resulted in a vicious cycle of her shutting down, him blowing up, and, more importantly, Cheryl *not setting compassionate and healthy boundaries* at work—a pattern she recreated when conflict arose at home as well.

How can we tell when we aren't holding compassionate boundaries?

- We say yes when we really want to say no.

- Other people's problems become our priority.

- We neglect important concerns related to home or work.

- We suffer physically because there is so much outward focus that we aren't listening to our self-care needs, like sleep, meditation, exercise, or taking breaks.

- We accept abuse in our relationships.

- We are overly apologetic and don't say what we are truly feeling and needing.

What is setting a compassionate boundary? It is the act of turning toward whatever difficulty you're feeling with compassion and listening to the underlying need that is both compassionate to yourself and the other person involved. How skilled are you at creating healthy and compassionate boundaries? Boundaries define us. They define what is you and what is not you. A boundary shows you where you end and someone else begins, leading to a sense of sovereignty. Knowing what your nos and your yeses are gives you the opportunity to take personal responsibility and practice good self-care, and it will ensure you need less armor because your boundary has been named and asserted.

What are some examples of boundaries?

- skin

- words

- truth

- emotional distance

- geographical distance

Outer Game Practice
CREATING A COMPASSIONATE BOUNDARY

To create a compassionate boundary, follow these five steps.

1. Tune in when you feel a boundary has been crossed. What physical sensations arise in your body? Where do you feel the most physical sensations in your body? What feelings are here?

   I had the opportunity to do some coaching with Cheryl on how to cultivate a compassionate boundary. For her, the physical sensations that were most present were in her hands and her belly. She identified the feelings as anger and fear, but she mostly felt anger.

2. Turn toward your feelings with compassion and kindness.

In order to stay with the difficult feeling of anger, I encouraged Cheryl to talk to her feelings of anger with a kind and accepting tone. Cheryl came up with this statement: "Anger, I appreciate that you are pointing out that my boundaries have been crossed and that you are looking out for me." She was able to say this statement over and over again to soothe herself when she really wanted to push the feeling of anger away.

3. Investigate the needs connected to your feelings.

In Cheryl's case, she was feeling anger, but with mindfulness she was able to watch it, be with it, and in an open and curious way ask it, "What needs to be protected? What needs to be restored?"

4. Acknowledge your compassionate boundary.

Cheryl identified that she needed to feel safe at work, and especially in relationship to her boss's requests. She needed a more calm and respectful communication style so she could be more centered and productive at work.

5. Cultivate a compassionate boundary using words.

Start with the good. (You can use the examples below at work or at home.)

"I appreciate how much you have contributed to the team."

"I treasure our friendship and appreciate how much you have always cared for and supported me."

Cheryl's statement: "I value working with you and supporting our department initiatives."

Be direct and specific.

Cheryl's statement: "I would like for us to find a more effective way of communicating around urgent work tasks."

Lead with compassion.

Cheryl's statement: "I understand that you have a lot of deadlines and need a quick turnaround. I am here to help you, but this is what I request going forward. If you have something that is urgent, please send me an email with what it is, what you need, and the timeline of when I need to get this back to you. I don't want to receive texts from you a few times a day because I feel startled and off balance and don't know how to respond right away. This causes less efficiency for us both.

Consider the other person.

Ask for the other person's viewpoint and invite feedback: "How does this sound to you? Do you have another suggestion that would work better for you?"

Be willing to let go of the outcome.

You may not get what you want, but it is important that you share what is true for you in an authentic, kind, and direct way. If we don't honor our truth, our boundaries continue to be violated and we aren't being compassionate to ourselves or the other person.

Anger, when channeled honorably, can set healthy boundaries without destroying the boundaries of others. This is living with a courageous and compassionate heart, something our world needs much more of. I have seen again and again that one person who leads with compassion at work can create an entire revolution of greater kindness and well-being. Will you be that person today? Yes!

To finish this practice, I invite you to first identify what boundaries you have for work and for home. What are you willing to accept and tolerate and what you are not? We need to know what our boundaries are before we can commit to creating healthy and compassionate ones. Next, go through the exercise above with a person in mind and write out your answers to each of the five steps.

Outer Game Practice
OFFERING COMPASSION TO THE DIFFICULT PERSON

"How can I offer compassion to someone who is difficult?" This is always a hot topic at my trainings and workshops and is one of the most frequent questions participants ask. Here are three things you can do that I have found get results:

- See if you can imagine a friend or loved one having an experience similar to the one this difficult person is going through. Try offering imagined compassion to the friend or loved one and see how this feeling might then transfer to the difficult person.

- Offer a compassionate verbal pat on the back. This soothes the stress of the individual, activates the reward center in the orbital frontal cortex, and makes one feel safe and willing to take risks.

- Make good eye contact and use appreciative speech.

Offering Compassion to the Difficult Person

You can probably imagine that developing the inner game of compassion can translate into an outer game of offering compassion to colleagues and team members who you may find to be difficult from time to time.

Compassion at Microsoft

Satya Nadella, CEO at Microsoft, was ranked by Business Insider as one of the top fifteen CEOs of 2019. Satya believes human beings are wired to have empathy, and that empathy is essential not only for creating harmony at work, but also for making products that will resonate with customers.

You have to be able to say, "Where is [my customer] coming from? What makes them tick?" [. . .] "Why are they excited or frustrated by something that is happening, whether it's about computing or beyond computing?" [. . .] In these times only two things really matter as a leader. The first is that we stand for our timeless values, which include diversity and inclusion. The second is that we empathize with the hurt happening around us. At Microsoft, we strive to seek out differences, celebrate them, and invite them in . . . Our growth-mindset culture requires us to truly understand and share the feelings of another person. Together, we must embrace our shared humanity and aspire to create a society that is filled with respect, empathy, and opportunity for all.

The Power of Compassion

Though he doesn't use the word *compassion,* when I hear Satya speak this way, I hear his compassionate inner game leading the way with love and care, not only for his company, but for everyone in the world. This kind of leadership pays big dividends. Since 2013, when Satya came on as CEO at Microsoft, the company has had a revenue increase of $820 billion (as of November 2018) and is one of the most profitable companies in the world.[11]

A University of Michigan research study found that employees thrive when working in an atmosphere that is "positive and virtuous," and that includes being treated with respect and compassion as well as being appreciated for the value of their contributions. Kindness can reinforce competence and lead to greater success.[12] People who are treated kindly and with respect operate more from their prefrontal cortex—which is associated with nuanced decision-making, creativity, and abstract thinking—rather than their amygdala, which is associated with the fight-or-flight response.[13]

Imagine a World with Enough for Everyone

Now we will explore the third piece of leading from love: *gratitude.* When we are thankful for what we have and share an appreciation for those on the journey with us, we take care of one another, collaborate well together, and draw even more opportunities to ourselves. No matter where our company is as a business or what is happening in our lives, it's important to lead from a place of "enough" versus "not enough." Why? Because the feeling of "not enough" triggers the inner critic and—bam!—we're back in survival mode, as we previously discussed.

Not only is the energy of scarcity contagious, but it does not support positive change. Scarcity looks like layoffs, competition, fear, manipulation, a lack of authenticity, and power struggles. If we're operating with a scarcity mindset, we can't lead from a compassionate, wise, or adaptive place. As a result, our companies and colleagues are going to sink, not swim.

What does scarcity have to do with gratitude? The two are polar opposites. In a scarcity mindset, we can't be grateful or show appreciation for what we have. We believe that "more is better." We compromise quality for quantity. A good example is buying a big house and then not having time to really enjoy life in it because you're working to pay for the home rather than savoring your life. You might have thirty pairs of shoes but only wear five pairs consistently, or you might be constantly scrolling your screens or be in "go" mode, when your soul is craving in-person connection, slowness, and play.

The belief in "more is better," in our companies and our nation as a whole, is the root cause of war, corruption, and exploitation of the Earth and our limited resources. The desire for more oil, more land, more possessions, more technology, and more money is causing economic and ecological debt all around. There is a better way, but it requires a shift in our internal thinking concerning what we judge to be enough on the inside and reflecting that point of view on the outside. A gratitude practice can shift us from "not enough" to "I have more than enough," which lends itself to generosity and an outlook of abundance—both aspects of the inner game of leading with love.

When you or your colleagues are leading from "not enough" or scarcity, everyone feels it. But conversely, when you shift that mindset to one of appreciation, everyone feels it and caring, innovation, and, ultimately, success can flow.

Inner Game Practice
LOVING WHAT YOU HAVE

Here's a practice you can engage in throughout your day to ensure that you don't fall into the scarcity trap.

And it's very simple. Start noticing and articulating everything you love, big or small.

For example:

- I love that I got an easy parking spot today.
- I love that my colleague smiled at me when I got to work.
- I love that I have healthy food available to me.
- I love that I am being really kind to myself today.
- I love that I have a lot of love in my life.
- I love that I am working with bright, incredible people.

When you direct the mind toward what you have, you can begin to appreciate what you have both on the outside and on the inside. Gratitude is powerful because it helps you become aware of abundance in the world. When you come from an attitude of abundance, it's easier to let go of a scarcity mentality because you know you have enough. And when you let go, something better almost always arrives.

Gratitude as a Daily Practice

Aaron Tartakovsky, the cofounder and CEO of wastewater technology company Epic CleanTec, has a daily gratitude practice that he learned from his father that keeps him shining brightly. Aaron is trying to solve a big problem in the world by transforming the way people think about water and sanitation. The problem he has applied himself to is that 2.4 billion people in the developing world have no access to sanitation, and using clean water to flush human waste makes no sense.

Here's what Aaron told me about his plan: "Rather than sticking with the antiquated status quo of flushing all wastewater into sewers and treating it in plants far away, Epic CleanTec is showing how to turn each building into its own treatment plant." His inspiring mission has landed him in the fast lane of entrepreneurship—seeking funding, talking to investors, and finding balance. And appreciation and joy are the qualities he needs to keep his energy and spirits high.

Whenever Aaron notices negative thoughts around the day-to-day work of building a company, he brings his focus back to gratitude. He is grateful for the opportunity he has and his desire to create real change in his lifetime. The world is not a perfect place, he observes, but his purpose is to make the world more humane and to move things in a better direction. He practices the inner game of love by practicing gratitude and highlighting three good things at the beginning and end of every day.

You can see the positive and successful effects of this practice reflected in his outer game. Aaron and Epic CleanTec won a first-place award in 2018 at the Global Climate Action Summit out of hundreds of leaders and businesses with a variety of ideas about addressing problems related to inclusive economic growth, sustainable communities, and transformative climate investments.[14] They were also selected for Fast Company's 2020 World Changing Ideas Awards.[15]

Leading from Love: The Outer Game

We have been developing the inner game of leading from love with loving-kindness, self-compassion, and daily gratitude. Now we will begin to see how leading from love can be expressed in our outer game.

Compassion in Action at Work

Over the last six years, Jane Dutton at the University of Michigan has studied an array of organizational settings, ranging from hospitals to universities to businesses like Macy's and Cisco. She found that when employees who are distressed receive acts of compassion—for example, emotional support, time off from work, or flowers—they demonstrate more positive emotions such as joy and contentment and feel a greater commitment toward their workplace. And here's a remarkable finding: these results were found regardless of whether employees received compassion directly or merely *witnessed* it.[16]

Stress inevitably spills into the workplace, contributing to lower productivity and higher health-care costs, but with a dose of compassion in that environment, people are far better able to bounce back from the ups and downs. Kindness and empathy build strong teams and collective intelligence. Here are some tips to help you bring more compassion to your workplace.

- Take notice of your fellow coworkers' psychological well-being. For example, if someone has experienced a loss, such as a divorce or death in the family, reach out to that person and offer your help.

- Encourage more positive contact among employees and display it yourself. Many workplaces have meeting spaces that can be used for informal gatherings. See if you can encourage weekly or monthly meetups to create more opportunities to notice when people need help or support.

- Invite greater authenticity and open communication into the workplace. If you can keep the lines of communication open with respect and kindness, you allow for time to talk about situations that may call for attention or empathic connection.

- Take on the perspective of the other person by reminding yourself, *This person is just like me.* This is also known as cognitive empathy, or simply knowing how the other person feels and what they might be thinking. This type of empathy can help when negotiating with or motivating people to give their best effort.

- Start with self-compassion. Remember, in order to truly have compassion for others, you must have compassion for yourself.

Gratitude in Action at Work

Research shows that gratitude drives "prosocial"—kind and helpful—behavior more than happiness or empathy. People who are grateful are more likely to volunteer to take on extra work, take time to mentor coworkers, be compassionate when someone has a problem, and encourage and praise others.[17] In one study, practicing gratitude was found to produce higher levels of positive emotions that are beneficial in the workplace—such as joy, enthusiasm, and optimism—and lower levels of destructive impulses like envy, resentment, and greed.[18]

The practice of gratitude is foundational in the leadership and development courses I offer at workplaces. Here are a few ways that I have shared with my clients to express gratitude at work:

- **Offer gratitude at the beginning and end of a meeting.** Offering appreciation to others, in group settings and individually, is one way to express gratitude. Such acknowledgment is often welcome, but not everyone likes public praise or can receive it in the same way, so be mindful of how and when you do this. Try approaching individuals whose work you appreciate after a meeting ends to personally express your acknowledgment and gratitude.

- **Aim for quality, not quantity.** Be specific about what you are giving praise or acknowledgment for. It should be much more meaningful than, "Great job." For example, "Megan, I appreciate how you thought outside the box and tailored the company's mission in the social media marketing campaign. Nicely done!"

- **Find the silver lining.** When I'm supporting organizations that are going through a major change, I often do an exercise where I invite participants to find the silver lining of the situation. Nobody wants layoffs, budget cuts, or extra work, but I ask them, "What is the learning or the hidden gem here?" This question invites a growth mindset amid the challenge. It also brings a mindset of seeing each other in the same difficult situation, rather than being in competition. It's we, instead of me.

Companies that Care

The organization Great Place to Work uses a list of criteria to rank the top fifty companies in the US that care. In 2018, Salesforce ranked number one on this list. (In chapter 8, we will look at how Salesforce demonstrates caring not just about their employees, but about the world, as demonstrated by the ways in which they give and some of their sustainability commitments.) At the end of the day, leading from love is the way forward.

Businesses that have a social purpose and want to make a positive contribution to society are being invited to tackle some big problems, so creating a culture in which love, compassion, appreciation, and gratitude are firmly embedded is essential. It has been shown again and again that employees who feel cared for report higher levels of satisfaction, invest more in their workplaces, and reciprocate care around them.[19]

Leading with Love Recipe

- I have everything I need.
- I am kind to myself and others.
- I am a compassionate leader.
- I am grateful for all I have.

Creating Your Recipe for Well-Being
Healthy You, Healthy Company, Healthy Planet

> Our food system is flawed, with preservatives, chemicals
> being present in whatever we eat. Today's youngsters are
> aware of this. We are at the beginning of a paradigm shift.
> Not eating meat is not a personal choice, it's a social choice.
>
> —DAVID YEUNG, founder and CEO of Green
> Monday, Green Common, and OmniFoods

Because their identities and values are so closely tied to their work, entrepreneurs, leaders, and hard-charging professionals can be at serious risk of burnout. But you can't bring your whole self to work or shine your greatest gifts as a leader if you're running on empty. In this chapter, I'll lay out options, point to research, and give examples from other countries for how to live and work with zest and balance. I will be incorporating the inner game qualities you cultivated in chapters 1 through 4 to examine what it means to have good self-care, focusing on the link between well-being and burnout while prioritizing how to take the best care of your body. We'll also explore the ways in which creating sustainable business practices supports individual and collective well-being at work and in the world.

Since there are no one-size-fits-all prescriptions for health and vitality, this chapter will inspire you to develop your own recipe for well-being by looking at how some established conscious leaders create routines to feed their body and soul. And speaking of well-being recipes, we'll even visit countries where people savor life to the fullest, and we'll look at how taking care of your body is intrinsically linked to the health of your workplace and the planet.

Staying Sane in the Fast Lane

My mission at REBBL is to ensure that this company and the foods we make have a positive and transformative effect at every level, on every human being that we touch.

—SHERYL O'LOUGHLIN, former CEO of Clif Bar & Company and REBBL and cofounder of the Women on Boards Project and the J.E.D.I. Collaborative

As the former CEO of Clif Bar & Company and REBBL, Sheryl O'Loughlin learned how to stay sane in the fast lane of leadership by prioritizing self-care. She has strengthened her inner game of well-being by meditating most days of the week, getting active in nature first thing in the morning, eating a healthy diet, and spending a lot of time with her family and circle of friends. She also checks in regularly with her intensity level because she can often go from zero to one hundred in a flash when she feels passionate about work. Sheryl has learned that she must honor and listen to her body.

Sheryl is also a cofounder and chairwoman of the Women on Boards Project, which works to increase the number of women on company boards, and she is a cofounder of the J.E.D.I. Collaborative (which stands for Justice, Equity, Diversity, and Inclusion). One of her stronger motivations as a conscious leader is to link sustainability and social justice with business. As a result, REBBL started off as a cause looking for a company, not a company looking for a cause.

Nourishing Your Heart and Soul

Jen Freitas works as the director of people learning and engagement at Clif Bar & Company, where she started as a kickboxing instructor twenty years ago. After moving her way up to managing the company's wellness program, she received another promotion into her current leadership role. Jen told me that she was looking for an opportunity where she could bring her whole and best self to work and align her personal and professional values. After she heard the company's founder, Gary Erikson, speak about the "five aspirations" (Clif Bar & Company's values and mission statement), she knew she had found her people.

The company's five aspirations are:[1]

- **Sustaining our people.** Working side by side, encouraging each other, our company is our people.

- **Sustaining our communities.** Promoting healthy, sustainable communities, locally and globally.

- **Sustaining the planet.** Conserving and restoring our natural resources; growing a business that operates in harmony with the laws of nature.

- **Sustaining our brands.** Creating brands with integrity, quality, and authenticity.

- **Sustaining our business.** Building a resilient company, investing for the long-term.

Jen believes that the spiritual, physical, social, and emotional aspects of life need to be expressed at work. Since Clif Bar & Company hires employees whose personal and professional values are aligned with their mission, it has a low turnover rate of between 3 and 5 percent—*whoa!* Clif Bar & Company does more than chase long-term profits: it invests in sustaining people, community, its brands, and the planet. I hope Jen's story and the brand's mission inspire you to find balance in your "soul's calling" for what matters to you personally and professionally. Once you do, you'll find it easier to lead from your heart in a sustainable way.

Personally, I really enjoy Clif Bars, especially when I'm hiking in the beautiful Bay Area, because they give me the energy I need to keep trekking. But sometimes we can turn to food when what we're really hungry for is something else entirely. The word *hunger* normally refers to the desire for food, but the truth is that our heart and soul need nourishment too. One question I ask myself and my clients in order to find that deeper wisdom is *What are you really hungry for?*

The answer is different for each person at every moment, but it's rarely about fried food or sugary drinks. You might have a hunger to play, to take a dance break or a nap, to speak up about a cause that matters to you, to sing, to volunteer, to go for a walk in nature or your urban park, for dark chocolate, for intellectual stimulation, for affection. The better we are able to identify our true hunger, the better we will be at satisfying it.

Inner Game Practice
MINDFULNESS OF PHYSICAL HUNGER

Oftentimes we mistake emotional hunger for physical hunger. If we want to be healthy, it is important to be mindful of these two types of hunger and how to satisfy them. The sensations of physical hunger include emptiness in the belly, lightheadedness, low blood sugar, a desire for food, or fatigue. Emotional hunger is the desire for something that may comfort or soothe an emotion (such as sadness, boredom, loneliness, or anxiety) but that has nothing to do with physical hunger. I find that when I push away or deny what I'm truly hungry for, I end up not performing my best. But when I honor what I'm truly hungry for, I am so much more present, connected, and focused.

In order to get better acquainted with the experience of physical hunger and fullness, I invite you to join me in the following exercise. Please read through it first, and then try it.

- Find a comfortable seated position. Close your eyes.

- As you sit, feel your body's contact with the floor or the chair. Notice where your hands are resting.

- Now start to notice the rhythm of your breath. Begin to breathe slowly in and out through your belly.

- Try placing one hand on your stomach, and as you breathe in, feel your stomach rise. As you breathe out, feel your stomach fall. Practice deep belly breathing for one to three minutes.

- After a period of breathing in this way, bring your awareness to the physical sensations of your belly.

- On a scale of 1 to 10 — 1 being you don't feel any hunger and 10 being you feel very hungry — ask yourself, *How hungry am I? What are the physical sensations that tell me I am hungry or not hungry?*

- Disregard any thoughts about when you last ate or what time it is now. Just listen to your body.

- Based on your hunger level, what amount of food do you need right now? What would be the most nourishing food or combination of foods?

- After you have taken in that information, return your awareness to your breath and your body, and open your eyes.

Paying attention to your hunger before you eat might inform you of when to eat, how much to consume, and most importantly, what might be most nourishing for you at this time.

Say No and Listen to Your Yes

Cultivating healthy boundaries is part of a good recipe for well-being. Leaders generally want to say yes; we are helpers by nature. The word *yes* has a forward momentum in the body. *Yes* propels us into the next thing, while *no* is a backing up, a slowing down. It requires energy and a pause to listen to your no and then align your actions around it.

You may have a history with the word *no*. Perhaps there were times in your life when your no wasn't honored, listened to, and respected, or you saw nos not being acknowledged or respected in those around you. As a result, you may feel more hesitant to say no. Following, is an example of the power of no that you can hear and feel in your body.

Start Now

It is important to act together, but you don't have to wait on anyone to begin to be the change. You can start now.

—RHEA SINGHAL, founder and CEO of Ecoware

Ecoware is India's largest sustainable food-packaging company. Rhea Singhal started Ecoware at the age of twenty-eight because she felt a big no to all the plastic that was being used in India, a country that has no formal waste segregation system—all trash goes into one bag and then into a landfill. In 2019, India's population was 1.3 billion people and its waste was still not being recycled. The country generates nearly 26,000 tons of plastic waste every day, making it the fifteenth biggest plastic polluter globally.[2] Ugh!

Rhea maintains that it makes no sense to invest in organic food if the plate or bowl you're putting it on is not safe and clean. And if there are no composting or recycling systems in place, massive amounts of plastic contaminate the water and soil. Rhea felt the need to create something that was easy to eat from and safe to throw away. This was her soul's calling, and when she got behind her no, she aligned with her yes.

Ecoware's products are 100 percent sustainable and compostable, and they are made from the agricultural waste of wheat, rice, and sugarcane. Once they're used, they will biodegrade safely in soil within ninety days. Amazing!

Rhea cultivates her inner game of well-being by walking for forty-five minutes to an hour a day. She has also developed stronger boundaries between work and home. By incorporating "unplugged" time, she's found a balance between switching on and switching off. Learning to say no so she can prioritize her yes is new to her, but Rhea is cultivating her inner game of well-being and you can see it in her outer game as she leads the way in supporting greater well-being and health in India and by being part of the solution in the disposal of plastics.

How to Say No

When we say no, we are expressing our belief in the abundance of the universe; that what is meant to be will come to us—not without effort and action, but it will come. When we say no, we give our yes so much more power. A simple exercise to strengthen your no is to identify five ways you will say no in the future and write them down.

When someone asks something of you, one way you can make space for no is by saying, "Can I get back to you on that?" By giving yourself time to think about the answer, you have time to reflect on what you really want. We'll look at how to name, claim, and lead from yes in the next chapter.

There is actually a relationship between nutrition and the choice between saying yes and no. When we aren't well-nourished, we are more susceptible to burnout and stress, which hurts our ability to be mindful in making the choice. When we feel full, on the other hand, we are more resilient in the face of stress and tend to have more ideas and energy to share.

Inner Game Practice
EMBODYING YOUR YES AND NO

Most of us have become expert jugglers at work. We feel pressured to make quick decisions while supporting numerous projects and people. Navigating these tornadoes of activity can sometimes leave me feeling disconnected from myself. So, I developed a way to better handle the pressures in my work and personal life; to slow down so I can hear my yes and no. This exercise will support you in hearing them clearly, too. You will need about five to ten minutes of quiet to experience the benefits. Ready? Here we go!

- Think about a time when you wanted to say no to something or someone but instead said yes. Imagine this experience in full color. Who was involved?

- Now go back in time and give yourself permission to say no. Say it out loud. Is it a little no or a **big no**? Where does the no live in your body—chest, hands, belly, throat?

- Now honor your no fully. How does it feel to say no instead? If your body could make a physical gesture of no, what would that look like? Is your hand facing away like a stop sign? Make the gesture now. After you've gotten the physical sense of your no, shake it out.

Now let's shift gears.

- Imagine a time when you didn't acknowledge your yes. For example, you really wanted to go to a certain event or wanted to choose something different than those around you but thought it would be easier to go along with the group instead. Go back to that situation and give yourself permission

> to name and claim what you want. If it feels right, say yes out loud. "*Yes*, I want this!"
>
> - How does the yes feel in your body? What physical sensations do you experience? What emotions come up—joy, excitement? Find a movement for your yes. Are your hands up in the air? Are you nodding your head and laughing?
>
> Don't be embarrassed; it's all welcome here. Once you get connected with your yes and no, you'll stop overcommitting and you'll be empowered to implement and enjoy healthy work-life boundaries.

Burning the Candle at Both Ends

Elon Musk, CEO of Tesla, said that the most difficult year of his life was the year he and his team built the Model 3 on very little sleep, which resulted in some erratic behavior. Entrepreneurs, leaders, and those in startup cultures face intense cycles of business development, marketing, and funding, all while creating a unique product. The result is high levels of stress, which trigger high cortisol levels—the perfect recipe for burnout.

The higher our levels of cortisol, the more impaired our decision-making and our ability to manage our emotions will be. High levels of stress can also compromise our attention, health, and well-being. Research reports that employees lose the equivalent of 31.2 working days per year due to health-related issues. Mental and physical health account for more than 84 percent of the direct effects on productivity loss.[3]

Chronic workplace stress can result in burnout. The World Health Organization describes burnout with these symptoms: feelings of energy depletion or exhaustion; increased mental distance from one's job, or feelings of negativism or cynicism related to one's job; reduced professional efficacy and lack of motivation; difficulty with sleep; lowered immune system.[4]

A startling conclusion of a Centers for Disease Control and Prevention study was that your immediate supervisor is more important to your health than your primary care doctor.[5] People don't leave organizations; they leave their managers or supervisors. Jeffrey Pfeffer, professor of organizational behavior at Stanford Graduate School of Business, puts it this way:

> Workplaces are making people sick (along with the managers who also do the same thing), adversely affecting people's ability to work. Interventions to improve health that do not attack the root causes of ill health are going to be less effective or ineffective.

The inner game of well-being starts with you as the leader. It's prudent to focus on health as an important imperative and to show the cost of ill health and its effect on productivity—but it's even more critical to look at the impact on people's well-being.

Your Recipe for Well-being: The Resilience Factor

As I mentioned in an earlier chapter, the first five years after I started my business, I worked too much. I was in a constant state of giving and serving. I was not very good about receiving in my personal life to refill the well. For those first five years, the vacations I took were silent meditation retreats or professional learning and development workshops. These gave me a boost to keep going and serving, but what I really hungered for was rest and play. I developed burnout and knew I needed to work smarter, not harder, to create compassionate and healthy boundaries around work so I could have more "Carley time."

In the process of creating these changes, I developed a course on being a resilient leader and manager, called Flourish. My strategies for resilience include delegating more, stating clear expectations of what I want my team to do, working in my zones of genius rather than trying to do everything, and enjoying a "slower" work week in which I often work from home on Mondays and Fridays and do more intense work meetings midweek. I like to call this the "yoga" week because I picture an image of yoga's Downward-Facing Dog, a triangle-shaped pose that showcases Monday's slow start (hands on the mat), Wednesday's peak (hips up), and Friday's return to a slower pace (feet on the mat).

I've also developed "Carley time" to include nurturing personal relationships, a daily yoga and meditation practice that I've maintained for twenty-plus years, and a once-a-month float in a sensory deprivation tank. I enjoy a mostly plant-based diet, and I prioritize exercising in nature and walking barefoot on the earth every day, a practice known as "earthing" or "grounding." I also like to take spontaneous dancing and singing breaks to increase my creativity and sense of joy. I've discovered that unless I'm taking in love for myself through good self-care, I have less love and energy to give. So, whenever I get off balance, as I often do, I gently forgive myself and find some movement to re-ground myself, and then get back on track.

Well-being is key to preventing the burnout that plagues so many leaders, entrepreneurs, working professionals, and managers. The first step in tackling burnout is to understand your energy levels. I developed this upcoming assessment when I needed to nurture my well-being, and now I invite you to use it as a self-assessment to cultivate greater well-being. Where are you now—a level 1, 2, or 3?

Inner Game Practice
WELL-BEING QUIZ

- **Level 1, Low energy.** You feel stuck and unmotivated, and you likely have limiting beliefs. Often, something difficult that you didn't expect or prepare for takes the wind out of your sails. But with the right resources, you can bounce back.

- **Level 2, High-level destructive energy.** You have been going full steam ahead for some time and are responding mostly from fight or flight in all areas of your life. You lose your cool and engage in unhealthy habits such as not getting enough sleep or drinking too much caffeine.

- **Level 3, Restorative or reflective energy.** This energy level allows you to be in flow, working at a more contemplative and slower pace while being productive and performing well in life. Attaining and then sustaining this kind of energy can best be achieved by engaging with the various pillars of well-being each day, whether this takes the form of meditation, exercise, a long walk in silence, or just unplugging.

To get to level 3 you need to master:

- **Healthy Food.** What foods bring you up or down?

- **Exercise.** What are you doing each day to move your body?

- **Sleep.** How much sleep do you need to flourish?

- **Meditation.** How often are you taking time to disconnect and just be?

- **Playtime.** What activities are you doing for the mere joy of it—activities where you don't need to accomplish anything?

- **Love, Community, and Relationships.** Do you feel you have a strong connection with friends, community, or family to support you through the ups and downs of life? If not, you'll want to put some additional energy into your relationships.

Cultivating your inner game of well-being supports you in being a conscious and resilient leader. The fuller you are on the inside, the more engaged and reliable you will be for your team and organization. If you start to feel burned out, go back to these questions and reassess what is out of balance. This is a good way to start, and it's usually the first tool I use when coaching executives and leaders around working smarter, not harder.

Plat du Jour

In the summer of 2018, I took a month off for my first sabbatical. France felt like the perfect place to nourish my well-being and discover how another culture works, lives, and plays. *C'est la vie!* I enjoyed a month of savoring life and saying yes to living with more ease and enjoyment—total soul food. While traveling in France, I discovered that almost every restaurant offers a *plat du jour* during lunchtime, usually consisting of a main dish, a coffee, and sometimes a small starter or dessert. It costs between ten and fifteen euros and is often paid for by one's employer; in France, employees receive compensation or coupons to order a nice lunch, then come back relaxed and ready to focus again.

In the US, our relationship with food, especially during the workday, is the opposite. Many startups and technology companies cater lunch or offer free or subsidized food in the company cafeteria, but most companies don't offer this perk. But the catering and free cafeteria food doesn't seem to be the answer—just ask any Google employee about the "Google 15," the weight people gain during their first year because of all the free catered food.

Most white-collar workers still eat at their desks, shoving food down while trying to multitask. Workers who take a lunch break often busy themselves with their screens while they eat instead of savoring and digesting their food. When we are using technology, our sympathetic nervous system (fight/flight/freeze) is activated, which isn't conducive in allowing our parasympathetic nervous system (rest and digest) to come online and support us in enjoying and digesting our food.[6] There's also the increasing trend of working from home, where it may feel even more trying to find a regular, healthy eating schedule amid child-care tasks and virtual meetings across time zones.

While I was in France, I found that the culture and design of the French workweek supports a life in which people can lead and live with more ease and joy. French employees work an average of thirty-five hours a week and have six to eight weeks of paid vacation, depending on their job and industry. The workday in France normally starts around 9:30 a.m., with most people taking a one- to two-hour lunch break. That kind of rhythm in the workplace is much more conducive to well-being than the current US model, and I think the sooner we can move to more flexibility in our work schedules and a prioritization of quality work time over quantity, the healthier our workforce will be.

HUMAN BODY=EARTH BODY

Your body is a really good model of the Earth, which makes it the perfect illustration to describe why prioritizing people and planet with a socially responsible business model and mission just makes sense.

The Earth is mostly water and so is your body, 60 percent, in fact. Your body is a living system made up of interdependent living systems, and so is the Earth. Your circulatory system is the "rivers and oceans" that move oxygen and nutrients through the body and cool you down. This is why you sweat, and it's why there is more water in the atmosphere and melting of ice as the planet's temperature rises—to cool the planet down.

Your digestive system and kidneys are just like the nutrient cycles of the planet, cycling energy into a usable form. Toxins like high-fat and sugary foods clog up digestion just as toxic substances disrupt the Earth's nutrient balance. Your respiratory system is like a forest that helps circulate oxygen and carbon. Even the musculoskeletal system mirrors the geological structures of mountains, valleys, and ridges.

The way we take care of our bodies, what we eat, and our consumption habits affect our individual bodies and, more importantly, the planet body. We want clean water, air, and soil, but if we aren't taking care of the planet, how can this be supported? Rivers are part of the planet's circulatory system. Like our body's circulation system, the planetary one doesn't work very well when it's clogged. Enter: plastic. Right now, it's polluting our entire world. Scientists have found that 90 percent of all seabirds have plastic in their stomachs, and fishermen find plastic inside many fish and other types of seafood.[7] Microplastic is now found in everything from beer to drinking water, from seafood to human stool, which means plastic is also in our bloodstreams, lymphatic systems, and livers.[8] If we are disconnected from our bodies, we are likely to be disconnected from our impact on the Earth body.

The Benefits of Spending Time in Nature

As you will learn in the following pages, spending time in nature and regularly connecting to the Earth offers many benefits including improved concentration and mood, lower inflammation, decreased stress, improved circulation, enhanced short-term memory, and greater creativity. As I mentioned earlier in the chapter, I enjoy the practice of earthing. I also do forest bathing—spending time among the trees, simply listening and sensing—a few times a week, and I feel the benefits of both practices immediately afterward. Let me take you on a quick tour of a few of the studies that support the varied benefits of spending time in nature.

- In a study at the University of Michigan published by *Psychological Science*, students were given a brief memory test and then divided into two groups. One group took a walk around an arboretum, and the other took a walk down a city street. When the participants returned and did the test again, those who had walked among trees did almost 20 percent better than they did the first time. The group who had taken in city sights did not consistently improve.[9]

- A 2010 study observed that "green exercise," or activity in nature, substantially improved self-esteem and mood. If there was water close by, there were even greater benefits for mood and self-esteem.[10]

- A study sponsored by the United States Environmental Protection Agency found that the average American spends 93 percent of their time indoors.[11] In industrialized societies, we rarely go barefoot outside or even wear natural leather shoes that would allow us to absorb the ground's energy. For the last fifty years or so, we've been walking in plastic-soled shoes that act as a barrier to the earth's energy. It is projected that by 2050, 66 percent of the world's population will live in cities, with fewer opportunities to be in nature.[12]

These are some of the ways we have become disconnected, ungrounded, and out of touch with the Earth. To reconnect to your body with the greater Earth body, I would like to invite you into a practice I first began teaching at Stanford University. During the exercise, the students and I walked barefoot on the lawn outside a lecture hall.

Inner Game Practice
LISTENING TO THE EARTH

This practice will help you reconnect to your roots. Head outdoors to a park or another natural setting and find a spot where you can move mindfully in nature for fifteen minutes. Leave your technology behind, or put your phone or device on airplane mode. If you can, find a space that is relatively quiet, with little stimulation or distraction.

Take off your shoes and socks and walk slowly on the ground. As you walk, notice what comes in contact with your feet. Is it grass? Dirt? Mud? What is the texture—wet, hard, dry? Feel the coolness of the earth.

- Invite your feet to rest on the earth. You can even dig your feet and toes into the ground if you want to.

- Notice the sensations in your physical body as you arrive here in nature.

- Breathe in slowly and breathe out slowly for a few minutes.

- Allow yourself to release all thoughts, feelings, and tension into the earth as you breathe in and out.

- Let your belly become soft and let your shoulders and upper body relax. As you walk, I invite you to do any kind of movement that comes to you so you can shake off the day.

- Continue to explore this natural setting by becoming aware of the sounds around you, the temperature of the air on your skin, the colors you see, and the smells you notice.

- See if you can allow the energy from your head to drop down into your belly and pelvis. You can imagine the energy being lowered so you can ground more into your body and the earth body.

Listen to the sounds that greet you. Breathe in a slower rhythm and notice the intricate details around you, from the smallest ant to the swaying of leaves. Notice the trees around you, some of which may have been in this natural setting for dozens or even hundreds of years, and acknowledge their resilience and grace. They have been through many ups and downs and changing seasons—through the dying off of winter and the rebirth of spring, through storms, and even through fires. There is harmony in the natural world that is balanced, intuitive, graceful, and allowing.

It feels quite the opposite of the go, go, go mentality of our "always-on" culture, doesn't it? While you are in nature, reflect on what you love about it, and feel the nourishment from this experience. What are the things the Earth gives you that you feel grateful for? Clean air, clean water, clean soil, food? Receive this nourishment. If there is anything you're holding that feels too much to carry, like sadness, fear, rage, or uncertainty, you can place both hands on the Earth and give your emotions to her. She will carry them for you.

When your retreat into nature winds to a close, take as much time as you need to slowly come back and awaken to the present moment.

As a way to bring this inner game practice into your outer game daily life, you might acknowledge your gratitude and appreciation for what the Earth and nature provide every day. For example, I feel especially grateful for clean air. See how this inner appreciation of the Earth could translate into actions that support nurturing the planet through what you choose to eat and buy.

> A question you can ask the Earth in nature is "How can I serve and protect you for the greatest good?" Listen to the Earth's answer and notice what inspired action might come from listening. With awareness, we can make different choices that are more aligned with our wisdom and values. I've heard Van Jones, a CNN political contributor, say, "It's in the convergence of leaders becoming socially responsible and spiritual people becoming leaders that humanity is awakened."

Be Mindful of Consumption

As I am writing this on September 1, 2019, the Amazon is ablaze with forty thousand fires, and Iceland has held a funeral for its 700-year-old glacier, Okjokull, or "Ok" as the glacier was known. For the people mourning Ok, the funeral was not just a symbolic display, nor did they grieve it just because climate change is a threat to their well-being. Their grief comes from a place of deep relationship. They held a funeral because they knew their glacier was once alive. Their world has "livingness."

Scientists tell us we have entered a new epoch, the Anthropocene, an age marked by the human-caused decline of ecosystems. A great dying of species is upon us. Our relationship with the beings and cycles and systems of life on this planet has been deeply ruptured. There is a feeling that business as usual is over, and it's my belief is that leaders and businesses can create solutions to heal the rupture.

An important place to start being part of the solution, is to be mindful of consumption. Our society often conditions us to look outside of ourselves for happiness. The notion that this moment is not okay encourages "wanting" minds, which can lead to overconsumption.

Our culture feeds greed by teaching us that more is always better. This is demonstrated by the greedy thirst for power, success, profit, and gain throughout the world. The focus on fossil fuels for our increasing energy needs, the collapse of our environmental systems, and the emergence of climate chaos are the direct result of a human mind that sees everything as an object to be owned and exploited or simply taken for granted. Climate change is being driven by the actions of humans and is one of the most pressing topics of our time. But by training the mind to see that our desires are fleeting, we can make wiser choices.

Being *aware* that desire is a normal part of being human without *acting on* every desire gives us more freedom to respond, not react. When we feed thoughts of greed, they cultivate more greed. But letting go of such thoughts gives rise to generosity. To support us in a simpler life and a more sustainable workplace and environment, let us practice how to be mindful of consumption.

Inner Game Practice
BEING MINDFUL OF DESIRE

In this practice, we will cultivate "enoughness" and choose generosity. To increase your motivation to be mindful of consumption, take on this practice as a way to benefit all beings, at work and in the world. The best way to begin is to come into a relaxed and comfortable seated position. Close your eyes or shift your gaze inward so you can bring your attention inward. Feel your belly rise and fall. Place your hands gently on your lap and feel your feet making contact with the floor.

- **Bring to mind a beautiful object you would love to have.** Something you want—that you *really* desire.

The first thing that comes to mind is the best. Imagine you are at a store or an art gallery and you see the object there before you. Go ahead and admire it for a few minutes. As you focus on it, notice any feelings of desire. How does this feel in the mind, the body? Imagine yourself *almost* having what you want. Feel the tension there as you notice the feeling of desire in your mind and body. Notice what arises now that you are so close to having your desired object. It is almost within your grasp.

- **Then, let it go.** Take a deep breath and let those feelings go too. Embrace the object for what it is. You don't need to own it in order to feel complete, to be enough, or to be satisfied.

- **Now shift your awareness to something that you feel grateful for in your life right now.** It could be your health, your loved ones, the appreciation of the present moment—just notice how this feels. Take a minute to feel and receive this abundance.

- **Then, let go of this image.** When you let go, how does it feel in the mind and the body?

Reflect on the ways in which these experiences felt different. Compare how you felt in your mind and body when you were grasping for something compared to when you knew you had enough. Say this sentence and listen to the words: "I have everything

> I need right now." Focusing on gratitude for what you have diminishes the thoughts and actions of greed and desire, which cultivates the ability to become mindful of your consumption.

Savor and Sustain

Food production takes up almost half of the planet's land surface, and 40 percent of the Earth's land is given to agriculture.[13] Did you know that 60 percent of all the mammals on Earth are livestock? The other 36 percent are human, and only 4 percent are wild animals. This means that the harmony between species is lessening while farming animals for food is increasing.[14]

As the global population grows from seven to ten billion people and socio-demographics change, there will be increased pressure on the world's resources to provide not only more food, but different types of food.

Increased demand for animal-based protein, in particular, is expected to have a negative environmental impact, generating greenhouse gas emissions and requiring more water and more land to produce. Avoiding dairy and meat is one of the most effective ways we can be mindful of consumption and reduce our environmental impact. We need to create and choose sources of protein that are more diverse and sustainable. Research prepared by the University of Oxford's Oxford Martin School shows that balancing meat consumption with alternative sources of protein can lead to significant health and environmental benefits.[15]

Several of the leaders profiled in this book choose to eat a mostly plant-based diet. For example, David Yeung eats a vegan diet and has created businesses to support the rise of plant-based eaters. Yeung came across the Meatless Monday movement, an American concept that urges citizens to give up meat for one day a week, and started the Green Monday spin-off in Hong Kong alongside a vegan grocery store called Green Common.

My diet is 90 percent plant based; I eat mostly fruits, veggies, beans, nuts, sustainably caught fish once a week, and some really good raw cacao (Honey Mama's is my favorite).

One of the most important things we can do to nourish and care for our bodies and the planet is to become mindful of our food choices. We can do this by eating a "flexitarian" diet and limiting our meat consumption to a small number of meals per week. It has been found that people who eat primarily plant-based foods are the healthiest.[16] By being mindful of what we are eating, we can live in harmony with our available resources, each other, and the planet.

Young people are already going this route. Thirty percent of young Swedes are already eating more plant-based food in order to reduce their environmental footprint, while in Denmark 8 percent of Millennials identify as flexitarian.[17] Over forty countries are incentivizing the habit of committing to one meat-free day a week, including South Africa, Brazil, Germany, and Belgium.[18]

Well-Being at Work

There are many ways we can engage with well-being and self-care at work. In the next few sections, I will share some game-changing outer game practices that will help you shine in your pursuit of well-being.

Encourage Sustainability Goals at Work

A business that puts people and planet first realizes that in order to do innovative and effective work, basic requirements like clean air, water, and soil—all of which benefit from reducing waste—must be met. When you commit to less waste, it positively impacts your individual well-being, the well-being of everyone at work, and the world. Actions include participating in trash cleanups, living a more minimalist lifestyle, sharing rides or biking rather than driving a car, and replacing meat, dairy, and eggs with plant-based foods.[19]

Outer Game Practice

SUSTAINABILITY AT THE OFFICE

I suggest setting two short-term sustainability goals (for a period of twelve months) and two long-term sustainability goals (for thirty-six months) with your team to shift the company culture. Make them quantifiable and actionable.

Here are some easy-to-implement ideas:

- Replace vending machine drinks in plastic packaging with beverages in cardboard-based containers from smart packaging brands like Tetra Pak, which uses completely renewable products and packages.

- Limit business air travel to reduce carbon impact. Instead, use Zoom for team meetings, coaching, and goal setting (OKRs—objectives and key results) with remote and distributed teams.

- Install trash bins that separate regular trash, compost, and recycling.

- Host green events such as Bike to Work Day, Earth Day, or Zero-Waste Holiday.

- Encourage and incentivize carpooling, using public transportation, working from home, and add bicycle parking options to lower your carbon footprint.

- Support and/or start a green team where employees can come together to plan sustainable events or initiatives, such as cleaning up a beach or planting trees.

SUSTAINABLE SOLUTIONS

Salesforce is a sustainability trailblazer. With Dreamforce, the four-day annual event that Salesforce hosts, the company brings 170,000 people to San Francisco to learn about technology, small businesses, climate change, and to encourage diversity and belonging at work. At Dreamforce 2019, Marc Benioff, cofounder and CEO of Salesforce, announced that in 2020 the company will donate $17 million to align with the seventeen worldwide Sustainable Development Goals the United Nations has established and will encourage one million volunteer hours of Salesforce employees to go toward these SDGs.[20]

According to the UN website "The Sustainable Development Goals are the blueprint to achieve a better and more sustainable future for all. They address the global challenges we face, including those related to poverty, inequality, climate change, environmental degradation, peace, and justice. The seventeen goals are all interconnected, and in order to leave no one behind, it is important that we achieve them all by 2030."[21] (See a complete list of these seventeen goals in chapter 8, where we will talk more about sustainability and conscious leadership.)

I was invited to attend Dreamforce in 2018 and 2019, and I found it focused on sustainability in many intriguing ways:

- The lunches at Dreamforce were 100 percent beefless, conserving an estimated ten million gallons of water.
- All lunch packaging for the conference was 100 percent compostable.
- The goody bags given to attendees were made out of cloth and contained reusable glass water bottles.

- Recycling and compost stations were provided.

- Earthforce, a green resource group of more than seven thousand Salesforce employee volunteers, sifted through segregated waste to make sure that trash was put in the appropriate place.

On another note, the Salesforce Tower is the second tallest building in California and the tallest building in San Francisco. Many of its forty thousand employees work there. The design and architecture of the building took into consideration the severe droughts California has suffered, and a blackwater recycling system saves 7.8 million freshwater gallons a year. Keep shining, Salesforce!

Redesigning Work

One area where workplaces are already making changes to support well-being (and attract the best talent) involves space and time: the design of the workplace and the workday. More and more companies are promoting practices like desk sharing, working from home, increased focus on results (over clocked hours), and more flexible ways to structure teams. In other words, they're allowing people to be in charge of their own lives. It doesn't matter so much anymore when, where, and how people work—only that they get good results.

Economists like Stanford University's John Pencavel have identified what they call a "productivity cliff." Pencavel found that productivity drops quickly after a workweek exceeds fifty hours and drops off a cliff after fifty-five hours. Exhausted employees are not only unproductive, but they are also more prone to costly "errors, accidents, and sickness." Furthermore, reams of research suggest that people who work long hours are not more productive or successful than people who work shorter hours and lead more balanced lives with family and other interests outside of work.[22]

Business leaders talk a lot about work-life balance, but rarely are any substantial changes put into practice in the US. We work among the longest hours of any advanced economy, but we are not the most productive per hour. We talked a little about the French approach earlier in this chapter. Luxembourg, Norway, and Denmark have some of the most efficient workers and they work very differently than employees in the US. With a twenty-nine-hour workweek, Luxembourg largely allows workers to organize their work hours to make time for outside commitments and interests. All employees have a minimum of five weeks of paid time off per year, and workers must be compensated for overtime. Norway, at twenty-seven hours, has one of the shortest workweeks, while Denmark consolidates thirty-five hours of work into four days.

When we look at the data, it's clear that productivity increases as hours spent in the office decrease. In August 2019, a Microsoft subsidiary in Japan closed its doors every Friday, leading to a *40 percent* increase in productivity compared to August 2018.[23] Full-time employees still received their full pay despite the reduction in hours. In addition to making employees happier and more focused, the company conserved valuable resources and reduced its impact on the planet; the number of pages employees printed decreased by almost 60 percent and electricity consumption was down by 23 percent.

I believe it is the responsibility of business leaders to initiate change to benefit people and the planet. Between the statistics on productivity and the fact that Millennials place such a high value on flexibility and work-life balance, my forecast is that over the next few years more companies are going to explore the thirty-hour workweek. In addition, embracing a remote, distributed-team approach to work will offer corporations added benefits. Cost savings in the form of office space and the use of supplies and furniture is one benefit, but that's not even the best part. Redesigning work to accommodate a more remote workforce will support happier and more engaged workers who experience greater well-being. This will in turn increase people's sense of belonging and performance, as a diverse talent pool work together from all over the world. We can create an agile workforce and empower employees to do their best work because they have the freedom and flexibility to work in a way that fits their lifestyle and family.

We Are the Planet

In closing, it's time to pay attention to our bodies and feed our true pangs of hunger. The more nourished we feel on the inside, the less we will consume mindlessly and the more we will have to give, supporting our capacity to lead and inspire. However, our personal well-being can't be fostered in a vacuum. We have to align our outer game with ways of protecting the well-being of ourselves, our workplaces, and our planet.

Well-Being Recipe

- I say no with ease.

- I spend time in nature to nourish my body and soul.

- I have short- and long-term practices in place to reduce, reuse, and recycle.

- I am happy, healthy, and inspired.

Shining Your Authentic Light
Embracing All Your Parts

> When you feel you've cleared all the muck away so you can
> see the business risk clearly, there's something else you need
> to do: you need to look at yourself clearly.
>
> —SHERYL O'LOUGHLIN, former CEO of Clif Bar &
> Company and REBBL and cofounder of the Women on
> Boards Project and the J.E.D.I. Collaborative

Leading from vulnerability and courage is vital to being a conscious leader. Scott Kriens, whom we met in chapter 1, puts it this way: "Leading with authenticity means giving others permission to be vulnerable and more open." An authentic leader demonstrates to the team how to open to vulnerability— "the birthplace of love, belonging, joy, courage, empathy, and creativity," according to inspirational author Brené Brown. Your ability to have courageous conversations, what I call "brave exchanges," and create belonging will never exceed your ability to authentically shine your unique light.

In this chapter, you will grow your inner game of authenticity by listening to your inner voice, honoring what is most important to you, loving and embracing all parts of you, and then owning the freedom to choose your path. This might take the outer game form of speaking out against the norm or choosing a different route. The more you embrace all of your parts—the messy, shy, negative, positive, strong, and brilliant ones—the better you will be able to forgive yourself for the times you lost your way and celebrate the times you succeeded on your journey.

What if you knew that the way to access the best in yourself and shine your unique light required you to face your unique darkness? What if you knew that your greatest power could be found in the parts of yourself that you believe are the most shameful? As you learn to accept and care for the parts of your psyche you have long rejected, an extraordinary thing can happen: those darker aspects will become allies in your development as a leader and will even become guides. Embracing these traits on the inside will allow you to lead from authenticity on the outside. And that encourages deeper connection, confidence, teamwork, vulnerability, forgiveness, compassion, and belonging for your team and in all your relationships.

You bring powerful wholeness to work and the world when you embrace the dark and the light.

I have coached and supported some brilliant people who identify as women, men, and LGBTQIA+ in my career, and I've found that even the most successful and accomplished leaders and managers have a hard time recognizing and owning their unique power. As we've seen, we often get caught up in pleasing others; saying yes when we really want to say no, not giving ourselves permission to ask or go for what we really want, and feeling like we don't even deserve what we really want.

Our challenge in the workplace is to remain aligned with the goals of the company we work for without losing ourselves. Without losing *me* to support the *we*. Showing up authentically depends on feeling a certain degree of trust and safety on the inside so we can create a culture at work where the sharing of feelings, needs, and honest thoughts is invited and honored without fear of reprimand or punishment.

Getting Real

Adrian James, the cofounder and president of Omada Health, models authenticity at his startup by demonstrating empathy and kindness. He genuinely cares about his team members, and he knows that when he's open about what's going on with his internal experience, he's creating an environment of psychological safety for others. He knows that authenticity can be cultivated one on one, in small groups, and at larger roundtable meetings whenever managers are being "real" with one another. He gives people permission to speak honestly and informally, and he has seen that when managers do this, the attitude ripples down from the top. For example, when someone points out a problem or an uncomfortable situation, Adrian often says, "Thank you for speaking up." He knows it's important to acknowledge and appreciate people taking the courageous step to have brave exchanges and that this increases safety and trust.

Let's look at what it really means to be authentic—to be true to ourselves in the way we lead at work. There are four key elements:

- Developing kindness toward and acceptance of all parts of yourself
- Developing your capacity to forgive—both yourself and others
- Modeling authenticity with others
- Bringing your "wholeness" and whole self to work

What Prevents Authenticity

Brené Brown offers my favorite take on authenticity: according to her, authenticity is a *daily practice*. Choosing authenticity means cultivating the courage to be emotionally honest, to set boundaries, and to allow yourself to be vulnerable. Being authentic is one of the fastest ways to create psychological safety in the workplace.

Psychological safety is the sense that we can share our feelings, beliefs, and experiences openly with others at work without fear of reprimand, losing status, or punishment. Studies on psychological safety conducted in a collaboration between Google and the Massachusetts Institute of Technology found it to be *one of the most important factors* in creating successful teams and, thus, high-performing, innovative organizations.[1] Psychological safety supports moderate risk-taking, speaking your mind, and creativity.

What blocks authenticity for leaders or entrepreneurs is the feeling that we need to show others we have it all together and all figured out. If we don't, the thinking goes, other people, including investors and team members, might see us as weak or won't be inspired to follow our lead. This is understandable when entrepreneurship and leadership are about selling a vision. If you're the one establishing the vision of your company and you're perceived as weak, how are you going to sell that vision?

The conflict between the desire to save face and "being real" is universal. We all experience this conflict. Why? Because we fear that speaking up will threaten our status in the workplace—or even get us kicked out of it (which was a threat to our very survival when we were living as hunter/gatherers in more primitive environments and communities). If we fear that what we want to express will not be well received, we are disempowered from owning our truth, and that inhibits us from sharing our contributions and unique light.

As you work through this chapter, you'll develop an understanding of what it means to own your truth and shine. I can't promise that you'll never struggle with being authentic again or that you'll never waver in speaking up amid uncertainty or the fear of reprimand—as I said, we all experience conflict in this area. But with time and practice, you will learn that self-expression creates more safety and trust than self-protection does. That's why I support leaders in owning their truth by embracing all their parts.

Own It

There are two essential steps to owning your light and power at work. The first step is to see the *dark aspects of yourself*, such as blind spots and projections, with loving awareness. For example, do you have someone in your life who really triggers you? Perhaps it's someone you experience as being narcissistic and very selfish. Each time this person "takes up all the space," makes it all about them, doesn't ask about you, or offers no compassion or empathy, you feel frustrated and resentful inside. The moment when you notice your heart starting to race with anger, it's time to look at yourself and ask, *When am I selfish?* The more you can acknowledge and embrace your own selfishness, the less anger you will experience when you see that selfishness in others. In the next section you'll find an exercise to guide you in looking at yourself when triggers such as these arise.

The second step to owning your light and power at work is to *acknowledge all your shiny parts*—but it's important to balance this appreciation by embracing your weaknesses too. For example, your shiny parts might include beauty, kindness, grace, playfulness, humility, intelligence, and resilience. Yet you may also at times be impatient, judgmental, self-righteous, or stubborn, perhaps especially when you care deeply about something.

Like you, I have many parts. I try to embrace and accept all of them, with (I hope) grace and humility, because I acknowledge my innate goodness and that my deepest motivation in life is to be of service and support the greater good. To fully love and embrace your teammates, colleagues, and superiors, you have to love and embrace every part of yourself. The following practice aims to guide you past fear and into courage so you can embrace all of yourself and bring your wholeness to work and the world.

Inner Game Practice
EMBRACING ALL OF YOURSELF

Exercise 1: Dark and Light

As I outlined, there are two essential steps to cultivating your inner game of authenticity. The first is to witness your blind spots and projections through the lens of self-love and self-awareness. The beloved spiritual teacher Ram Dass calls this perspective *loving awareness*. Loving awareness means that wherever you look and *whatever you touch with awareness, you love*. Ahh, doesn't imagining that make your whole body relax? When you activate the inner game qualities of awareness (chapter 1) and love (chapter 4), you can lead from who you are instead of who you think others want you to be.

- Find a space where you can be quiet for several minutes.

- Take a few deep belly breaths in and out.

- When you are ready, imagine yourself standing in the middle of a circle of people who are supportive of you. They can be family, friends, colleagues, pets, guides, divine beings—anyone you like. As you stand in the circle, imagine that everyone around you is beaming feelings of love and acceptance toward you. Feel yourself soaking up all the good stuff.

- Now allow yourself to acknowledge a part of yourself that you struggle with or have disowned. It could be impatience, arrogance, shyness, fear of being unlovable, or anything else you might harbor shame around. Let's label these the *dark parts* of you; the shadow. There's nothing to feel ashamed about; we all have dark parts.

- If you're uncertain of what quality to focus on, an easy way to identify a fruitful one is to bring to mind a person in your life who triggers you. What is it that you do not like about them?

What quality in them do you struggle with? What is the trait that is the most challenging about this person? For example, let's pick someone at work: a colleague who always turns in her reports late. You notice feelings of anger or discomfort each time, as well as your own judgment about her behavior and lack of accountability.

- Now it's time to grab your metaphoric hand mirror, hold it up in front of you, and ask, *In what ways am I like this?* Or you can be more specific about the aspect that bothers you the most: *In what ways am I sometimes not accountable?* When you are aware of these parts of "the other" in yourself, you will likely feel some discomfort in your body or even an *ouch!* feeling. This is your opportunity to be with all that arises with loving awareness.

- Invite this dark part of you to come forward and allow it to be here for a few minutes. Acknowledge it, aloud or silently, with lovingkindness and presence. It might sound something like, *I can be selfish. I can be arrogant. I can be impatient.* The more openly you can acknowledge you have these shadow parts, the more you can integrate and embrace them and avoid being triggered by people who mirror your dark side.

- *The truth is that we need all our parts in order to shine our greatest light and potential in the world.*

- Now it's time to shift your awareness. Take a deep breath in and a deep breath out and get ready for the second half of this exercise.

Next you're going to focus on where you shine. These are the qualities you identify in yourself as positive or as strengths. These qualities describe your unique light.

- Choose one of these qualities and say it, aloud or silently, for a few minutes. This might sound like, *I am strong. I am smart. I am compassionate. I am resilient.*

- Invite this part of yourself to come into awareness with love and presence. Allow yourself and the circle of supportive beings you brought in at the beginning of the meditation to embrace it.

After you have acknowledged the dark and the light, strengthen your inner game with an affirmation such as, *[Your name], I embrace all of you. I love and accept all of you. I choose all of me. I am loving awareness.* As you repeat the affirmation, notice how you feel in your mind, heart, and body. Choose a phrase that resonates with you and repeat this affirmation as many times as you need to.

Now you can reinforce the practice and take this affirmation "to go" by integrating it into your daily meditation practice or calling on it multiple times during the day, especially when you feel like you aren't being very compassionate or kind to yourself.

Exercise 2: Body Integration

A very effective way to embody your whole and best self at work and in life is to get fully into your body. You can use movement to play with the polarity of your dark and light parts.

There are endless variations on how you might choose to do this, and I encourage you to experiment to find what works for you—you might even choose something different each time you do it. Here's one option to try:

- First, identify a dark part and a light part within yourself that you want to work with during this exercise.

- To embody your dark part, start by standing with your feet together. Then, come into a fetal position so your body is curled into a ball. Your fists are closed, and your heart is armored.

- To move into the lighter part of your being, say something to yourself about that light part. For example, if one of your light parts is resilience, you can say, *I am a strong, adaptive, resilient person.* Then, bring your feet hip-width apart, open your hands and arms at both sides, stand up tall, lift your chin, and take some deep breaths. Feel the power of the pose. If you'd like, you can add a sound, such as *ham,* a syllable known to activate the throat chakra, which is helpful for speaking one's truth and perfect for cultivating the inner game of authenticity. *Sat nam* is another affirmation you can say. *Sat* means truth and *nam* means "identity." Put together, *sat nam* translates into "Truth is my identity."

During this exercise, play with the movements you have selected. Toggle back and forth, moving from contraction to expansion and back again, noticing what movement helps you embody these shifts from dark to light. In the middle place between contraction and expansion, simply "be," standing tall and shining in who you are.

These two exercises will help you integrate and embody all parts of yourself, so strive to employ your whole mind, body, and heart during this process. As you attain a feeling of full acceptance in your inner game, your outer game will reflect this in how you present yourself as a leader—including how you walk, talk, and carry yourself in the world. You may not notice changes right away, but remember that developing any new pattern requires patience and persistence. In time, you'll feel more comfortable embracing and showing your whole self.

A thriving business is typically the result of trust and safety in the workplace. The more you develop the inner game of authenticity by embracing all your parts, the more authentic you will be as a leader or manager and the easier it will be for you to create a culture of trust, safety, forgiveness, and belonging.

Show Up and Share

Scott Kriens, the cofounder of 1440 Multiversity whom I mentioned earlier, has found that meditation enables him to listen to his heart and body by quieting his mind. "We've been told, from our early days, to go out into the world and discover who we are and what we want to be," he said. "There's a lot to learn out there, but only when we look within will we find the answers we are looking for."

Scott's definition of an authentic person? Someone who shows up and shares what *they* believe instead of what they want *you* to believe.

Inner Game Practice
FOUR QUESTIONS TO FOSTER YOUR AUTHENTICITY

Here are four questions designed to help you get to know and embrace all sides of yourself. To get started, find some space to be and reflect. Allow yourself to see and feel whatever arises with kindness and understanding.

1. What are the parts of you that you don't share at work? Why?

2. What is something you are grappling with that feels scary, painful, or embarrassing to say?

3. What really matters to you in how you show up at work?

4. What reflections have you been given, as a person and a working professional, about your strengths or about areas you could further develop?

Write your thoughts in your journal.

The last question refers to feedback you may have received from peers, direct reports, other senior leaders, and even yourself. I have found this kind of "360-degree feedback" very valuable in my work with professionals in helping them grow, learn, and develop into the best leader or manager they can be. Understanding how others perceive you helps you avoid your blind spots.

It isn't always easy to leave the inner critic at the door when you become aware of your weaknesses in this way, but this is where a growth mindset comes in. You can incline the mind toward seeing this new information as a way to learn and grow instead of seeing yourself as flawed or "not enough." On the contrary, if we let the inner critic lead, we may reject parts of ourselves, and this creates a wound of unworthiness. To fill or heal this wound, we often look outside of ourselves for acknowledgment and/or validation, and this can be a never-ending cycle. Once we accept all that we are, we strengthen our inner game of authenticity by turning toward ourselves with love, compassion, and forgiveness, another powerful practice we'll explore further along in the chapter.

Try on New Behaviors

If we are to embrace all of our parts and live authentically, we have to learn how to change our behaviors. This can require us to do the opposite of what we have been doing, so it can feel uncomfortable and messy at first, but you will reap the benefits. Try practicing one new behavior for a week and remember not to expect huge changes right away—establishing a new pattern requires patience and persistence. Following is a sampling of behaviors that may be new to you and that will help jump-start your authenticity. You can substitute other behaviors in order to address the four questions you just answered.

- Say no instead of yes.

- Ask for what you want, without guilt, without apology. Just ask and then be quiet and sit with any discomfort that may emerge as you wait for a response.

- Invite support. Ask for help.

- Be playful.

- Do the opposite. If you normally talk a lot, share the airspace and give others the floor to speak. Or if your preference is to be quiet, challenge yourself to speak up.

- Stop trying to make things happen—put in less effort. Practice patience and persistence.

- Take more time to gather information before making a decision.

If fear arises, lean into it and shower yourself with lovingkindness. You might tell yourself, *I am lovable just for being me* or *I love and accept all parts of myself.* Tap into your inner cheerleader, the voice that encourages you every step of the way and loves you unconditionally, regardless of performance.

Authenticity in Action

I remember talking with Amy, a leader I coached, about the practice of authenticity, and she shared the toll that not being authentic had on her marriage.

> So, here's how it goes for me. I feel afraid to share something with my husband—I'm afraid he will disconnect from me. I'm afraid of his reaction. So, I tuck it under the rug. Then it arises again a few days later and I put it off again. My resentment builds and I start to feel disconnected from him.
>
> After a week of this, a wall begins to form between us. I even start to feel less connected to myself. He notices that I seem distant and asks what's wrong. My feelings have built up so much that I explode in a fit of anger and frustration. We get into a fight. All of this could have been prevented if I had just had the courage to share what I was really feeling and needing that first time I felt afraid.

Easier said than done sometimes, but so true. How do we develop this courage?

Inner Game Practice
AUTHENTICITY IN ACTION

Before we try to be courageous in our interactions with others, we need the courage to understand ourselves and what's important to us. The following inner game practice focuses on cultivating this understanding.

Find a quiet space if you can and take out a journal. Take a minute or two to breathe and tap into your center. Now think of a recent experience you had with a partner, friend, family member, or coworker where you wanted to be authentic, but weren't. Imagine pausing at the height of this interaction and asking yourself the following questions:

- What am I afraid would happen if I shared my thoughts and feelings with this person right now?

- How will I feel if I don't share them?

- If I weren't afraid, what would I most want to say to this person right now?

- How can I be even more open and vulnerable?

When I asked Amy these questions, she responded this way:

What are you afraid would happen if you really shared your truth with your husband?

"I'm afraid he won't love or accept what I want to share, and this will create conflict and he will become defensive or distant, or both."

How will you feel if you don't share this?

"Angry at myself for not sharing my feelings and needs. Angry at him. Down the road, resentful, or aggressive, or distant with him."

If you weren't afraid, what would you most want to say?

"Well, in the situation the last time this happened, I'd say, 'Sweetheart, I know your mother is coming for a visit next month, and I would prefer she stay with us for three days instead of a whole week. I understand you have a close relationship with her, but I often feel so overwhelmed by her demands on top of our full work schedules. I feel the duration of her visit puts a strain on our relationship and makes it difficult to enjoy the time she's here. I feel it would be easier and more enjoyable for everyone if she spent half the time with us and the other with your sister, or maybe there's a way that you can take some time off to spend with her by yourself?'"

How can you be even more vulnerable and open?

"I can be honest and say, 'I felt scared to share this with you and I want us to have a good visit with your mom. I don't know what the solution is, but I'd like your support and I welcome your thoughts. Could we come up with a plan for her visit that works for both of us?'"

It takes emotional resilience to be able to feel and embrace all our scared and vulnerable parts so we can have authentic, brave exchanges like this one.

I shared this example of a conflict at home with you because it's true that what happens at home goes to work and what happens at work goes home. Part of embracing all of who we are is being able to bring our whole self forward in both places.

Leading from the Inside Out

As leaders and managers, it's important that we're the first ones to model how to be authentic in the workplace. Josh Tetrick, cofounder and CEO of JUST, Inc., and I talked about his process of hiring for resilience and developing a resilient culture by leading with authenticity. First and foremost, Josh makes it clear in his communications what he cares about most. JUST's mission is to increase the consumption of plant-based foods and to reduce animal and forest degradation. Josh has found that the more confident he is in his mission and who he is, the more vulnerable and humble he can be when he makes mistakes.

He now recognizes that when JUST was just starting, he projected more self-assurance—to the point of arrogance—than he really felt because he wanted to sound more confident than he really was. But as he's stepped into leading, he's learned that he's good at some things and not so good at others, and he knows and accepts that. This frees him from feeling the need to overcompensate and allows him to be his authentic self.

Josh let me in on some of the things he says when interviewing new hires: "This is the kind of company we are—this is the mission. If you gave me a 100 percent chance to get bought by an investor or a 20 percent chance to stay in the ring and get closer to achieving our mission, I'd choose the 20 percent probability."

Then he tells potential new hires he wants them to ask themselves if they're willing to get dirty, step into the unknown, and stay focused on that mission for the long haul. Sharing his truth upfront in this way weeds out people who aren't the greatest fit. He takes the same approach with investors.

Josh also asks job candidates questions that are designed to assess their resilience, because he's found that those who are the best fit for his company are inherently resilient. Josh offers a great example of cultivating a strong inner game of authenticity and sharing your truth and confidence as a leader on the outside.

Leading from authenticity sometimes means leading from vulnerability. According to Brené Brown, vulnerability entails uncertainty, risk, and emotional exposure. As a leader, you have the opportunity to create conditions that support naming the fears that come up around being vulnerable. Once they're named, you can get past fear to the place where courage arises and encourage more confidence, teamwork, and connection.

Be Forgiving

We can't expect perfection—either in ourselves or our businesses. That's why, in order to bring our whole and best self to work and the world, we need to learn to forgive our own imperfections and those of others. Deciding to forgive is making the decision to free ourselves from taking personal offense and blaming, which keep us mired in a cycle of suffering.

It's easy enough to say, but forgiveness is not easy. It often involves many feelings and layers. Forgiveness is also finding comfort with the word *no*.

Inner Game Practice
"DEAR SELF, I FORGIVE YOU"

For this practice, I invite you to write yourself a letter of forgiveness, beginning with the statement "Dear Self, I forgive you."

If you're wondering what you might need to forgive yourself for, here are some common categories: all the times when you didn't speak up; when you

---

didn't take good care of yourself; when you didn't give yourself permission to name and claim what you wanted; when you didn't maintain healthy boundaries and said yes when you wanted to say no.

If you need a little more guidance, you can listen to the forgiveness audio at my website.[2]

If you are struggling to forgive yourself (or another), you can add a—yep, you guessed it—loving affirmation. Try one of these or make up one that feels true to you:

- I am a loving person and deeply want the best for others. I forgive myself.

- I am willing to try to forgive myself.

- I forgive myself . . . I forgive myself . . . I forgive myself.

Leaders and managers often share with me that they have found self-forgiveness to be a powerful practice. Leaders and managers who are women often feel more pangs of guilt than men when they leave their children and families for work. Rhea Singhal, whom we met in the last chapter and is the mother of two small children (ages eight and ten), is no exception. She practices forgiveness for that and forgives herself for all the things she didn't know in her business's early years. As a result, she is able to move between work and home with better compassionate boundaries.

The first feeling you might experience when you explore forgiveness is anger. Anger alerts us that a boundary has been crossed. Anger shares important information: that we want protection from disrespect, harm, and reprimand. But this doesn't mean an angry response, such as shaming or blaming, is called for. To create a culture of safety, trust, and belonging, it's important to instead cultivate compassion, understanding, and forgiveness.

Forgiveness is an inside job—you have to start by forgiving yourself and then move on to others. We often need to forgive ourselves for those times when we didn't listen to, protect, or take good care of ourselves. When we can acknowledge the times we failed to honor ourselves, we gain the opportunity to offer ourselves compassion and gratitude for the lessons we are learning.

Forgiveness Is a Choice

Forgiveness is a decision based on motives, and it's also a choice about resilience. Deciding to forgive increases resilience in a relationship, while choosing not to diminishes resilience.

Forgiveness researchers Michael McCullough and Everett Worthington often distinguish the act of forgiveness as separate from pardoning an offense, dismissing it, or opening yourself up to further abuse due to your choice of forgiveness.[3] Instead they define forgiveness primarily in terms of shifts in motivation. They write:

> We define interpersonal forgiving as the set of motivational changes whereby one becomes (a) decreasingly motivated to retaliate against an offending relationship partner, (b) decreasingly motivated to maintain estrangement from the offender, and (c) increasingly motivated by conciliation and goodwill for the offender, despite the offender's hurtful actions.

Make no mistake: forgiveness doesn't mean that the person who caused the hurt necessarily gets invited back into your circle. It simply means you are choosing to forgive the wrongdoing, the action. Personally, I have forgiven someone in my life, but based on their level of consciousness, personal responsibility, and development, I chose not to have any connection or contact with them and have stated this boundary either implicitly and/or explicitly. To move into this kind of action, I took the time to feel the disappointment, grief, loss, and anger—whatever feelings needed to be felt, and then moved into a space of acceptance and letting go.

You can also decide whether a person you forgive for a certain action is someone you wish to have in your life. In this case, you can instead practice holding a compassionate boundary: I have compassion for myself and compassion for you, and this is my boundary of what is an acceptable way of relating and what is not acceptable.

The Path to Forgiving

We may be more ready to forgive than we think. In most cases, we just need to know the tools required to do it. I've found, personally and professionally, that the most difficult things we experience—loss, abuse, betrayal, discord—are also filled with chances to grow. It's not just a cliché that we should be thankful for challenges that help us grow—it's the truth.

I first started teaching forgiveness at Stanford University several years ago with my friend and colleague Fred Luskin, who did his dissertation at Stanford on forgiveness and also wrote a bestselling book on the subject called *Forgive for Good: A Proven Prescription for Health and Happiness.*[4] During my years teaching solo and with Fred, and through my own personal experience, I developed the following practice.

Outer Game Practice
THE PATH TO FORGIVING

To get started, identify someone at work who you have difficult feelings for and see if you can walk yourself through the following six steps:

1. Acknowledge and turn toward all your feelings about this person's behavior and how it has pushed a boundary or doesn't make you feel respected or acknowledged.

2. Offer compassion and understanding to these hurt feelings.

3. See the bigger picture. Recognize that your primary distress is not the person's behavior. It's the hurt feelings and the stories you have created about what is happening. Ask yourself, *What is my story?* and *What is the story of the other person?* Ask yourself, *Can I bring in a sense of compassion for myself and the other person?*

4. Try not to take it personally. Usually when a person is violating a boundary in some way, it's more about them than it is about you. It is important to name what is and isn't okay with yourself and this person, but try not to hold onto the offense. Let it in and then let it go.

5. Identify anything you can appreciate about the situation or the other person. Can you bring in a sense of gratitude for some kind of silver lining? Even a small sliver will do.

6. Take back your power with care. Accept full responsibility for your life. Give up on expecting things from other people. What can you do for yourself that will give you what you need? You might want to create stronger boundaries or have a courageous conversation in which you assert your limits. Put your energy into what you can do for yourself without trying to change the other person. I've found this phrase to be helpful in this step: "I care about this situation, but it is the way it is."

Because it's so important, let me emphasize one thing again: forgiving doesn't mean forgetting or pardoning an offense. It means *acknowledging* the grievance, *feeling* your feelings, putting appropriate *boundaries* in place, *letting go*, and *moving on*. It means recognizing the imperfection in everyone, including yourself. We all consciously and unconsciously hurt one another, and if we can accept that this is part of relationship, we can forgive more easily. You can choose to keep someone you have forgiven in your life or establish a new boundary that keeps them out of it. When you honor yourself, you will make the best choice.

Forgiveness in Action at Work

So, what does forgiveness look like in the workplace? When we cultivate the practice of forgiveness on the inside, this essential part of building our inner game of authenticity is reflected on the outside. Let's look at an example of how this works:

Nancy is a leader at a large bank and works out of the Portland, Oregon, office. Deirdre is a vice president in the Omaha, Nebraska, office. The majority of their communication takes place over email or phone.

Nancy has noticed that Deirdre is often very short with her, and that she gets defensive when Nancy asks a clarifying question. Nancy also senses that Deirdre doesn't have any particular interest in getting to know her. As a result, their phone calls are short and to the point, and when she speaks up, Nancy often feels rejected. Over time she has found herself asking fewer questions of Deirdre and has gotten to the point where she's begun to dread their calls. She's always received great performance reviews when it comes to teamwork, but she feels a lot of anxiety every time she has to interact with Deirdre.

Nancy acknowledged during our conversation that she had created a story about Deirdre that was getting in the way of working smoothly with her. It was also zapping her confidence at work, particularly in relation to Deirdre, but not exclusively.

I encouraged Nancy to bring compassion and gratitude to the situation, both of which facilitate forgiveness. I then asked her to tell me what she learned when she did. This is how she described it:

I can feel compassion when I see that I am imperfect, and that she is too. I think Deirdre may be having some difficulty at work or maybe at home that's causing her stress. I don't really know what is going on in her world, but I'm going to believe that her intentions are likely good. I still don't like the way she interacts with me, but this new story helps me understand what her internal experience might be, and it makes it easier to forgive her brusqueness on the phone. Plus, I have to admit that I am not always the most pleasant or talkative person to be around when I feel stressed, and maybe she's picking up on that too.

As far as gratitude goes, I decided that before I get on the phone with Deirdre, I'm going to ask myself what I could be thankful for about this relationship. I've already discovered that I'm thankful that she supports me in any decisions I make and that she doesn't micromanage me.

All this inner game work has taken down the temperature for Nancy. She's less stressed when she has to speak with Deirdre now, and she realizes she doesn't need to take Deirdre's behaviors as a personal insult. They might never become best teammates, but Nancy no longer dreads their phone calls.

The essence of forgiveness is the notion that we are all imperfect. Because we will never be perfect, forgiveness is an essential part of creating safety, trust, and resilience in our relationships at work. We all have challenges and difficulties with others from time to time—that will never change—and the more forgiving we can be, the more of our energy and power we can liberate to focus elsewhere.

The story above reflects the fact that many of the skills that support forgiveness are those we have already been fostering in this book: mindfulness, emotional intelligence, compassion, gratitude, and authenticity.

Bold Humility

In every conversation I've had with Sheryl O'Loughlin, former CEO of REBBL, I feel struck and deeply touched by her enthusiasm and authenticity. I once asked Sheryl what supports this authenticity, and she told me that "bold humility" was one of her core values. Sheryl described it this way:

At REBBL we were constantly learning, and it is a messy journey. We have to have the humility to say, "I don't know everything." We've been taught to believe that asking for help is a sign of weakness, but it's really such a strength because not only does it offer us as individuals a chance to learn, but it helps the whole team. It's a way of saying, "I care about this so much that I need you to help me so I can help the team."

The Psychology of Safety

Business is all about relationships. We can make or break a sale, develop an outstanding product or a flop, or expand or downsize as a result of the quality of our business relationships and corporate culture. And all of these outcomes depend on how safe we feel about bringing our whole selves to work. A thriving business is usually the result of a foundation of trust and safety in the workplace culture; the creation of an environment where people can be their authentic selves.

So, what is trust? Psychologists and researchers John and Julie Gottman have written extensively on the topic of trust in relationships. To them, trust is evident when someone can bear witness to another person without getting defensive when they are showing negative emotions. The Gottmans have also found that the number one predictor for success in a relationship is a ratio of five expressions of appreciation to every one of criticism.[5]

Outer Game Practice
THE BAROMETER OF SAFETY

The following questions will help you and the team gain an understanding of everyone's sense of safety in the workplace. Indicate agreement or disagreement with the statements by choosing one of the following responses: Not at All, Moderately, or Definitely.

- If I am about to make a mistake, someone on my team will tell me and give me an opportunity to change course before I get punished for it.

- I feel safe discussing mistakes and problems with my coworkers and supervisor.

- My coworkers will not consciously behave in ways that undermine or discredit my efforts or contributions, privately or publicly.

- My team and I take the time to prioritize speaking about conflicts in a timely manner; we don't avoid them for weeks or months.

- My team and I create shared agreements for how we want to work together when conflict arises, so we have a protocol for how to move forward with ease, authenticity, and resolution.

As we learned in chapter 4, a foundation of trust and safety can be built in the workplace by practicing gratitude. While each person is unique in regard to what combination of words and actions help them feel safe, there are commonalities. That's why when I consult with leaders and organizations on the principles of creating a culture of belonging, I start with a few standard questions to take the pulse on their current state of psychological safety.

I encourage you to ask these questions quarterly—and anonymously—to get the weather report on trust in your workplace. It will help you gauge whether psychological safety is rising or falling amid whatever ups and downs the organization may experience over time.

Outer Game Practice

CREATING THE SACRED WORKPLACE

After you have assessed the team regarding organizational safety, you can nurture this safety by creating agreements that support people in bringing their whole selves into the room. I think of this as creating a kind of "sacred space" wherever workers gather. The space can be built by having your team or organization develop a few statements supporting safety that everyone can agree to. Once you have those, you can ask someone to read them at the beginning of each meeting.

Following are some examples of statements that I have found to build safety in various workplaces. There are many choices here, but you only need four or five to create an agreement of safety. Choose the ones that work for you or create your own.

- I show up as a caring person.

- I will be patient and allow people the time they need to communicate.

- I come here with the intention to learn rather than debate.

- I will lead with inquiry and curiosity, not judgment and blame.

- I will value and encourage diverse opinions in the discussion.
- I will lead with empathy and seek positive intent.
- I will remember that I come into the room with my own unconscious biases.
- It is okay for me and others to be silent and not answer questions that are uncomfortable.
- I will respect the confidentiality of the room.

Then, you can end each meeting with these affirmations:

- You are safe here.
- You belong here.
- Your voice matters.
- You have a place here.

It takes very little time—just a handful of seconds—to reinforce common agreements such as these. And doing so can powerfully shift everyone's sense of safety for the better. I also encourage the leaders and managers I serve to bring in similar agreements of psychological safety into one-on-ones with their direct reports. This supports greater connection, efficiency, and candor.

Outer Game Practice
ZOOM IN/ZOOM OUT

Once you have nurtured safety in your team by creating sacred space, you can begin to model authenticity with them. Here's where the "Zoom In/Zoom Out" practice comes in. The Zoom In is a chance for everyone in the meeting to share what is happening for them right now. I find this practice to be especially important in creating more connection among remote and distributed teams.

As the leader and manager, it is important that you step into the ring first and share with honesty and vulnerability. So, start the process yourself, and keep it to one to two minutes per share so everyone has a chance to speak and listen. Using a timer supports focus. The practice itself is simple: just name your current experience. Avoid referring to anyone else in the room—this is all about you revealing your own experience. Your Zoom In might be any of the following:

- Sharing an internal state, such as feelings of excitement or dread.

- Reporting on an internal goal. For example, state that you're coming to the meeting with a desire to listen better. Or with the intention to practice better emotional intelligence by really paying attention to your own experience while staying connected to what might be happening for others.

- Speaking authentically about something challenging or wonderful that is happening on the home front; for instance, that you are about to celebrate your fifth wedding anniversary or that your mother-in-law has dementia and this has been a struggle for you.

Checking in authentically at the beginning of a meeting invites everyone to bring their whole self to work. Then, at the end of the meeting, just before saying your closing affirmations, it's time for the Zoom Out practice.

Zooming Out is a way for everyone to share a reflection that encompasses the whole of the meeting and allows you to end the meeting well. Your Zoom Out could be any of these:

- An expression of excitement, appreciation, or other feelings. For example, "I am appreciating [identify something you appreciate] about [a person or the team] right now."

- A request for others to support one another through encouragement or accountability.

- A practice you plan to continue to develop over the week.

The Zoom In/Zoom Out exercise allows people to practice focusing alternately on the "me" and "we" of the group, which creates a strong sense of community and belonging.

Integrating the Me and the We

Throughout this chapter, you have looked at increasing your authenticity from the inside out by owning your whole, messy, brilliant self from lots of angles. You have practiced showing up, telling the truth, forgiving yourself and others, and inviting others to be authentic too. You have been cultivating inner belonging: a belonging to yourself that supports belonging at work and the world by creating teams and cultures where people feel safe. As a result, you're building greater teamwork, trust, and innovation. Inner belonging creates collective and planetary belonging, which we will look at more deeply in the next chapter.

Authenticity Recipe

- I love and embrace all my parts.

- I forgive myself.

- I am my word in action, and others trust me.

- I lead with conviction, authenticity, courage, and vulnerability.

LEAD WITH YOUR LIGHT ON, AT WORK AND BEYOND

Now it's time to take all the inner game skills you've learned and practiced into your workplace and the world—where everyone can see you shine. In part II you'll learn about brave exchanges, read about some of the amazing successes the conscious leaders we've been following have accomplished in their organizations, and join with others in transforming businesses operations in ways that are sustainable and healthy for people and the planet.

Encouraging Brave Exchanges
Creating Trust and Belonging

> As a society, we are committing ourselves to belongings rather
> than what we really crave, which is belonging. Belonging to
> the community, belonging to the family, belonging to our
> circle of friends, belonging to our neighborhood.
>
> —LYNNE TWIST, cofounder of The Pachamama
> Alliance and founder of The Soul of Money Institute

In this chapter, we will see the ways in which developing a conscious inner
game and bringing our wholeness to work can enable us to have deeper
conversations that create an inclusive workplace. The six inner game qualities you have become familiar with—self-awareness, emotional intelligence,
resilience, love, well-being, and authenticity—have been preparing you to
lead with a confident outer game that will create belonging, psychological
safety, trust, teamwork, and connection in your workplace.

Clear, open communication is one of the most important qualities for
cultivating trust, collaboration, and harmony. You will learn how to bring
your whole and best self to conversations that support business objectives,
as well as important workplace issues such as gender equality, inclusive

cultures, and corporate social responsibility. Coming together in this way supports everyone in their quest to solve the larger problems of our world. You will practice pausing and listening to what is being said—and what is not being said—with the intention to learn, not necessarily to jump in and fix. Listening for the purpose of learning, growing, and giving and receiving vulnerable feedback with care is how you bring healthy boundaries into the workplace.

In the coming pages, you will discover how to shift shame by looking beyond the mask of your own assumptions and connecting to the unique experiences of individuals and teams so you can understand what they really want and need. In this way, everyone will feel invited to the table.

The Science of Trust

How much trust does your organization experience? That's the first question I ask when I do a culture assessment with the businesses I serve. Trust is the essential ingredient and foundation for all relationships and businesses. Without trust, you can't build anything that will succeed for the long term, and any kind of organizational change will be seriously challenged.

Organizational scholars define trust as our willingness to be vulnerable to the actions of others because we believe they have good intentions and will behave well toward us. In other words, we let others have power over us because we don't think they'll hurt us; we think they'll help us and have our backs. When the trust level is high within coworker relationships, it corresponds to trusting the company that employs us, and we feel confident it won't deceive us or abuse its relationship with us.

But what are the mechanics of this? *How* do we trust? In order to trust someone, especially someone who is unfamiliar to us—which means we haven't had the opportunity to develop trust yet—our brains build a model of what the person is likely to do and why. And there's a lot going on beneath the surface; we use both mindfulness and empathy during every collaborative endeavor. This means both people in an interaction are always assessing, *Should I trust you? How much do you trust me?* Some of us are innately trusting, naturally seeking positive intent and putting *we* before *me*. But in my experience, trust is earned. It is not wise to trust someone blindly until you have vetted that they are, in fact, trustworthy.

Inner Game Practice
BOLSTERING TRUST

Take out your journal and reflect on these three questions:

- What assignment can you follow through on today that will support you in increasing your trust in yourself?

- Identify someone in your life, at work or at home, who has violated your trust. After expressing your fears and concerns to this person, negotiate a task he, she, or they can do to rebuild trust with you.

- Invite an open conversation with someone in your life, at work or at home, whose trust you have violated. What happened? Did you break an agreement or break a boundary of theirs? After sharing your feelings of remorse and a desire to repair, make an agreement that begins to restore the original broken agreement. You can follow the two conversation frameworks later in this chapter to create brave exchanges.

Trust and Safety Requires Nuturing

The level of trust in an organization is influenced by how much psychological safety exists. Do people feel safe voicing their honest opinions? Do they believe that any criticism aimed their way will be fair and that their response to it will be heard? Teams that enjoy high trust levels have been shown to be more creative and to come to decisions faster. They're higher performing teams because they're willing to admit mistakes and to call out problems and challenges and ask for help.[1] If two teams are equally smart, why would a more trusting team be more productive than a less trusting one? Because they iterate faster. They learn faster. And why do they do that? Because they trust each other to be honest and point out the things they're discovering in real time. A foundation of safety helps these team members understand and develop those discoveries quickly, collaborate smoothly, and co-create with flow.

In the workplace, trust is highly influenced by leadership because leaders model the behaviors others will follow. When leaders lead with fear and dominance, trust and safety suffer in the long run. A boss who berates, threatens, or punishes you will affect your performance and ability to speak up authentically as you focus your attention on self-protection. This leads to feelings of "learned helplessness" as employees avoid the boss and/or remain as invisible as they can by doing the minimum. And face it: this kind of leadership behavior hurts, to the point of inflicting trauma.

Humans experience social rejection and social pain in the brain's pain matrix for longer than they experience physical pain. Research in neuroscience has shown this. We are wired to connect and belong. If we lack the trust and safety that are essential to belonging, we feel that our very survival is threatened, which prolongs our suffering.[2] To turn this around, we can consciously and actively work to create greater belonging using conscious leadership techniques at work and in the world.

Belonging means belonging to *yourself*, as well as being connected to a purpose larger than yourself. For a great example of a company that shines in just this way, we'll take a look at Salesforce.

Leading with Trust

> We are part of an integrated holistic system which is the
> global economy, and so Salesforce strongly believes that
> companies and CEOs have to be activists. As a CEO,
> if you're not doing that in today's world, you're making
> a mistake.
>
> —MARC BENIOFF, cofounder and CEO of Salesforce

When Marc Benioff founded Salesforce in 1999, he made his motivations
clear by outlining an agenda that looked beyond shareholders' needs and
included people and the planet, not just profits. From the get-go, he vowed to
donate 1 percent of the company's revenue, 1 percent of his employees' time,
and 1 percent of the company's product value to nonprofit organizations
each year.[3]

There are many ways Marc's conscious inner game is expressed in his
outer game—among them instilling trust, becoming a "male ally," and
encouraging brave exchanges. Later in this chapter, we will further discuss
the importance of "male allyship" as part of the new era and paradigm of
conscious business leadership.

In 2015, when the then-governor of Indiana, Mike Pence, signed a
bill that would allow companies to deny service to LGBTQIA+ customers,
Marc took a brave stand and threatened to withdraw his company's investment in the state. He encouraged other tech CEOs to help fight the bill
too, and Indiana quickly revised the law.[4]

In 2016, Salesforce bought thirteen companies, including e-commerce
platform Demandware, word processing app Quip, messaging startup
HeyWire, and the sales rep software company SteelBrick. With the purchase, all the employees at these companies moved under the Salesforce
umbrella, but their salaries had not been included in an earlier analysis the
company used to achieve equal pay for women. So, Salesforce went back
seven years and paid all the women in these acquired companies the money

they would have received if they had been paid the same rate as men and pledged to review the gender pay gap on an ongoing basis for the entire organization. As a result of these acquisitions and this policy, Salesforce has now spent $10.3 million in salary adjustments for its 35,000 employees around the world.[5]

But Marc didn't stop there in his mission to align his business with his values. He also implemented a policy that bans companies that sell automatic weapons from using Salesforce technology. This move was yet another example of Marc walking his talk, being his word, and placing the interests of society above profits. All of these actions instill a strong sense of trust and belonging among Salesforce workers, and as a result, since 2013, Marc has consistently scored above 90 percent in CEO approval ratings on Glassdoor, where the average approval rating is just 69 percent.[6]

Marc's motive transparency and concern for others have earned him the trust of employees, customers, and shareholders. And he believes instilling trust has to be the number one priority of a CEO. As he said in an interview on CNBC, "If trust is not your highest value, your employees and executives are going to walk out."[7]

This is how our need to trust and to be trusted—a fundamental, individual, human need—has very real economic impacts. But more than that, this need deeply affects the fabric of society. If we can't trust other people, we'll avoid interacting with them—and if we're avoiding each other, how can we innovate, solve problems, or build anything at all?

Being an Inclusive Leader

The importance of cultivating an inclusive workplace where everyone can thrive only increases as the world's workforce demographics continue to change. Millennials and the generation after them, Generation Z, are now 50 percent of the workforce. These populations have little patience for organizations that don't value diversity, inclusion, and belonging. They expect inclusive workplaces, and if companies fail to provide that they'll search for another company to support and serve. In the next decade in the US, the majority of workers will be people of color—already the new norm in the rest of the world.[8]

If we want a more just world, one in which less dominant groups and vulnerable people are heard and supported, we need to equalize the playing field. To do that, we must grasp the urgency of our own role and take responsibility for leading in this way.

By reading this book, you are already well on your way to learning how to lead inclusively. All of the inner game qualities you familiarized yourself with and practiced over the last six chapters support inner belonging, and with those skills and techniques now bolstering your inner foundation, you can create the outer game of belonging for others.

When we embrace who we are as human beings on the inside, we can invite our teams and organizations to support our outer belonging. As a leader, you'll step into the ring first. You'll instill trust in your organization by owning your truth, speaking up to injustice when you see it, creating allyship, modeling healthy boundaries, and putting new agreements and accountability processes in place that reflect what you value.

The first step toward creating belonging is *listening* and trying to *understand* another's experience.

Listen First, Listen Carefully

Nowhere is listening more important than in navigating a reorganization. Reorganizations can feel traumatic, but they happen for all sorts of reasons: a new CEO coming on board, a need for budget cuts and layoffs, the sale of one company to another, and more. Whatever the reason for it, reorganizational change has the potential to bring about a positive transformation—but this is very much dependent on how leaders listen and communicate about the changes taking place.

I was brought in to serve Bank of the West as a leadership consultant and culture builder. Nandita Bakhshi, the bank's first female CEO, had been hired only a few months before. One of the first things Nandita did in her new position was to go on a "listening tour" of the larger offices of the organization. She created a space where she could welcome groups of employees and invite them to speak with her so she could hear their concerns and share her vision with them. Prioritizing listening demonstrated her care for, curiosity about, and interest in the many employees she leads.

When any organizational change occurs, the first feelings commonly exhibited are fear and uncertainty. These feelings are natural, and acknowledging these fears aloud actually offers an opportunity to create belonging and a stronger workplace in its reorganized form. Listening well as a leader in this environment is your best friend. When the people you are responsible for feel seen and heard, you're creating an environment of safety, which builds the commitment and accountability needed to succeed and thrive. Listening is also the way to achieve dynamic collaboration. Bottom line: it's one of the most powerful skills a leader can cultivate.

Following is a practice to help you do just that.

Inner Game Practice
LISTENING WITH INTENT

- Come into a seated position and bring your attention inward. Push "pause" on all the outside noise, the tasks ahead of you, and everything you were doing just before this moment.

- Breathe. Breathe deeply in and out of your stomach.

- As you breathe in, allow your stomach to rise, and as you exhale let out a big sigh. Release anything that is not serving you right now: tension, tightness, difficult feelings—let them go.

- Now in your mind's eye bring your attention to someone with whom you interact pretty regularly and with whom you have had an obvious disagreement, a pause in communication, or have an intuitive sense that something between you is amiss.

- Bring your attention to the last few interactions you've had with this person. What did this person say to you? What did their nonverbal behavior show you (fear, anger, disappointment, avoidance, disdain, judgment)? Try to remove the story you've created about this interaction as much as you can. Instead, be curious; listen intently, using both your ears and your eyes. Pay attention to their words and what their body language said. Do your best to fully see the other person, hear them, and be interested in their experience, without judgment.

- Now ask yourself these questions:

  ‣ What might they be feeling right now?

  ‣ What might they be wanting or needing?

  ‣ What do I want for myself?

  ‣ What do I want for them?

  ‣ What do I want for the relationship?

  ‣ If I truly want these things for me, for them, and our relationship, what actions might I take?

- You might imagine yourself taking the next step to invite a safe connection by communicating, through your words and actions, that you care about and want to hear the other person's concerns, that you want to truly see their potential, and that you are invested in the mutual benefits of your relationship.

- Next, spend some time imagining how the person might respond to your invitation. Let yourself imagine changes in body language and anything you think they might say in return.

- When you feel complete, take a deep breath, knowing that you are taking the courageous step to repair the disconnection and owning your part in building a bridge.

- Take a few more deep breaths and when you feel ready, bring your awareness back to your body, open your eyes, and slowly integrate back into your day.

Listening starts by being curious about the other person. Then, you must be clear on what you want for yourself and for the relationship *before* you invite the conversation. With practice, you will learn to master this technique.

Of course, no matter how strong the intention, we can't expect all conversations to flow smoothly. What happens in real life will often, if not always, differ from what you've imagined, and sometimes it will involve conflict. We will move into how to have healthy conflict later in the chapter.

What Gets in the Way of Listening?

A number of things can break that listening connection: trying to fix a situation or control it, going too fast, having an agenda, feeling triggered and self-protective, a lack of receptivity, feeling distracted, and being overwhelmed with other tasks. All of these are normal responses and are nothing to feel ashamed about. When one of these obstacles to listening arrives—and it will, in some portion of your interactions—you have a number of tools. First, bring mindfulness to it; simply notice what has happened and get curious about it. Then, bring yourself back to your intention to listen with this simple question: *What would help me listen better right now?*

Here are some answers I've heard from other leaders:

- Ask more questions.

- Stay curious.

- Give myself time to digest what I'm hearing before going to the next thing.

- Seek to understand, rather than judge.

- Invite a beginner's mind; recognize there is something I don't know and I really want to know it.

- Embody empathy.

- Let go of my agenda.

- Assume positive intent on the part of the other person.

- Breathe deeply.

- Be less reactive to my triggers.

As we saw in the last chapter, when we slow down and listen to ourselves, we tap into what really matters to us personally—and then we can show up authentically. The more we can be fully, authentically present and able to listen and meet ourselves, even amid conflict, the more we can provide a caring and safe space for others to be present as they really are too. In this way, we create an invitation to openness, presence, and honesty.

Understanding Your Blind Spots

We are all biased—if you think you're not, think again. There are two types of bias: conscious bias, also known as explicit bias, and unconscious bias. Biases, conscious or unconscious, are not limited to race and ethnicity; they can exist toward any social group. Our age, race, gender, religion, orientation, weight, and many other characteristics are subject to bias. Our conscious and unconscious biases get in the way of our ability to see each other clearly and have real, open, and authentic discussions about inclusion and belonging. And they can perpetuate separation, disconnection, and a lack of trust.

Let's talk about unconscious bias. Unconscious bias is a blind spot—an assumption we are making that we may not even be aware of. When it comes to inclusion and exclusion in the workplace, unconscious bias takes the form of an implicit attitude or association about race, gender, or some other aspect of another person or group that flavors how we perceive them. Since upper-level leadership in the workplace is currently dominated by white men, unconscious bias on their part often means that they set a higher bar for women, people of color, or other less dominant groups, requiring more evidence to demonstrate their competence. If these leaders don't really *see* what is right in front of them—the talent, experience, native intelligence, or other qualities of these different genders, races, and/or groups—then there is a blind spot. Ultimately, a self-sabotaging one.

Of course, it's not just white male executives who have this limiting problem. Want an example? According to research, coworkers who judge a woman as competent often judge her as unlikable; this is an unconscious bias. That correlation doesn't hold true when it comes to perceptions about men. Additional research shows that men get promoted based on potential, while women get promoted based on performance.[9] Why? Because many male executives are overconfident about their abilities. They believe they're better—more savvy, more talented, more visionary—than they actually are, and they strive to persuade others to raise them to higher levels of promotion. The unfortunate result is that women who may be equally competent, but not *over*confident in their skills, get bypassed for opportunities. This is unconscious bias in all its pernicious glory.

As a leader, you can best influence diversity, inclusion, and belonging by committing yourself to becoming *aware* of your own inherent bias and the bias in the culture. Your inner game is there to serve you in this. The qualities of self-awareness, emotional intelligence, empathy, and a growth mindset can help you bring biases to the surface. Mindfulness and meditation have also been found to reduce unconscious bias because they support greater awareness of the projections, stories, and conclusions we have about a race, gender, or another less dominant group.[10]

Inner Game Practice
ASSESSING BIAS IN THE MOMENT

Let's break it down and build awareness so we can create new systems and guidelines that give everyone the same opportunities for learning and advancement in our organizations, regardless of gender, race, sexual orientation, age, and differing abilities.

To begin, it is important to understand what the dominant group identity is within any given workplace culture (which might be heterosexual, white, and male, for instance) and what the less dominant groups are. These could be people of color and people in the LGBTQIA+ community, for example, who might acutely feel their subordinate status as a group at work. Additionally, people on your team may struggle bringing their whole selves to work because they have different stigmatized identities. For example, a black woman with mental illness may struggle more in her role than someone with less marginalized identities. As a leader in this workplace culture, especially if you are in the dominant group, you can set out to understand the experience of individuals within any marginalized group or identities that may be present.

Answering the following questions can be helpful in assessing and increasing your awareness of bias in the moment when you are speaking to various coworkers:

- What assumptions or beliefs about the other am I aware of when I am speaking to them? Is this assumption or belief really true?

- How might this person be experiencing me (as a friend, an ally, an enemy)?

- What voice am I speaking from, dominant or subordinate? In other words, am I giving feedback differently based on this person's different background?

- What action can I take to be more inclusive right now?

When you make the effort to answer these questions and uncover your blind spots, prejudices, and biases, you give yourself the opportunity to overcome them. With newfound awareness and the desire to change, you can move into the role of advocate and supporter. In addition to exploring the above questions in the moment in the workplace, I recommend all leaders take Harvard University's Project Implicit (unconscious) bias test, so they know where they stand and can develop a more inclusive perspective.[11] The best place to start with this test is to take the race test and then bring self-compassion toward the results you receive. We all have biases and blind spots, and unfortunately we have been socially conditioned by the structures in place to believe certain things about different people, races, and groups within our culture. But with awareness we can change our biases.

The Ally Journey

A 2012 study by the Boston Consulting Group found that diversity among employees increases a company's bottom line, concluding that "increasing the diversity of leadership teams leads to more and better innovation and improved financial performance." This study looked at 1,700 companies across eight different countries of varying industries and sizes, so this is a widespread phenomenon. Companies with more diverse management teams enjoy 19 percent higher revenue, brought about by increased innovation. This finding is huge for tech companies, startups, and industries where innovation is the key to growth. It shows that diversity is not just a metric to be strived for; it is actually an integral part of a successful, revenue-generating business.[12]

Creating workplaces that support diversity, inclusion, and belonging requires leaders to lean into discomfort, embrace a different mindset, lead with heart, and instill safety and trust in their communications and behaviors throughout the organization.

One pathway toward creating a culture of belonging is to empower *allies* at work. What is an ally? It's someone who is not a member of an under-represented group but who holds a position of privilege and power and can advocate and take action to support that less represented group. For example, an ally will advocate for the well-being of that person or group without taking over the culture's voice. "Allyship" is incredibly important in making sure that everyone is not only invited to the table but is also heard, acknowledged, and recognized for their contributions. As an ally, you can take a strong stand against bias, even in its most subtle forms. And you can understand when you need to step in and use your voice to address bias as it occurs.

Inner Game Practice
YOUR ALLY ASSESSMENT

There are many models you can use to determine where you are on your journey toward becoming an ally, but my favorite is the one devised my friend and colleague Jennifer Brown. She has identified four stages of inclusion in her book *How to Be an Inclusive Leader: Your Role in Creating Cultures of Belonging Where Everyone Can Thrive*, ranging from "unaware" to "advocate."

Let's do an exercise based on this model. Read the following four stages and rate where you think you fall on the continuum:

- **Unaware.** You don't notice or understand that certain demographic groups, or those with specific backgrounds and experiences, have a much harder time thriving at work and in the world.

- **Aware.** You realize the playing field is not level in the workplace or in other groups or organizational contexts. You see your blind spots and are beginning to understand other people's perspectives and stories while working through your own stories and biases.

- **Active.** You are beginning to lean into discomfort, which may feel awkward and will require more personal and social responsibility. You are finding your voice and starting to speak against injustices, calling out microaggressions (comments or actions that subtly express prejudice), and sponsoring and supporting others at work who are different from you. When you are aware of your bias and have a desire to create positive change, you can move into the role of advocating for and supporting others; this is what it means to be an ally.

- **Advocate.** At this stage you are likely feeling more comfortable in taking action to create more equity, inclusivity, and belonging at work and in the world. You may be ready to take action for those who need support and begin to fight for the dismantling of systems that have kept oppression, racism, and inequality in place and you are taking more personal and social risks to create these changes. This stage is when your words and actions come into alignment as an ally and you suggest different strategies or ideas to create a workplace and world that works for everyone.

As you move forward in your journey as an ally, you may circle back to each stage—this is all part of the process. For example, you may find in certain situations and experiences you fall back into "unaware" and in some spaces you act courageously as an "advocate." Choosing to be an ally requires humility and heart, and you will make mistakes along the way. But we are all being invited to step forward into the path of allyship so we can individually and collectively heal and transform our workplaces and the world.

Becoming a "Male Ally"

As women and other disempowered and/or marginalized groups are painfully aware, the most dominant and powerful group in the workplace and the world are men. In order to create belonging and solve some of the larger problems in our world, we have to get more comfortable with the discomfort that naturally arises in having brave conversations about topics such as equal pay and equitable hiring and promotion for women, people of color, LGBTQIA+ and nonbinary people, and others.

This means enrolling men who hold positions of power—normally white men—in the effort so they can use their social capital (influence, knowledge, and resources) to support less dominant groups within leadership. Men who take up this role are called "male allies."

If you're a man in a position of power within an organization and you recognize you can influence the work culture for the better, here are some best practices:

- Declare yourself a male ally to yourself and to your team. (Take a cue from Vince Guglielmetti of Intel Corporation.)

- Listen. Be mindful of your bias and embrace a growth mindset.

- Understand the impact your words or actions have caused in the past, take responsibility for them, and course correct.

- Embrace the difficult emotions that arise when underlying power structures are surfaced, such as in discussions of equal pay or opportunities for promotion; these topics often elicit strong emotions on both sides.

- Go to the source. Ask women, nonbinary people, people of color, and other less dominant groups how you can help. Do they need sponsorship? More learning opportunities? Something else?

- Speak up and call out other people if you see them abusing their power with others. Stating what you see happening and taking a just action are key to change. Silence only perpetuates the cycle.

- Speak up, stand up, and show up.

THE CALLING UP OF MALE ALLIES

What does a highly placed male ally do in practice? I got my answer when I had the opportunity to interview Vince Guglielmetti, Intel's vice president of the Americas general manufacturing operations, on the *Shine* podcast while researching this book.[13] Vince has publicly claimed himself to be a male ally with his leadership team and direct reports. He sees himself as a balance of masculine and feminine qualities, "I am my mother's son," he often says. In his role as an ally, he is straightforward, asking women, people of color, and LGBTQIA+ people, "I know you need my voice. How can I be your voice?" He challenges and speaks directly to microaggressions and recruits other male leaders to take on male allyship roles and lend their voices to disenfranchised minorities. To accomplish these goals, Vince regularly assesses and educates himself on topics and issues related to disempowered groups.[14]

THE FUTURE IS FEMININE

The future is female, for we need to understand that we cannot succeed when approximately half of our global population is being held back.

—JOSEPH MUSCAT, former prime minister of Malta

A diverse workforce is a critical factor in improving not just the quality of a company's leadership and decision-making, but its overall financial, environmental, social, and governance performance—and ultimately, its sustainability. Companies like Credit Suisse, McKinsey & Company, and Catalyst have shown that the presence of women in the top levels of management and leadership correlates with better financial performance. Notably, companies with more women on their board of directors are more likely to be invested in sustainable operations and missions.[15]

The science is clear when evaluating the key predictors of good leadership, and women tend to outperform men. Why? Because they lead transformationally. One study found that women excelled in taking initiative, acting with resilience, practicing self-development, monitoring others' performance, giving unbiased critical and constructive feedback, empathizing with others, driving for results, and displaying high integrity and honesty.[16] In fact, women were thought to be more effective in 84 percent of the competencies we most frequently measure.

Additionally, numerous studies have demonstrated that as MBA students, employees, consumers, and investors, women are more aligned with and desirous of corporate sustainability. Yet, based on the January 2019 S&P 500 Index, women currently hold only twenty-seven (5.4 percent) of the CEO positions at those S&P 500 companies.[17]

Women are also less likely to lead passively. In other words, men in leadership positions communicate less around difficult matters, and this is an ineffective way to lead.

What's at stake? A study by McKinsey & Company projects that in a "full potential" scenario in which women participate in the economy identically to men, $28 trillion (26 percent) would be added to the annual global GDP when compared to the current business-as-usual scenario.[18]

This brings us back to male allies. How can we advocate for women and other less dominant groups so they can influence businesses to be more financially, socially, and environmentally sustainable? We need to enlist large numbers of men to assume the role. The unfortunate truth is that without the avid support of men, we're unlikely to make significant progress toward ending gender and other disparities in the workplace and world.

Outer Game Practice
STRUCTURAL WAYS TO ENROLL MALE ALLIES

When we raise our expectations on matters of inclusion, we can have deeper conversations on this essential aspect of workplace culture. Here are some structural ways to encourage this:

- Invite men to attend discussions and events around gender equity in the workplace. This will make efforts to increase inclusion, diversity, and belonging more successful.

- Encourage and facilitate more positive professional interactions among men, women, and LGBTQIA+ people. Research shows that the more positive interactions men have with women in workplace settings, the less prejudice and exclusion they tend to demonstrate.[19]

- Give men an important role to play in gender parity efforts. The motivation for this role can be tied to personal examples and a sense of fairness and justice.[20] Many men want to support women, different races, and other less dominant groups, but don't know how to step in and offer aid. This requires all people to ask men for what they need. Personally, I have learned the benefit of asking male leaders and mentors for sponsorship and mentorship in my life. I wouldn't be where I am if I hadn't had the courage to ask for the support of male allies in my life.

- Cultivate supportive partnerships with women and less dominant groups. Ask how you can support them. You might share your social capital through information, knowledge, and/or your influence with organizational resources or invitations.

Calling in Microaggressions

A microaggression is a statement, an action, or an everyday slight or incident of indirect, subtle, or unintentional discrimination against members of a marginalized group such as a racial or ethnic minority. "Calling in" microaggressions is a powerful way to become an ally. The term *microaggression* was most commonly used in academia and was originally coined in the 1970s by Chester M. Pierce, a Harvard Medical School psychiatrist. Since then, *microaggression* has been used widely in social media campaigns, and Derald Wing Sue, a professor of counseling psychology at Columbia University, has written several books on microaggressions, including *Microaggressions in Everyday Life: Race, Gender, and Sexual Orientation.* Individuals who have engaged in microaggressions are often unaware that they have participated in an offensive or demeaning way.

Here are some examples of microaggression:

- When a person showcases many different ethnicities or a skin color or nongender norm on the outside, some people may speak to this ambiguity by asking, "What are you?" This can feel offensive and aggressive to the person receiving it. If we don't speak up about a microaggression like this head-on, it can have long-term consequences on the individual's mental and physical health, and can erode psychological safety in the relationship, team, and workplace.

- Say a person (of either gender) who identifies as heterosexual learns that a female coworker identifies as lesbian and says, "Oh, you're lesbian! My friend Ann identifies as lesbian too—I should connect you two." The comment may seem completely harmless, but it can feel offensive. *Why do you think I need help with my friendships or my love life, and why do you think I need it from you? What makes you think all lesbians get along?*

- Another frequently encountered example of microaggression in the workplace is when a woman (or member of another less dominant group) is talked over or talked past by the men in the room, who speak mainly to each other instead. Still another example is when a dominant person in the group takes credit for an idea a member of a less dominant group has contributed.

If no one speaks up against microaggressions, it can become part of the culture, resulting in a lack of safety, trust, and belonging. We can eliminate microaggressions by bringing them into awareness with the correct language and gentle interventions. When we "call out" someone's behavior that is not healthy, people usually take offense and get defensive. Calling someone *in* is different because we are speaking directly to what they did but from a place of curiosity, strength, and a desire to shift the behavior. When we call in individuals and teams, we are inviting them to act with integrity, care, and personal responsibility.

How might you call in a microaggression?

- **Be direct.** Restate what you heard them say using reflective listening.

- **Ask for clarification.** "Could you say that one more time? Can you share what you mean by that statement?"

- **Acknowledge feelings.** Express empathy and compassion. "It sounds like you're really frustrated/nervous/angry . . ."

- **Share impact and request.** "I imagine you didn't realize this when you said it, but when you _____ (insert comment/behavior) the impact was that I felt hurt, disrespected, or _____ . In the future, I request that you do this instead _____ (insert different language/behavior)."

Then see how this person responds. If they still don't lean in, try this:

- **Encourage empathy.** Ask how they would feel if someone said something like that about their group or their friend/partner/child.

"How might you feel if someone said that about or did that to your sister or friend?"

- **Create a new agreement.** If after speaking up this person leans in and seems open to shifting their mindset and thus behavior, set a precedent and agreement for new behavior and accountability. If they continue to engage and communicate in the same aggressive and offensive manner, then it is important you continue to speak up, set a boundary, and find support.

Calling in people is a delicate process, and we have to be direct while also avoiding the shame or blame game which may cause the other person to become defensive. Ultimately, you don't have control over how the person responds to your call in, but it is still important that you speak up, or the behavior will never change. When we speak up, we are inviting transformation and a new pattern of communication and relating that reduces harm to ourselves and others.

. . .

In the last chapter, we spoke about psychological safety. Now we'll take that one step further. As a leader, what guidelines will you use to call in microaggressions? For example, what is each person's responsibility? The trick is to create agreements in advance.

If you notice the ubiquitous microaggression of a man speaking over a woman or speaking for a woman (or person from another less dominant group), also known as "mansplaining," your agreement as a group can be that any person in the group is free to say something like, "Hey, you're interrupting Karen and I want to hear what she has to say."

Your agreement can include the necessity of a response from the microaggressor, which can be as simple as, "Thank you for pointing that out." Such an expression of gratitude, rather than defensiveness or shutting down, conveys that you care and are willing to learn, and the dialogue as a whole indicates the willingness to bring biases to the surface and make a shift as a group.

Outer Game Practice for Men
BEING AN ALLY—
MINDFUL JOURNALING

Consider the following questions and write down your answers. This is a simple exercise, but it can prepare you to put your desire to be a male ally into practice.

- What agreements can we make at the beginning of a meeting to address instances of a woman, LGBTQIA+ person, or person of color being talked over so we can reduce the frequency of this happening?

- What are the responsibilities of each person in the meeting for creating safety?

- Where are there opportunities in my workplace for allyship?

Being an inclusive leader and manager means being comfortable with discomfort. It also means being willing to enhance your own self-awareness, growth mindset, compassion, and empathy so you can create more belonging for others. The most important part of being an ally is your willingness to try new ways of speaking and interacting at work. Being an ally is a lifelong learning process. You won't do it perfectly, but as long as your motivation is to help and grow, it's better to speak up than to be silent.

> Once you've ensured that the group has made the agreements necessary to foster inclusion, it is vitally important that people are held accountable to those agreements. Change happens at the speed of trust, and trust is what you're developing with these agreements.

From Conflict to Creative Breakthrough

Conversations break down all the time and for various reasons, many of which are outside of our control. Research shows that miscommunication adds up to $62.4 million in losses for large companies[21] and $420,000 for smaller companies.[22] So, what can we do about this? When a conversation breaks down, we can learn how to reestablish trust, create psychological safety, and resume the conversation to repair the rupture so it doesn't fester into resentment, gossip, or, worse, trauma.

Before you endeavor to set this in motion, I want to acknowledge that stepping into addressing conflict is *brave* leadership. We feel a sense of danger and fear going into this because we don't know how things will turn out. We hope a conversation that addresses the rift openly will bring greater understanding and a resolution, but there's a chance the discussion won't go as well as we hope. That means we have to be able to sit with and soothe any difficult feelings and triggers, as we learned to do in chapter 2 by growing our inner game of emotional intelligence. We are also entering into this conversation with our inner game tools of self-awareness, understanding how to create more safety and trust, knowing our blind spots, expressing empathy, and being willing to listen with curiosity.

After a communication breakdown, it is important to reestablish the connection and seek repair quickly. In the Brave Exchanges curriculum that I facilitate with teams, leaders, and managers, I outline the two practices below. First is a fifteen-minute frame for a short conversation to support you in the first step toward resolution. Later in the chapter, I will support you with a deeper follow-up conversation to give and receive feedback with courage and vulnerability. Ready? Here we go!

Outer Game Practice

CREATING CONNECTION IN 6 STEPS

Imagine that your direct report, Amar, didn't get a deliverable in on time and you need to give feedback to create accountability and a shared agreement. Here is a six-step process for creating a connection with Amar:

1. **Acknowledge your feelings first.** Being the first one to reach out and attempt repair can often bring up feelings of fear because we don't know how the other person will respond. You have the tools to make friends with fear (from chapter 2) so you can step through fear and into courage. Acknowledge the fear or discomfort with loving awareness, then shake it out and identify what you need and move forward.

2. **Invite a conversation to repair quickly.** Reach out and identify a time you can both talk within the next few days in person (virtually, if need be), but no more than a week from now. Be specific about the topic, but leave out any emotional content until you talk in person.

   - **You:** Hey, Amar, I know we have had a lot of deliverables in our department, and I have appreciated all your support. Yesterday, the capstone project was due and I didn't see the final presentation in my inbox. I am wondering if we can find time to talk in person in the next day or two for fifteen minutes? Let me know some times that work for you.

3. **Create context for the conversation.** State your motivation for the conversation and ensure it creates structure and safety and avoids blame.

- **You:** Thanks for making time to talk today. I wanted us to speak because I know we've had many competing projects lately and I want to understand how we can work together to co-create a system that supports us in meeting our deadlines and working effectively. Let's aim for fifteen minutes, and if we need to have a longer conversation, let's set that up for another time this week. Does that work for you?

4. **Lead with personal responsibility and authenticity.** Taking responsibility and naming the conflict head-on often disarms the other person's feelings of being threatened so they can relax, hear you, and be inclined to collaborate. When you take responsibility for your part, you can also try to put yourself in the other person's shoes to see how they might have been feeling when they missed the deadline. You also want to stay curious; gather information first and avoid assuming conclusions about their motivation until you fully understand.

- **You:** I want to first acknowledge that I know I've been asking for your support on many competing projects lately and I appreciate all of your effort.

We assured our client that the capstone presentation would be delivered yesterday for their quarterly review, and we didn't meet this commitment. You're the lead on this project, and I want to understand what happened so we can meet our deliverables on time in the future. What happened on Tuesday?

- **Amar:** Well, Rosa needed help on the other project, and I got pulled into working with her on it. There were too many conflicting projects and I wasn't sure which one had priority.

5. **Find your shared reality.** We need to leave the conversation with more empathy and understanding about where we agree, disagree, and/or feel uncertainty. Here we use active and reflective listening, which is repeating what we heard the other person say. This creates understanding, a shared reality of what the other person is feeling, what happened, and a chance for the other person to clarify if what you heard wasn't what was said or meant. It's also important to express empathy here. Empathy for the person's experience is one of the most important ingredients in understanding and collaboration.

- **You:** I hear that you felt torn about what project had priority and there were too many competing tasks. Is that accurate?

- **Amar:** Yes.

- **You:** I imagine you might have been feeling frustrated and overwhelmed. I feel compassion for your experience. I've often felt like that when I had too many competing tasks on my plate. Going forward, I have a suggestion. Are you open to hearing it?

- **Amar:** Yes, I would like to hear your suggestion.

- **You:** Great. Next time you face a situation where there are too many projects and you feel unsure of where to put your time and attention, can you check in with me and share what your status is and any questions you have? I welcome you to share transparently where you are with everything so I can best support your process. This way we can address the most pressing deadlines. Does that work for you, or do you have a better idea?

- **Amar:** Yes, that sounds good. I can do that.

6. **Make requests and agreements.** It's important to speak up, share specific requests, and develop new commitments and agreements for next steps at the end of the conversation. You can develop several options and then pick the one you can both agree to. This will keep you both accountable for the solution toward which you are both working. Try to be sure that both of you own what you'll do to support the project or relationship. Then find time within the next week to check in on your progress.

- **You:** I feel like we found some resolution, and I want to keep checking in on this new process during our weekly meetings so we can tweak and make adjustments. Let's put a time on our calendars to meet next week to check back. What's best for you?

- **Amar:** Friday at noon.

- **You:** Great, that time is clear on my calendar too. Thanks, Amar, for your time today.

This is an example of a conversation going smoothly, but if for some reason one of you becomes triggered, you can rely on what you learned in chapter 3 on page 69 in the section titled Shifting the Mood of the Team and invite a time-out.

For a handy visual summary of these six steps, see appendix B.

More Love, Less Conflict

Being able to give positive and constructive feedback as a leader and manager is essential for influencing team members to enhance their best qualities and address their worst so they can excel at leading.[23]

Delivering feedback around performance and evaluations requires a growth mindset so we can inspire positive change and growth in our teams. Before giving feedback, it is important to create a safe space in which to do that, because if there is no safety, the other person's capacity to receive the feedback will be limited. If a person isn't ready to receive another's thoughts or concerns and/or there's no foundation of trust, effective communication cannot take place.

Outer Game Practice

11 STEPS FOR GIVING AND RECEIVING FEEDBACK WITH COURAGE

Let's dive into how to give and receive constructive feedback. This can be done in your regular one-on-ones, and I invite you to set aside thirty minutes to an hour for a successful session. I also suggest practicing this conversation alone or with a trusted friend or colleague so you can feel confident and comfortable when the time comes. Let's run through the eleven steps:

1. **Set your intention for the conversation.** What kind of feedback do you want to give? Appreciation, coaching, or evaluation?

2. **Give feedback in person.** There's too much room for misunderstanding when we communicate by email or text. We need to be able to see the other person's nonverbal behavior and observe how our feedback was received and what "impact" it made upon the listener.

3. **Be open.** Sit with an open and receptive body posture.

4. **Focus on cultivating growth.** When inviting and delivering feedback, you might share the context for your statement by saying, "My motivation for sharing this is that I want you to have the best possible chance to advance, and I know your growth in this role and this company is important to you."

5. **Model vulnerability first.** As we learned in the last chapter, leading with vulnerability models how the other person can join in the conversation. For example, "I am sensing some fear in myself as I approach this conversation with you because I want it to go well. I am wondering if you might be feeling that too?"

6. **"Presence" what you see.** If you notice that the other person (or people) is demonstrating body language that alludes to not feeling safe, like crossed arms or looking down or away, name it. For example, "Vanessa, I notice that your arms are crossed, and your answers are pretty curt. Would you be willing to share more of what might be happening for you? Or can you think of a way I can support you to make this conversation easier right now?" Find the language that feels authentic to you. Acknowledging the emotion inherent in the conversation—yours or the other person's or both—will ease tension and create more psychological safety.

7. **Be specific with details and requests.** For example, "It was really helpful when you made our deadline for the report on time, but what created a problem was that you got to the new-client meeting late, and we had to wait for you before we could begin the presentation. Going forward I need you to be on time for client meetings. Can we agree to that?" Speak in specifics when possible. For example, "When you did _____, I felt _____, and I would like _____."

8. **Focus on behavior or performance, not personality.** Focus on an employee's behaviors (what they do) rather

than on their personality traits (what they're like). For example, "You act self-righteous in meetings and it is causing a problem" addresses personality traits. Saying something like, "When you interrupt others to get your point across it causes a problem. Can we find another way that is more inclusive?" describes behavior and its impact. One type of feedback is helpful and the other is not. This goes back to creating psychological safety. The more you can create a space where the other person feels safe, the more likely you are to find collaboration and a solution.

9. **Stay on your side of the net.** This means your thoughts, feelings, intentions, and desires are yours; own your experience and don't project them onto the other person. Remember, you don't know what's going on inside the other person. Let them tell you, and then listen when they do.

10. **Practice active and reflective listening.** Active listening is a great tool to use when there is conflict or disagreement. Active listening is listening without judgment and showing interest and presence in what the other is saying through the nonverbal cues of eye contact, nodding, and an open and receptive body posture. Reflective listening goes one step further; it's paraphrasing what you've heard the other person say (content, meaning, and feelings) and asking for clarification. For example, "I hear you saying that you feel overwhelmed and really don't understand the next steps in this project. Am I getting this right or is there anything else?" An instance where your colleague

or team member is getting defensive or presenting as triggered is a very good time to employ active listening. It gives you a way to stay centered and nonreactive so you don't meet his, her, or their defensiveness with your own defensiveness. How does this work? In two ways: it gives your mind something to do and it slows the conversation down. These characteristics create more space for you to be present with what you're hearing.

11. **Invite feedback.** You want to understand how your thoughts, observations, and comments have impacted the recipient. Asking for feedback at the end illuminates blind spots and develops trust. Here are three ways to ask for feedback on your delivery:

   ▸ What worked and what didn't in my delivery?

   ▸ How did it feel or impact you to hear this message?

   ▸ How could I have presented it more effectively?

   I've included a quick visual summary of these eleven steps in appendix B.

Cultivate Belonging

Belonging is a human need, and in my experience, it is just as important for our ability to flourish as having healthy air, food, water, and shelter. We need relationship and belonging to thrive. We want to belong to ourselves, to others, to our workplace, to our home, and to the world. What gets in the way of creating belonging everywhere is that we have committed ourselves to *belongings* instead—valuing stuff and accomplishments over connection.

As we discussed in chapter 6, belonging is developed from the inside out. The more we can accept and love every part of ourselves, the better we can feel and heal any shame for the parts of ourselves we don't embrace. If we don't love and accept parts of ourselves, we can often project our inadequacies and insecurities as judgments on the other, which creates a feeling of "not belonging." In healing and transforming our internal belonging, we can extend acceptance and healing to those around us, no matter what our perceived differences may be. As Brené Brown said, "Our sense of belonging can never be greater than our level of self-acceptance."[24]

Cultivating belonging in ourselves, the workplace, and our greater world takes time and requires a strong commitment. This particular skill set courageously looks beyond the mask of what someone is presenting and connects to what the person actually wants and needs.

Outer Game Practice
FOUR ACTIONS THAT CULTIVATE BELONGING

Belonging is at the root of our ability to be calm yet powerful. To belong is to feel safe. It's about being accepted and cared for and feeling at home. Here are four key actions to cultivate belonging in your workplace and the world:

- **Get to know others from a beginner's mind.** Who is this person? What's important to them? What experiences may we have in common that I can use to build a bridge?

- **Bring awareness to your own biases with kindness.** It is normal to have biases. See it and turn toward it without shame; then shift to curiosity.

- **Spend time with other kinds of people.** This is helpful for learning and understanding different groups and experiences beyond your own.

- **Help people connect with their communities.** Within your company or organization, encourage the formation of groups based on shared identity and experience, whether it's the millennial group, the environmental group, the people of color group, or a male allies group.

Many people feel lost and disconnected right now. We hear in the media and from our politicians that we're more divided than ever. But I don't believe that's true. I believe what saves us in anxious times like these is our sense of community and belonging. The challenge before us all is this: Will we continue to rail about who does and doesn't belong? Or will we pause and look around and see our neighbors as ourselves? Now is the time for us to calm our collective spirits and start to see that we are one community and one world—and to create organizations that affirm this understanding.

Belonging Recipe

- I close my mouth and learn to listen.

- I choose to see other people with a beginner's mind.

- My voice matters and is welcome, seen, and heard.

- I create belonging at work by inviting all voices and perspectives to the table.

Remeasuring Success
Putting People and Planet First

Salesforce is one of the biggest tech companies in San
Francisco. We can unleash a power onto this city. All of
these people can go into the public schools and volunteer,
and they can work and make the city better. They can
improve the state of the city, improve the state of the world.
All I have to do is give them permission to do that.

—MARC BENIOFF, cofounder and CEO of Salesforce

In this chapter we will look at measuring success differently from the way
traditional business models have done it. Rather than limiting ourselves to
standard metrics such as revenue growth, market share, productivity, and
profit, we can add an entirely new dimension to the definition of success.
In light of the great challenges we are grappling with globally, *we can measure how well we are creating ethical and conscious companies that are aligned
with creating a sustainable world.*

Conscious leaders create conscious companies because they feel a sense
of purpose to be of service to the world. This means these leaders take all
stakeholders into account in their operations, decisions, and strategies, and
have a long-term vision that keeps them motivated beyond profit.

If you aim to put people and the planet first in your business, it's time to ask questions that go deeper than your balance sheet:

- What is my company's highest value?

- Why are we selling what we're selling, and how does it impact the greater good?

- How can businesses shift the idea of competition so we're in competition to be the best for the world?

To explore these questions, I will share research on and rationales for mission-driven leadership and corporate social responsibility efforts that enhance the bottom line. We'll also get better acquainted with the nine conscious leaders you've already met in your travels through this book—leaders who bring their whole and best selves to work and, as a result, *shine* their unique torch of leadership and manifest positive impacts worldwide.

Two Important, Newsworthy Moments

March 15, 2019 brought with it a stunning event. It was the date of the School Strike for Climate, a movement organized by sixteen-year-old Greta Thunberg. Millions of kids from 123 countries took part in a massive demonstration, demanding that adults take action to address the climate change emergency. Greta became a household name overnight. She has since been nominated for the Nobel Peace Prize and was chosen as *Time* magazine's "Person of the Year" in 2019.[1]

A fierce advocate for urgent solutions to climate change, Greta spoke at the World Economic Forum, a gathering of prominent business and government leaders, that same year. Unafraid to confront this privileged and powerful group, she spoke truth to power.

> Climate change is an existential crisis that some say we
> have all created . . . But that is not true because if everyone
> is guilty, then no one is to blame. And someone is to blame.

> Some people, some companies, and some decision makers, in particular, have known exactly what priceless values they've sacrificed to make unimaginable amounts of money, and I think many of you here today belong to that group of people. The future of humankind rests firmly in your hands.

August 19, 2019 was another pivotal moment. One hundred eighty-one CEOs and Business Roundtable members from the most powerful companies in the world—JPMorgan Chase, Apple, BP, PricewaterhouseCoopers, ExxonMobil, Amazon, and The Carlyle Group among them—released a statement on "the Purpose of a Corporation" that committed their companies to operate for the benefit of all shareholders.[2]

The Business Roundtable committed to these principles:

- Respect communities and the environment by embracing sustainable business practices.

- Deal with suppliers and partners fairly and ethically.

- Invest in our employees, fostering diversity and inclusion.

- Demonstrate transparency and effective stakeholder engagement.

You might not expect such commitments from major banks, oil companies, and tech companies, but even leaders at this level and with these track records are beginning to realize that paying attention to the big picture—to how their companies are perceived and to the social consequences of selling their products—is good business.

The two events I've highlighted here indicate that we have reached a watershed moment at the intersection of social and environmental activism and business. We can no longer deny the fact that the environment is a key stakeholder for every business and for everyone who inhabits this planet. And this realization arrives without a moment to lose. The world needs a clean energy economy if we want a shot at building a more inclusive, prosperous society and avoiding catastrophic climate change. Conscious business practices can lead the way.

THE PLANET IS OUR
LARGEST STAKEHOLDER

For too long, companies have ignored or brushed off the environmental impacts of their actions, claiming that it would be "too costly" or "logistically impossible" to build sustainability into their culture, their practices, and their business models. But these excuses no longer hold water. If you aren't serving the interests of your biggest stakeholder, the planet, then you aren't serving the interests of your other stakeholders either.

—MARC BENIOFF, cofounder and CEO of Salesforce[3]

Conscious Leadership Just Makes Cents

Now let's investigate the concept of corporate social responsibility (CSR). CSR initiatives have been shown to align a sustainable economy and future with bottom-line results.

A hefty study launched in 2015 by the Campbell Soup Company and Verizon measured the benefits of environmental, social, and governance programs within businesses. Titled, "Project ROI: Defining the Competitive and Financial Advantages of Corporate Responsibility and Sustainability," this study was conducted by IO Sustainability and Babson College. It found that the highest drivers of return on investment for any company are providing high-quality products and services and effective CSR practices that augment and boost business performance, delivering a higher return on investment than similar companies without such strategies.[4]

The report also found that companies that fully integrate CSR in their long-term business strategy reap the most financial benefits. Effective CSR can increase the market value of a company by 4 to 6 percent. For example, for a company in the S&P 500 Index this translates to on average

$1.28 billion in additional shareholder wealth (an average of $85 million per year) for a cumulative return of 133 percent over a fifteen-year period (1991–2006).

Also, engaging in meaningful CSR could avoid revenue losses of up to 7 percent of market value and reduce employee turnover rate by a staggering 50 percent.[5]

Beyond statistics and return on investment, one of the common attributes of companies that have high-performance workplace cultures is having a clear, well-specified purpose that addresses both *how* and *why* the company makes a positive impact in the world. This is their fundamental reason for existence, beyond just making money, and is not just a feel-good statement. It actually works toward uniting people, especially during difficult times. A clear, positive purpose also allows people to make better decisions and generates tremendous alignment and energy toward a common cause. It's been reported that 75 percent of Millennials will take a pay cut in order to work at a purpose-driven, responsible company.[6]

A company that is mission-driven and "on purpose" also creates a high-performance environment. According to Imperative's research, purpose-oriented employees are 54 percent more likely to stay at a company for more than five years and 30 percent more likely to be high performers than those who work solely for a paycheck. Employees who love their jobs are more productive and loyal, and cost the company less over the long term.[7]

Inner Game Practice
AWAKENING YOUR PURPOSE

This practice will help you discover the work you are here to do. It's about listening for your deeper calling and then putting the answers you hear into committed action. Have your journal close by to write down your thoughts at the end of the exercise. You can choose to experience this practice indoors or outdoors, and I encourage you to try both. When you're outside, take in all the elements of nature around you: the air caressing your skin, the pulse of the earth underneath your feet.

In this example, we'll do the exercise seated in a chair indoors:

- Find a quiet spot and assume a comfortable seated position. Stretch, roll your shoulders back and down, and bring your neck and spine into a neutral posture.

- Let go of everything that has transpired over the day.

- Now bring your awareness to your body and your breath. Allow your eyes to close, or rest your gaze on the floor, whichever best allows you to bring your attention inward.

- Pause.

- Take a few deep breaths, releasing anything that doesn't serve you on the exhale.

- Now move your body in any way that feels natural to help release any pent-up energy. You may even feel inclined to make some sounds to release fully.

- Next, exhale in a way that feels comfortable, relaxed, and authentic to you. Then, as you breathe in, feel your stomach rise. As you breathe out again, feel your stomach fall. Breathe naturally and notice your breath.

- Now bring some movement to your body while remaining seated on the chair. Breathe in as you slowly move your hips and pelvis back and push your belly out.

- Then, exhale out and bring your hips back to neutral and push your low back into the chair. Do this a few times at your own pace.

- Now you're going to make some statements. If you're alone, you can say them aloud. If you're not, you can say them silently to yourself:

  ► I love …

  ► I love …

  ► I love …

- Let whatever you love arise and then observe it passing by. Do this for one minute. It might be, *I love my family. I love nature. I love my home.*

- Allow what you love to take up space.

- From this loving state, ask yourself, *What do I love so deeply that I would fight to protect it? How can my life be of service to whom and what I love?*

- Choose one way to be of service right now—you can always do this exercise again—and focus your attention on it. Feel your love and your commitment to protecting what you love in your heart. Feel it in your whole body. Let this feeling radiate outward.

- Next, get in touch with your gifts. Ask yourself, *What gifts has life given me?* Is it deep caring? Contagious enthusiasm? A quiet commitment that wants to get things done? Creativity? Identify at least one or two.

- Now, ask yourself, *What holds me back from the fullness of what I can contribute to this world? What if I were bold? What if I didn't play small? What if I let my gifts out and expressed all that caring in constructive ways?*

- Showing who you are makes a difference.

- Ask yourself, *What is the first step I can take today that would support me in listening to this deeper knowing and in living and giving my gifts in service of what I love?*

- And finally, ask yourself, *What can I let go of so I can step into this deeper calling and purpose?*

Slowly come back to the present moment. Take a deep breath. Stretch. Then, when you are ready, begin writing. Write down one or two things you love most of all. Then write down an action step or steps you can take today to be in service of who and what you most love.

Now, go a little further and let your imagination lead you in beginning to put your discoveries into action. Visualize:

- What would it look like to engage in this action on a weekly basis?

- What would it look like to engage in this action on a monthly basis?

This practice will give you the confidence you need to translate your gifts into action with courage and commitment. And you can increase the power of this practice by sharing this commitment with three other people in your life. When we are witnessed in our commitments, we gain a sense of support and accountability that helps us follow through on our actions. We have to name it to claim it! And who knows—someone you share this with might be inspired to join you!

When I do this practice myself, the wisdom that arises for me is that my deeper purpose is to support the awakening of business—and by extension humanity—to create a sustainable and harmonious world and planet that supports everyone to thrive. My motivation for writing this book stems from this commitment. I can't bring my commitment to fruition alone—serving people and the planet is a big job, and it will require a lot of us to change the tide—but I can do my part and feel hopeful that we can shine a path forward together!

The Path to a Sustainable World

A report issued in October 2018 by the Intergovernmental Panel on Climate Change, a group of scientists convened by the UN to guide world leaders, reveals that the emissions path we are on will likely take us to 1.5 degrees Celsius of warming by 2040.[8] This means that as temperatures rise, many of the biggest cities in the Middle East and South Asia will become lethally hot in the summer. As soon as 2040—a period well within the lifetime of many who are reading this book and much of the global population—the world will experience worsening food shortages, wildfires, megastorms, and a massive dying-off of coral reefs.

The UN advises that to prevent this from happening, we must reduce greenhouse gas emissions by 45 percent from 2010 levels by 2030.[9] That is less than ten years away.

The economic losses that will result (and already have resulted) from the mega-storms, mega-fires, and millions of deaths expected from vector-borne diseases and air pollution are clear. Ten of the hottest years on record have occurred since 1998.[10] In 2016, the US experienced fifteen weather- and climate-related disasters costing over a billion dollars.[11] In 2017, Hurricane Harvey cost $100 billion-plus.[12] And in 2018 mega-wildfires swept through parts of California costing untold millions—with all these losses falling on taxpayers.[13] From my experience working with thousands of individuals and organizations on behavior and change management, I've seen that things don't really change unless there is a certain level of suffering. Until then, people choose to clean up the mess and go back to business as usual.

It is understandable to feel alarm, fear, rage, and even despair when confronted with global warming, but I'd like to inspire a sense of enthusiasm and spur wise action.

We can feel inspired by this mandate to change while watching the bottom lines of our businesses triple if we move the needle in the right direction now. The additional investment required to limit warming to 1.5 degrees Celsius is overwhelming—nearly $1 trillion annually from now until 2050. A recent report from The New Climate Economy shows that this level of investment will not only protect us from devastating impacts, but will also deliver $26 trillion in economic benefits by 2030—and that is a conservative estimate.[14] As my friend and colleague Alicia Seiger, the director of Stanford University's Sustainable Finance Initiative, said, "Climate change will need to be factored into every business decision going forward."

Sustainable Development Goals

Luckily, we have a fantastic blueprint to help us accomplish this and more: the UN's Sustainable Development Goals (SDGs) we touched on earlier. Incorporating these goals into our business strategies and operations can help our companies achieve a better and more sustainable future. These seventeen goals address the global challenges we face, including those related to poverty, inequality, climate change, environmental degradation, peace, justice, and prosperity for all. The goals encompass 169 targets, are all interconnected, and have been created to leave no one behind. Leaders from all United Nations Member States adopted them in 2015 and they are set to be achieved globally by 2030.[15]

I believe that out of the seventeen goals, the key is number thirteen: climate action. If we can target climate change with appropriate action now, we will be able to address and account for all the other goals.

So, what specifically are these SDGs? Here's the list:

- Goal 1: No poverty

- Goal 2: Zero hunger

- Goal 3: Good health and well-being

- Goal 4: Quality education

- Goal 5: Gender equality

- Goal 6: Clean water and sanitation

- Goal 7: Affordable and clean energy

- Goal 8: Decent work and economic growth

- Goal 9: Industry, innovation, and infrastructure

- Goal 10: Reduced inequalities

- Goal 11: Sustainable cities and communities

- Goal 12: Responsible consumption and production

- Goal 13: Climate action

- Goal 14: Life below water

- Goal 15: Life on land

- Goal 16: Peace, justice, and strong institutions

- Goal 17: Partnerships to achieve the goals

Take another look at this impressive list and read the last one again: partnerships. There is literally an unlimited number of ways conscious business leaders can move the world toward meeting these goals. The World Bank has estimated that in order to achieve these goals by 2030, trillions of dollars of private capital must flow into enterprises across the world that deliver strong social, environmental, and economic impacts.[16] Many of these will need to be for-benefit enterprises—businesses whose purpose is to deliver such impacts—rather than traditional profit-maximizing firms. This "fourth sector" economy—the emerging sector of the economy consisting of "for-benefit" organizations that combine the market-based approaches of the private sector with the social and environmental aims of the public and nonprofit sectors—is coming, and it's a chance to build an economic model that will benefit all.[17]

Now that we understand the magnitude of the challenges we must solve together, we have a sense of the potential that business leaders have to move us all in the right direction. Next, let's take a closer look at how they're actually doing it.

Nine Leaders and Companies Who Are Rockin' It for People and Planet

The conscious leaders I've talked with and interviewed for this book embody the conscious, inner-game leadership qualities we have been cultivating:

self-awareness, emotional intelligence, love, resilience, well-being, and authenticity. As we've seen, these inner-game leadership qualities support a strong outer game of socially responsible leadership that can bolster emerging conscious businesses. In the remainder of this chapter, you will see how a conscious inner game supports these leaders in using business as a platform for good and in committing to practices that align with the Sustainable Development Goals.

Salesforce: Technology, When Used for Good, Can Change the World

You've met Marc Benioff, cofounder and CEO of Salesforce, a couple of times so far. Marc has advocated for business as a force for good for most of his leadership journey, and he participated in the 2001 World Economic Forum to discuss the nature of globalization and the consequences it will have on economies, welfare, and the environment.[18] When he worked at Oracle, he learned that when you start a business, you have to start philanthropic efforts immediately so generosity becomes part of the culture. It's also important, he said, that a company's philanthropy has a clear focus and is modeled from the top down so it becomes a cornerstone of the culture.

Since its inception, Salesforce has given $240 million in grants and provided product donations for more than 39,000 nonprofits and institutions of higher education, while employees have donated more than 3.5 million volunteer hours to the community.[19] On top of that, more than 8,000 companies have adopted the Salesforce 1-1-1 model of corporate philanthropy—devoting 1 percent of their time, 1 percent of their profit, and 1 percent of their product to make a difference in the world around them, both locally and internationally. Personally, Marc and his wife, Lynne, have overseen $500 million in personal charitable giving and serve as "impact investors" in for-profit companies they believe are doing good things for the planet.[20]

As we learned in chapter 5, at Dreamforce 2019 Marc announced that in 2020, Salesforce would donate $17 million to align with the seventeen worldwide Sustainable Development Goals (SDGs). The company is also encouraging one million employee volunteer hours to go toward actions that support those goals. Dreamforce's latest effort to spark awareness of SDGs included a keynote speech by Barack Obama.

Marc and Lynne have focused their personal philanthropy on specific SDGs. In 2016, they established the Benioff Ocean Initiative, donating over $15 million dollars to support ocean protection. He partnered with the Coca-Cola Company to develop and deploy a physical plastic waste capture system in rivers throughout the world. Additionally, Salesforce was one of the twenty-one companies at the Global Climate Action Summit in 2018 that signed on to the launch of the Step Up Declaration, a new alliance dedicated to harnessing the power of the fourth industrial revolution to help reduce greenhouse gas emissions across all economic sectors and ensure a climate turning point by 2020.[21]

As part of Salesforce's commitment to this declaration, they are on track to achieve 100 percent renewable energy in their operations by 2022 by taking the following three steps:

1. **Avoid.** Salesforce avoided two million metric tons of emissions last year alone.

2. **Reduce.** Salesforce invested in green office spaces and improving data center efficiency while continuing to drive energy savings.

3. **Mitigate.** Salesforce signed two virtual power purchase agreements for a combined 64 megawatts of wind power, offsetting and producing more than the company's total electricity use for years to come. The company plans to be fully renewable by 2025.[22]

Marc and Salesforce paved the way for other CEOs to make bold commitments to solving climate change. On February 17, 2020, Jeff Bezos, CEO of Amazon, announced he would commit $10 billion to solving climate change with a new initiative called the Bezos Earth Fund.[23]

With Marc's leadership, Salesforce is committed to achieving SDGs 4, 5, 7, 8, 11, and 13: quality education, gender equality, affordable and clean energy, decent work and economic growth, sustainable cities and communities, and climate action.

MARC'S CONSCIOUS LEADERSHIP

For all his trailblazing, Marc maintains a daily meditation practice. He's installed meditation rooms throughout Salesforce Tower to support his employees and their culture with tools for greater self-awareness, resilience, and wisdom. Marc has been highly influenced by Zen Master Thich Nhat Hanh, the wise Vietnamese Buddhist monk, and often invites monks from Plum Village monastery to annual Dreamforce events. Marc believes having a beginner's mind informs his management style.

> I'm trying to listen deeply, and the beginner's mind is informing me to step back so that I can create what wants to be, not what was. I know that the future does not equal the past. I know that I have to be here in the moment.

Omada Health: Ensuring Healthy Lives and Promoting Well-Being

Adrian James is the cofounder and president of Omada Health, whose corporate mission is to inspire and enable people everywhere to live life free of chronic disease. Omada has developed a digital, evidence-based, behavioral-intervention software to help participants change their habits, improve their health, and reduce their risk of chronic disease.

Adrian became passionate about chronic disease after losing his father to such an illness over a five-year period. His father was predisposed to chronic illness through a combination of genetics and bad habits that caused extreme weight gain, high blood pressure, and diabetes. Then, while still fairly young, he was diagnosed with advanced prostate cancer. When Adrian's father passed away, leaving five children behind, Adrian thought, *Wow, no one knows how to eat!*

At the time, Adrian was working at IDEO, and he realized that even his most intelligent colleagues didn't know how to eat either. So, he started to read books on nutrition, discovering along the way that food is *medicine*, and that it can transform people's quality of life and help them live longer. When I met with Adrian at Omada's office in San Francisco, he had this to say:

> I feel the food system is an injustice that in some cases is unwittingly and unwillingly put on massive numbers of people. There are powerful lobbying groups that protect the interests of companies that counter the effects of public health, to the degree that the federal government spends a lot of money both creating poor health and paying for the impact of that poor health at the same time. There is no one saying, "Hey, that doesn't make sense. How can we possibly do that?" This is real money we are dealing with that could be used for other things, like teachers' salaries and sustainability initiatives. It's a messed-up system and the people that get impacted the most are immigrant families, the economically disadvantaged, and/or those with low literacy. These populations all have more trouble navigating the system.

To practice what it preaches, Omada inspires healthy eating in the office by stocking lots of fruits and veggies in on-site kitchens. The company's culture also promotes eating plant-based foods by labeling every conference room with the name of a fruit or vegetable, and the company encourages employees to take running or biking breaks during the day.

Omada is committed to Sustainable Development Goals 3 and 4: good health and well-being and quality education.

ADRIAN'S CONSCIOUS LEADERSHIP

As you might expect, Adrian maintains a daily practice of eating healthy foods. He also exercises regularly by walking to work or taking walking meetings with his colleagues. He has a strong inner game, practicing all the inner game qualities you've read about in this book. I've seen them all in action in the conversations I've had with Adrian. His employees praise him for being an authentic leader, one who always strives to lead from vulnerability so that his team feels safe. Adrian doesn't avoid conflict but embraces it, and as a result he's able to have the difficult conversations that support a culture of belonging.

JUST Inc: Just for All

Josh Tetrick, CEO of JUST Inc., is on a mission to make the food system healthier, sustainable, and just. Like Adrian, Josh didn't have the best access to healthy foods as a kid, but his motivation to start JUST came from his love of animals. He aims to help people eat in a way that is kind to animals and that allows everyone, regardless of income, access to a healthy diet. His company does this by turning plants into proteins, which reduces global warming by reducing the production of animals for food.

Josh believes most people are kind and compassionate, even when their food choices are not, which motivates him to create products that make it easier to make kind and compassionate choices. Examples are cookies, eggs, and mayo that are created in ways that don't harm animals, waste water, or deplete rainforests.

In one of our conversations, Josh shared this:

> There are a billion people around the world who are living on under a dollar a day—you've got to figure out how to make nutritious food affordable for them. We have identified a plant that can be made into a source of protein—and it's really, really inexpensive—and we imagine distributing that through the World Food Program to achieve zero hunger.

Josh has a strong vision and is passionate about his mission. He has dedicated his life to making sure that everyone eats well while reducing meat consumption and global warming. He aims to create food choices that are nourishing to the body and also affordable, and he wants to ensure that the entire system of intensive animal agriculture is dismantled before he dies.

In 2018 I visited the JUST headquarters in San Francisco; the million-dollar lab where they make plants into proteins. I was eager to try out their newest concoction, JUST Egg, a plant-based egg substitute. JUST Egg debuted in Hong Kong and now has demand in China, Dubai, and Singapore.

WHAT'S WRONG WITH CHICKEN EGGS?

Did you know that every single egg you eat requires an average of fifty-three gallons of water to produce? Chickens also require water-intensive grain feed (about two pounds of water for every pound of chicken protein produced) as well as water for drinking and irrigation. With temperatures rising and greater risk for mega-storms, fires, and drought, a high-protein substitute for eggs that requires much less water to produce is a welcome addition to the food supply.

I can attest to the tastiness of the JUST Egg and I loved their nondairy ice cream! My field trip to JUST happened to take place on the same day they announced a new partnership with Eurovo Group (Europe's leading producer and distributor of packaged, pasteurized, and dried eggs) to assist in a massive expansion of vegan scrambled eggs in Europe.

JUST's clean-meat team of scientists has big goals: they're working on creating plant-based tuna, chicken breast, and Wagyu steak too. "Chicken" nuggets are coming next year! And after its successful debut in Hong Kong and Singapore, JUST hopes to enter China and Japan.

This early-stage startup is committed to Sustainable Development Goals 2, 3, 4, and 12: zero hunger, good health and well-being, quality education, and responsible consumption and production.

JOSH'S CONSCIOUS LEADERSHIP

Josh cultivates his inner game of conscious leadership through well-being. He has a daily practice of walking his dog through the streets of San Francisco and eats a vegan diet. Josh values resilience and empathy and said he learned these qualities growing up with a single mom and used them during the entrepreneurial process of creating a startup. In fact, Josh values these inner game qualities so much that he screens for them in the hiring process. Leading from authenticity, Josh aligns what he says with his actions to create a trustworthy, mission-driven outer game to support people and the planet.

Green Common: Common Good, Common Sense

Green Common is a vegan grocery store with six locations in Hong Kong that recently expanded into Singapore. Its customers are treated to delicious vegetarian food that riffs on Chinese classics—think Hainan chicken, minus the bird—and can take home the newest plant-based groceries. Founder David Yeung tells me many customers eat at Green Common several times without realizing everything is vegan. They just like the food! David is also the founder of OmniFoods and its OmniPork, a plant-based alternative to pork that has been served all over Asia and in Michelin and fine dining-style restaurants as well as at Green Common.

David also started Green Monday, a multifaceted social-venture group that aims to tackle climate change, global food insecurity, public health, and animal welfare issues. Green Monday champions a sustainable food system by advocating for a once-a-week plant-based meal philosophy. In 2008, David was living in Hong Kong and shared with me the shocking news that Hong Kong was ranked as one of the world's highest meat-eating regions per capita. This information motivated him to make plant-based eating fashionable while standing by his commitment to do no harm.

How would he do this? He likes to call it the "Swiss Army knife of Green," because the plan was made up of the following four "arms":

- Start a movement where eating healthy is fashionable.

- Consult with companies to help them become greener.

- Invest in companies that want to go green.

- Use the retail model to encourage the consumption and purchase of the newest plant-based foods and groceries.

Green Common's nonedible items are great too—and include reusable water bottles, green cleaning products, skin-care products, cookbooks, and vegetable-growing kits.

David also wants to create an international alliance that includes investors, change agents, and innovators such as Beyond Meat and JUST Inc., and has been recognized for his role in helping 1.6 million Hong Kong residents shift to a more plant-based diet. His work earned him the Social Entrepreneur of the Year award from the World Economic Forum and the Schwab Foundation for Social Entrepreneurship.[24] Other honors and recognitions include JCI's Ten Outstanding Young Persons, *Fast Company's* 50 Most Innovative Companies, and Idea of the Year by Hong Kong media.

Green Common is committed to Sustainable Development Goals 2, 3, 4, 12, and 13: zero hunger, good health and well-being, quality education, responsible consumption and production, and climate action.

DAVID'S CONSCIOUS LEADERSHIP

David's daily meditation, mini-meditations, and mindful vegan eating support his inner game of self-awareness, emotional intelligence, resilience, and well-being. As a father of two with a very busy schedule, he makes sure to pause and practice good self-care, supporting his ability to be with the ups and downs of life and entrepreneurship with strength and humility. He enjoys great personal and professional support from his friend Josh Tetrick.

David's heartfelt commitment to supporting people and the planet comes from his inner game of love and authenticity. Because he wants young children to thrive, he works with more than 2,000 schools to increase healthy food options for children.

REBBL: The Power of Plants and Regenerative Business

Sheryl O'Loughlin is famous for contributions that led to the creation of the Luna Bar while working as the CEO of Clif Bar & Company. But she just as passionately led REBBL, a plant-based, organically sourced beverage superfood, for many years as the brand's CEO.

REBBL was a cause looking for a company and was born out of Not for Sale, an organization dedicated to creating a world without human trafficking, the fastest-growing illegal industry in the world.

How does REBBL stand against human trafficking? Two-and-a-half percent of net sales goes to Not for Sale, and that money is used to aid victims of human trafficking with counseling, education, and additional resources. REBBL started in 2012, and as of March 2019, the company has given $1 million to Not for Sale.[25]

Sheryl believes economic instability coupled with global warming and climate challenges are fueling human trafficking. Most people who live in poverty are farmers, and when they can't make a living growing food, they become desperate and turn to human trafficking. REBBL supports farmers by sourcing more than seventy organic ingredients from over thirty-nine countries to make their products. In this way, the company has become a part of many cultures worldwide.

Sheryl shared the following with me:

> Farming organically is great, but farming regeneratively goes even further. As we broaden our perspective and develop more holistic and comprehensive solutions, our positive impact will grow. We can work collectively with our consumers, partners, and retailers to create even

more change and add more value to their lives and, in
community with other entrepreneurs and manufacturers,
we will learn together and multiply our positive impact.

REBBL's efforts to support its growers and those in their supply chain
stem from a desire to build community resilience, which involves understanding inclusion, belonging, and diversity. To advance this aim, the
company connects for-profit organizations with nonprofits. Sheryl believes
business can be a force for good when organizations come together in such
partnerships. And these efforts are being recognized. In 2019 REBBL was
ranked one of the Certified B Corporation's Best for the World.[26]

Since then, Sheryl has stepped down from REBBL to become a
cofounder of the J.E.D.I. Collaborative, a community in which natural-
product companies and leaders come together for justice, equality, diversity,
and inclusion.[27]

REBBL is committed to Sustainable Development Goals 2, 3, 5, 12,
13, 16, and 17: zero hunger; good health and well-being; gender equality;
responsible consumption and production; climate action; peace, justice,
and strong institutions; and partnerships to achieve the goals.

SHERYL O'LOUGHLIN

*In a paradigm of connection, we view ourselves not as
conquistadors or demigods but as representatives and care-
takers of ourselves, one another, our communities, and the
Earth. In this paradigm, we take full responsibility for seeing
the bigger picture—as much as we are able—and thinking in
terms of far-ranging impact.*

SHERYL'S CONSCIOUS LEADERSHIP

Sheryl has developed her conscious leadership through regular meditation, a healthy diet, exercise, and a morning gratitude practice. She's one of the most authentic leaders I've met, and she shared with me in one of our conversations that she is not proud of REBBL's plastic packaging. She encouraged me to share the fact that if customers ask for what they want—for example, reusable instead of disposable containers—companies will listen and cater to this desire, even if it costs more.

1440 Multiversity: Exploring What Matters to You

Scott Kriens and his wife, Joanie, founded and launched 1440 Multiversity out of a passion and commitment to live well through personal and professional growth and development. The name comes from the fact that we all have 1,440 minutes in a day that we can be present for. I love that! At 1440 Multiversity, which is located on seventy-five acres in the Santa Cruz Mountains of California, guests can choose from courses and trainings conducted by thought leaders who are focused on engaging the whole person to achieve health and well-being, both personally and professionally.

When Scott and I met, he told me, "I think the growing call in the world today for connection, meaning, and making a difference all indicate that there is an unmet need in many of us. The true mark of 1440 Multiversity's success will be that we can offer a welcoming and inspiring place to serve the loud need for quiet time and invite each person to find their own answers to the questions that matter most."

1440 Multiversity delivers on its mission by offering inspiring classes in a gorgeous redwood setting that includes a beautiful spa, yoga and movement classes, on-campus nature trails, and a sustainability-focused cafeteria and buildings. As the largest consumer of produce in Santa Cruz County, 1440 Multiversity has set up a win-win agreement with local farmers, buying the leftover fresh produce from local farmers' markets, which helps growers maximize their income. The 1440 Multiversity chef then creates the day's menu based on available fresh ingredients.

I've attended 1440 Multiversity a few times to engage in my own growth and development, as well as to speak at conferences about conscious leadership and business. The food is definitely made with love for people and the planet. I also find that the community is a wonderful place to connect and learn. It's a tranquil place to recharge, receive support, and tap into what's possible for you and your gifts.

1440 Multiversity is committed to Sustainable Development Goals 5, 8, 9, 10, 12, 13, and 15: gender equality; decent work and economic growth; industry, innovation, and infrastructure; reduced inequalities; responsible consumption and production; climate action; and life on land.

SCOTT'S CONSCIOUS LEADERSHIP

Scott has been meditating regularly for the past ten years, is an avid hiker, and appreciates savoring sustainably sourced foods. He leads with authenticity and love from the inside out. Additionally, he has committed to his own personal and professional growth as a leader and in life, drawing upon the wealth of spiritual and transformative teachers and workshops available at 1440 Multiversity.

Bank of the West

> Your money has the power and purpose to finance the
> change you want to see in the world.
>
> —BANK OF THE WEST TAGLINE

Until recently, Linda Lockwood was senior vice president of human resources at Bank of the West. We've been tuning in to her story throughout the book. Linda felt drawn to working in human resources because she cares about the human condition and wants her team members, colleagues, and direct reports to have the opportunity and platform to do their best work. While things are always shifting, the fact is that most of us don't like change. Whether we're experiencing illness, loss, a move, or even a promotion, change stirs us up, and often we want to turn away from the discomfort that arises. One of the core skills of conscious leadership is to turn toward that discomfort so you can adapt, see the bigger picture, heal, grow, and take wise action.

Linda reached out to me a few years ago when she was diagnosed with breast cancer. She wanted my counsel, not only as a coach and advocate, but for my expertise on the subject of cancer treatment and recovery, as I'd written my master's thesis on how to best support the quality of life in cancer patients undergoing chemotherapy and radiation treatment.

I moved quickly to ascertain the right and most effective treatment protocol for her—surgery, chemo, physical exercise, and emotional and nutritional support. We talked frequently during this time and I was on the phone to support her right before the nurse wheeled her into surgery. Her ability to stay focused during this frightening process, and to accept the gifts of each day, was incredibly inspiring to me. Once she stabilized in her recovery, I helped her process the impact of her cancer and its treatment on her life and explore how this difficulty could be used as an opportunity for healing and change in her work and home life.

During her recovery, Linda and I did an exercise in one of our coaching sessions where she envisioned the life she wanted, and then I invited her to create a vision board of this new life. As a result, she made many changes and upgraded her inner game to manifest her new vision of work, life, purpose, and balance.

Shortly afterward, Linda's company embarked on a massive change: it hired a female CEO, who implemented a large reorganization. The company's work methods and culture needed a new and improved infrastructure to withstand the coming changes, and Linda and her senior leaders and stakeholders invited me to design, implement, and facilitate new learning initiatives, leadership trainings, and well-being programs for cultural transformation. Bank of the West began to *shine*. A little over three years after implementing these programs, the company was voted the best place to work for LGBTQIA+ equality. Additionally, Bank of the West took its commitment to people and planet seriously by implementing a new checking account for customers that will automatically donate 1 percent of the net revenue from the account to environmental nonprofits, through 1 percent for the Planet.[28] Customers' debit cards are also made from completely compostable material, so when you throw it away it, the card expires for good. I feel so proud of this mission-driven company and bank.

Bank of the West is committed to Sustainable Development Goals 5, 12, 13, 14, and 17: gender equality, responsible consumption and production, life below water, and partnerships to achieve the goals. Paris-based BNP, the parent company of Bank of West, also has a strong commitment to people and planet and has made a commitment to twelve of the SDG goals.

LINDA'S CONSCIOUS LEADERSHIP

Linda ignites her inner game of conscious leadership with weekly yoga classes, mini-meditations, healthy eating, spending time with her family, and gardening. She's able to give love to her company, friends, and family by prioritizing self-care. Linda cultivates her inner game of authenticity by sharing honestly and directly and leading with integrity, which is why she's been a trusted advisor to senior leaders in two of her roles serving as chief of staff.

Epic CleanTec: Do Epic Shit

Aaron Tartakovsky is the cofounder and CEO of Epic CleanTec, a company that is revolutionizing the future of water and sanitation.

According to Aaron, "Buildings worldwide use 14 percent of all potable water and very few buildings recycle it. The best place to start the change is where people live and work. Once you change the public's perception, that change can reverberate outward beyond cities and to other industries."

Epic CleanTec is creating a patented, on-site treatment technology called Living System that quickly converts wastewater solids into a high-quality soil product. This carbon-rich and endlessly renewable soil can be used to grow crops, enhance gardens, and beautify green spaces. The on-site approach will decrease the cost of wastewater operations for buildings and municipalities, mitigate environmental damage, and curb greenhouse gas emissions.

Epic CleanTec is also connecting green technology pioneers in California and Israel. The company is starting their operations in San Francisco but wants to extend this wastewater technology to developing countries, where revolutionizing the future of water and sanitation means the difference between life and death. This reflects Aaron's belief that if things aren't right in the world, you have to act and create change.

Aaron invited me to observe the Epic CleanTec process at a facility in downtown San Francisco, and it was pretty amazing! I saw first-hand how they convert waste into clean soil and fertilizer that can be sold and used for growing food (including their own garden). Aaron told me the company has been gathering the waste of Stanford University students to pilot their technology and are in conversations with larger corporations, like Salesforce. With our shared Stanford connection, Aaron and I laughed about the program saying, "Wow, Stanford has some seriously smart shit!" As you might imagine, Aaron has developed many fun taglines to describe the business, such as "Epic CleanTec—Do Epic Shit" or "Your Number 2 Is Our Number 1!"

Epic CleanTec won the "Innovation Showcase" at the Global Climate Action Summit in 2018, an international gathering of 4,000 world leaders, executives, investors, and activists that enacted a follow-up to the 2015 Paris Agreement. The company has also been recognized by other leading organizations, including the Bill & Melinda Gates Foundation, the Cleantech Forum, and the United States Environmental Protection Agency.

Epic CleanTec is committed to Sustainable Development Goals 6, 11, 12, and 17: clean water and sanitation, sustainable cities and communities, responsible consumption and production, and partnerships to achieve the goals.

AARON'S CONSCIOUS LEADERSHIP

Aaron supports his conscious inner game through gratitude, well-being, emotional intelligence, and self-awareness. He eats a healthy diet, exercises regularly, and pauses during the day to notice what he is feeling and what he needs. In addition to spending time with family every week, the Jewish tradition and faith is a cornerstone in his life. Aaron celebrates Shabbat Friday night through Saturday, completely unplugging from technology and focusing within for reflection and reset. You can see Aaron leading consciously from the inside out in his motivation to change policy and make a meaningful impact in the world while creating significant revenue for his business.

Ecoware: Packing Made from Plants

Rhea Singhal is the founder and CEO of Ecoware, India's largest sustainable food-packaging company. Rhea's background as a pharmacist and her understanding of disease gave her the perspective and motivation to become part of the change India needs in order to achieve responsible consumption and production. Ecoware is a biodegradable alternative to single-use plastic that has a lasting societal and environmental impact. The company's products are 100 percent recyclable and will decompose within ninety days, leaving nothing harmful in the soil, air, or water.

Rhea moved from England to Mumbai, India, when she was twenty-eight years old. In her new home, she saw trash everywhere, an alarming amount of single-use plastic consumption, a lack of recycling, and the absence of waste segregation. Rhea felt the need to create something that was easy to eat from and safe to throw away.

The world produces more than 400 million tons of plastic each year. In 2015, plastic packaging waste accounted for 47 percent of the plastic waste generated globally, with half of that coming from Asia.[29] In India at the time of this writing, there are 1.3 billion people. Just imagine the amount of trash that is not being recycled or composted and the health hazards and catastrophe that can cause. It is not a pretty sight.

India is a biomass-rich nation, which means there is a lot of agricultural waste, including that of wheat, rice, and sugarcane. Ecoware has created a positive, threefold impact: it gives agri-waste to farmers; employs eighty low-skill workers (the majority of whom are women) who are educated and given pension and health benefits; and has created a brand-new industry and sustainable business model that reduces tons of plastic in India.

Ecoware has also completed a voluntary environmental and social audit that estimates an impact of $2.74 for every dollar spent on Ecoware products.[30] The company has been going strong since 2010 and counts Indian Railways as one of its largest customers. The railway was already on a sustainable path, and now any food sold on this national train system (currently *one million* meals a day) is served on Ecoware tableware. Wow!

Ecoware is committed to Sustainable Development Goals 5, 11, 12, 13, and 17: gender equality, sustainable cities and communities, responsible consumption and production, climate action, and partnerships to achieve goals.

RHEA'S CONSCIOUS LEADERSHIP

Rhea enhances her conscious inner game with daily exercise, healthy food, time spent with her family, getting enough sleep, and leading with authenticity from the inside out. Rhea aims to ensure sustainable consumption and production patterns for all, but especially within India.

Being a Conscious Company

Those are some serious success stories! In them, we have seen the inner game qualities these nine leaders cultivated translated into outer game skills and used to lead powerfully from the inside out. These are shining examples of inner and outer game practices manifesting in business missions, commitments, and communication to support transparency, trust, and accountability among companies, shareholders, and customers.

As a leader who wants to do good in the world, I invite you to follow in the footsteps of these nine leaders. Start creating brave exchanges and consistent outer game actions to better align your businesses with the sustainability goals that matter to you. Can you imagine a future in which CEOs and leaders around the world apply the same focus, effort, and creativity to challenging business problems and use that same motivation to solve social and environmental problems? Can you see it, feel it? I can. In our last chapter, we'll see how.

Conscious Leadership Recipe

- I am aligned with my purpose and in service of the greatest good.

- I honor my commitments in word and action.

- I lead courageously and take a stand for what matters to me.

- I am a conscious leader.

Honoring the Mother
Waking Up the World Together

All living systems heal in true relationship. We need a "deep
revolution" in how we relate to the rest of life—not as
dominators of nature, but as partners in an evolutionary
process that is much greater than ourselves. Only love can
give us the kind of courage and willingness to offer ourselves to the more beautiful world we know in our hearts
is possible.

> —CHARLES EISENSTEIN, public speaker and
> author of *The More Beautiful World Our Hearts Know
> Is Possible* and *Climate—A New Story*

We are at a pivotal moment in time, one that requires us to wake up and let
go of old ways of thinking, being, and responding. This final chapter charts
the way forward so we can create a world that includes, honors, and pro-
tects all beings. We'll review the conscious inner game skills you acquired
in earlier chapters, which inform your ability to bring your wholeness to
work and to cultivate compassionate, mission-driven, and profitable work
cultures. We'll shine a light on the interconnectedness of the natural world,
our workplaces, and ourselves so we can begin to heal what our greed and
lack of consciousness have harmed. The new, transformative era of business

we've been discussing has tremendous potential to be in service of one another and of life.

To explore your role in this transformation from a place of wisdom, you will assess:

- What do I stand for?
- What do I stand against?

Answering these questions will help you create a vision that honors all life and invites collaboration for a harmonious world. Acting on that vision begins with understanding what makes you unique and then tuning in to those gifts. Then, with hope and a sense of possibility, you can move to boldly shine your light to benefit all beings, at work and in the world.

The Gaia Theory: Connecting the Dots

The Gaia Theory suggests that all the components of Earth, organic and inorganic, have evolved together as a single, living, self-regulating system. This living system automatically controls global temperature, atmospheric content, ocean salinity, and other factors that maintain its own habitability. The theory was developed in the late 1960s by James Lovelock, a British scientist and inventor, shortly after his work with NASA resulted in the conclusion that there was probably no life on Mars. Lovelock's research led to profound new insights about life on our planet. Since the Gaia Theory was conceived, more and more research has emerged that supports it, and it has shown that what happens to us individually affects us collectively and environmentally.

Of course, Gaia, our beautiful planet, cannot self-regulate if we trample it. Once we understand that all life is interconnected, we start to see that environmental and social issues are interrelated facets of the same crisis. We can understand the connection between our climate change problems and our own high levels of stress, burnout in the workplace, and increasing loneliness, anxiety, depression, and a lack of meaning. A disconnection between self and nature and self and other lies at the root of these problems.

Otto Scharmer is a senior lecturer at Massachusetts Institute of Technology and founding chair of the Presencing Institute, an organization he created to engage 100,000 leaders and practitioners across the globe in letting go of old systems and listening for what wants to emerge. He speaks to the way forward as being threefold: open heart, open mind, and open will. The MIT Sloan School of Management has dedicated itself to this work, and other business schools have followed its lead.

We can see the interconnection between our individual suffering, the suffering of our workplaces, and thus the destruction and depletion of the Earth's resources as all stemming from the same mindset. To change our behaviors to benefit our planet, a shift of mindset is required:

- Replacing greed with generosity

- Replacing delusion with wisdom

- Replacing judgment and hatred with love

Change Your Mindset, Change the Game

Those of us who are educated in the West are taught that success is based on what a person has on the outside, *not* the inside. We compete to stay ahead of other people so we can show off what we have or what we've accomplished. This unfulfilling, delusional approach impacts how we lead and run our organizations, and the result is a mindset based on scarcity instead of generosity.

My friend Lynne Twist, thought leader, cofounder of The Pachamama Alliance, founder of The Soul of Money Institute, and the author of *The Soul of Money: Transforming Your Relationship with Money and Life*, put the problem with this approach succinctly: "Our drive to enlarge our net worth turns us away from strengthening and deepening our self-worth."

We can see the ways in which greedy, averse, and delusional thoughts are very much responsible for the behaviors we see in our world. In the original Buddhist texts, these pervasive qualities of the mind are named the "three defilements." They are the origins of the scarce inner game that creates a scarce outer game. Let's examine these qualities:

- **Greed.** We look for something pleasant because this moment is not enough as it is, or we are not enough as we are.

- **Aversion.** We create a story that this moment is either unpleasant, not neutral, or pleasant. For example, we think *I don't like this meeting or this coworker*, which can lead to hurtful speech or disengagement.

- **Delusion.** When we are faced with something uncomfortable—a layoff, a loss, an illness, a warming climate—our thoughts jump to *This isn't happening* and we put our head in the sand.

All of these kinds of thoughts are normal—that's why the Buddhist texts address them. Having them doesn't mean we're "bad." But the fact that we have them requires us to remain aware that our scarce inner game is leading to a scarce outer game and also to make the effort to consciously shift our thinking to encourage different thoughts and, thus, different behaviors.

Let's say I'm a leader at a company and the thoughts I keep encouraging reflect scarcity: *I want more. How can I make more money? How can I gain more power?* What kind of actions will result from these thoughts? Actions that lead me to possess and to dominate.

The resulting behaviors can be seen in big corporations and are often the driving force behind war, corruption, and exploitation. The endless push for more oil, more land, and more profits have begun to collapse as the urgent need to move toward a clean energy economy has become clear. Yet delusion still abounds. For example, we have created the Great Pacific Garbage Patch, a huge mass of trash twice the size of Texas floating between California and Hawaii. But, disconnected from that reality, we still overconsume plastic.

This never-ending drive for *more* has workers experiencing burnout and work-life imbalance. To interrupt that cycle, a shift in mindset is required. The underlying thoughts pressuring workers to keep pushing past what is necessary and adequate toward "more, better, faster, harder" are *I don't have enough* or *I am not enough*.

When we begin to train our mind to turn away from thoughts of greed, aversion, and delusion, our hearts begin to open; first to ourselves and then to others. And when that happens, a transformation occurs. An inner game of generosity, love, and wisdom displaces the three defilements and we become able to lead from the stance that there is enough for everyone.

Let's spend some time with these opposite mindsets.

Generosity

Generosity is the opposite of greed. Shifting thoughts of greed to thoughts of generosity is really very simple; the trick is to remember to do it. Notice when you find yourself thinking *I don't have enough* and tell yourself *I have everything I need right now*. We explored this in the practice of being mindful of consumption in chapter 5. Another benefit of shifting your inner dialogue this way is that gratitude supports more generosity, as we discovered in chapter 4.

Love

Love is the opposite of aversion. There is a connection between aversion and fear, and you can vanquish fear through the practice of replacing fear-based thoughts with loving ones. Whenever you notice fear-based thoughts creeping into your inner dialogue, you can ask yourself the question *What would love do?* and listen for the answer. The inner game practices of loving-kindness (chapter 4), forgiveness, and embracing all your parts (chapter 6) will support this shift in mindset and "heartset."

Wisdom

Finally, wisdom is the opposite of delusion. There will be times when discomfort makes us not want to be with a current experience or present moment. At such times, we can notice that we're pretending the situation isn't happening and engage in some self-inquiry by asking ourselves *What is happening right now?* in order to see more clearly. Then we can ask *What would wisdom say or do?* The inner game practice of self-awareness will support an outer game of wise action. When we see things as they are, as opposed to how we want things to be, we can choose wise responses in our speech, efforts, action, and choice of livelihood. This is what it means to be a conscious leader, and it's the reason an awareness practice is integral to shifting scarcity mindsets to abundant mindsets and behaviors that reflect an expansive inner game.

Inner Game Practice
MINDFUL JOURNALING— CHOOSING WHOLESOME THOUGHTS

Take out a pen and a piece of paper. Identify a thought and then an action that has arisen for you in each of the three categories of greed, aversion, and delusion. Following is an example of what the completed exercise might look like, but I invite you to create a list of your own.

THOUGHT	ACTION
Greed	Eating more than I need.
Aversion	Acting hostile toward a coworker.
Delusion	Refusing to see and respond to a coworker's microaggression.

Now do the same exercise with the opposites of these thoughts. What actions arise when you have thoughts of generosity, love, and wisdom? Examples follow, and I invite you to see what emerges for you. Which thoughts and actions do you want to encourage?

THOUGHT	ACTION
Generosity	I give appreciation freely to my team members. I use my privilege and social influence to help others.
Love	I create safe, compassionate, and caring spaces where people can be their authentic selves.
Wisdom	I look at the big picture to see whether the products and ethos of my company are living in harmony with the planet.

THE SHIFT FROM SCARCITY: A CONVERSATION

What can we do individually and collectively to shift away from scarcity thinking and all that flows from it? When I asked Lynne Twist this question, she shared an example of what she might say to the CEO of the Chevron Corporation if given the opportunity. She told me she would thank him for the enormous gifts that the oil industry has given to humanity, to technology, and to the energy sector and acknowledge how difficult it must be to let that go. She then said:

I would give honor to this dying industry with love, respect, and gratitude. We honor what came before, acknowledge its usefulness, and then let it die. The oil industry gave us an opportunity—the chance to find new alternatives. We let go with love, not hate, and move into developing new systems and structures. People can't find their way to accountability when they are being attacked, but they will show up when we affirm their intentionality, listen, and make our best efforts to understand.

Being with Discomfort

To develop clarity around your relationship with discomfort, draw on your awareness practice to notice your thoughts when they arise. Over the last fifteen years, I've taken on the challenge of pushing my limits in how I relate to discomfort by spending one or two weeks in silence. While I'm on these silent meditation retreats, I don't have access to many of life's temptations and stimulations (such as technology, conversation, chocolate, coffee, sex, alcohol, and comfort foods). The practice of separating oneself from these distractions purifies the mind, heart, body, and soul.

A few years ago, I went on a week-long silent retreat, which was focused on watching the three tendencies of the mind we've been exploring—the three defilements—arise and pass. During this time of reflection, I gained some insights. I noticed that the more I focused on thoughts of greed, aversion, or delusion when discomfort with the present moment arose, the more these thoughts turned into unwholesome actions. For example, if I kept thinking, *It's so hot, it's so hot, it's so hot* or *I don't want to be here*, I found myself looking for ways to leave the retreat instead of finding a way to be with that discomfort and surrender to the moment. In contrast, when I embraced the heat, I found peace and joy.

Life is always changing, and discomfort is often part of those changes. Simply being alive means you will have a variety of experiences, and sometimes you won't know what's going to happen to you next. You can look for what is comfortable and safe, but you can never avoid the ups and downs of life. And that means that in order to live and lead consciously, you need to develop a relationship with discomfort, or you will be vulnerable when unpredictable changes happen.

Emotions like rage, sadness, jealousy, fear, and despair can feel uncomfortable, but with the right tools, we have the opportunity to stay with these emotions. And when we grow our capacity to be with discomfort, we have more choice in how we respond. It becomes possible to be with these big feelings and access joy by relaxing in the midst of chaos. By resting in the uncertainty of the present moment, over and over again.

We began learning how to be with our emotions in chapter 2 by developing our inner game of emotional intelligence and agility. To take that a step further, becoming more comfortable with difficult emotions allows us to be more skilled in how we conduct ourselves, take care of our emotional health, and protect what is sacred. This is a skill that becomes more fluid with time and practice.

What do I mean by "what is sacred"? I'm talking about our minds, our bodies, our hearts, our relationships, each other, and our planet. All of life is sacred. Honoring the sacredness in the world has never been a more important priority than it is right now. If we can understand that what is happening individually is congruent with what's happening collectively, we will be better able to develop our capacity to respond in ways that celebrate and protect life.

This next exercise will support you in being with intense emotions so you can create a practice to honor what is sacred.

Inner Game Practice
TURN EMOTIONAL UPSET INTO INSPIRED ACTION

This meditation takes thirty-five to forty minutes and consists of four stages. I practice it to help me lean into discomfort around topics that have often felt too uncomfortable for me to be with and fully experience. It has been a game changer for me, so I'm excited to pass it along to you. During one particularly difficult period in my life, I practiced it every day for a month. You can think of it as an emotional cleanse.

The practice is adapted from Osho's Dynamic Meditation, but I created a shortened and more joyous version that resonates with me. "Be your own guru" is my motto. I encourage you to do this practice once or twice a week; the early morning before breakfast is a good time or at another time in your day when you have more spaciousness. Just make sure you're in a place where you're free to move your body and make some noise.

I understand the challenge of clearing thirty-five to forty minutes for this practice, but if you try it just once you'll enjoy the benefits and understand how worthwhile it is. It will become a conscious leadership habit you look forward to, a way to achieve more joy, freedom, and capacity.

- **Breathe heavily (5 to 10 minutes).** In a standing position, breathe heavily in and out through your

your nose or mouth. Now pick up the pace and breathe more quickly, focusing on the exhalation. You want to move energy out of your body. Allow your breathing to become intense, deep, and fast.

- **Let go! (10 minutes).** Allow all *big* emotions to come out—rage, fear, grief, doubt, agitation. Let out whatever has been stirred up by your intense breathing. Give your body the freedom to express whatever it wants to express. You can scream, shout, cry, jump, kick, shake, laugh, or run around. Hold nothing back; just keep your body *moving*. You can let the mind focus on the things in your life that have felt too challenging to be with during your day. Or your week. Or your life! All your emerging difficult feelings are normal and valid, and the idea is to express these emotions so you can face the discomfort of them head-on. The challenging things you focus on during this time could range from personal to global, from a situation at home to the mass extinction of species in our world or the division and discord between Israel and Palestine.

- **Dance (10 minutes).** On the other side of discomfort and pain is—joy! Take these ten minutes to allow yourself to feel the joy that bubbles up after the physical release of challenging emotions. Play your favorite music to tap into joy. Laugh, smile, and stay with this experience, noticing the physical sensations that arise in your body.

- **Drop (10 minutes).** Now turn off the music, drop to the floor, and just rest. Allow yourself to feel the sensations in your body and listen to the silence. Relax in stillness. During the last minute of this rest period, bring your awareness to a sense of gratitude.

After you do this practice, ease slowly into your daily routine and see if you can stay connected to the joy you felt. It's easier to align with what matters when you live in a state of joy. Fear and uncertainty, on the other hand, can cause you to lose focus and make it more challenging for you to remember your purpose for being here.

As you resume your day, contemplate:

- What's the most important action I can take right now?

- What emotion do I want to feel as I am doing that action?

Clarity and inspired action come from being with things as they are, finding some space to appreciate what is present, listening to the wisdom within, and then acting on your awareness. This way of honoring the sacred in your life is an act of self-respect as well as an act of service to help support and protect all you hold dear.

Emotional Resilience=Climate Resilience

At the 2019 Planet Home conference I presented on the topic of emotional resilience as the pathway to climate resilience. Planet Home is a gathering of change makers, scientists, Hollywood activists, and musicians who are working to bring greater awareness to climate problems and their solutions. My talk stemmed from my belief that the more emotionally resilient you are, the more climate resilient you will be.

I led the participants of my workshop on a nature hike in the Presidio of San Francisco. First, I invited everyone to notice what they love about nature. Then, based on that love, I asked them to notice what feelings arose when they thought about the Amazon burning, the glaciers melting, and the massive numbers of species threatened every day. In other words, I led them straight into their deepest discomfort. People shared profound grief, anger, fear, and uncertainty—and hope. Embracing discomfort in this way gives us the chance to inform ourselves about how we want to act in service of the Earth. If we avoid or deny such discomfort, we will never have the opportunity to discover that.

Inner Game Practice
RELEASING AND RECOMMITTING

I invite you to do what the Planet Home conference-goers did as a weekly practice. Take yourself out into a natural environment and walk barefoot on the ground. Listen to the Earth, allow yourself to feel the nourishment from your connection to nature, and notice your love and appreciation of your surroundings.

If there is a tree nearby, sit with your back against it and receive its support. Acknowledge the extension of the roots that are being held by the Earth. These roots give life and support to the tree, just as they are supporting you with security, shelter, and nourishment. Allow yourself to receive these gifts right now, and notice that there is no separation from your well-being and the Earth's well-being.

Then let yourself think about all the destruction taking place on our planet. Let yourself experience all the feelings that arise from that—the fear, grief, and rage. If it becomes too much to bear and you aren't already sitting, you can drop down on your hands and knees and let the Earth hold some of the emotion for you. Make some noise if you have to, and let the emotions release out of your body; you don't need to hold them in. From this place of deep feeling, ask yourself, *How do I want to be in service of the Earth?* You may even go one step further and ask the Earth, "How can I best serve you? What you do need?" Whatever answer arises, follow it. And when you do, you will be standing in your commitment to honor life and Mother Earth.

WOMEN ARE THE LEADERS OF THE FUTURE

The Dalai Lama said:

In the West, you have education. This is good. You have technology. This is good. But you do not educate your people in values of the heart, of compassion. This you must do . . . It does not matter whether you are Buddhist or Christian. Compassion lives in the heart, beyond religion. Even me, a Buddhist, can say that you do not need Buddhism. All you need is the compassion of the heart. Women know this because peace is implicit in women. You put boys together, they make war. You put women together, they make peace. Women are the leaders of the future.[1]

Belonging in the World

Through our individual and collective efforts, the cultivation of belonging at work extends to the greater world. We can turn to nature for an example of this. An aspen grove is one of the largest single living organisms on Earth. Above ground, the aspens appear to be individual trees, but below ground, unlike many other trees, they share a single root system. Above ground, we walk around as individuals with different ideas, feelings, experiences, and histories. But underground, we share the same roots. If the water, soil, and air are contaminated in India, you have to care because they're your water, soil, and air too.

When we are leading consciously, we can tap into the roots we all share. This altruistic mindset generates the motivation to bring all voices and perspectives into the room so we can access the greatest collective wisdom and consciousness to create the solutions our world needs now. This is embodying interconnectedness, and it means relating to social justice and environmental justice as one interrelated issue. As Kenny Ausubel, founder and CEO of Bioneers said, "Taking care of nature means taking care of people, and taking care of people means taking care of nature."[2]

As a conscious leader, it's important for you to know that alternatives exist to the current "more is better" business model. We can look to the field of biomimicry, which uses bio-inspired materials and chemical engineering that's focused on the design of products and processes that minimize the use and generation of toxic substances. Three universities (Stanford University; University of California, Berkeley; and Singularity University) have all dedicated research areas to bio-inspired material innovation. For example, the San Francisco–based IndieBio is a new incubator program that matches PhD-level material scientists with business strategists, entrepreneurs, and investors to bring greater bio-innovations to the market.

Find Your Allies

Leaders perched at the tops of their organizations can often feel lonely, so it's important to create alliances. We're stronger when we tackle problems together. Remember Josh Tetrick, CEO of JUST and David Yeung, founder and CEO of Green Monday, Green Common, and OmniFoods? Josh and David are friends, and they've created a partnership that helps their missions and businesses thrive, with Josh creating plant-based products that David can sell in his vegan grocery stores. Sheryl O'Loughlin, the former CEO of REBBL, is part of OSC²'s Climate Collaborative program, a group of sixteen CEOs who meet monthly to find ways to partner and support one another in their business and climate-related initiatives. Sheryl and the rest of the natural food companies in the alliance are committed to creating products that live in harmony with nature and with the United Nation's Sustainable Development Goals.

How can you find your tribe? For starters, you can reach out to some of the leaders in this book or others in your community who share your vision. Why not abolish plasticware and utensils from all your meetings, off-sites, and cafeterias? Instead, use Ecoware or other compostable options. Follow Marc Benioff's lead and create a foundation to donate to and support causes that matter to you, or reach out to Aaron Tartakovsky at Epic CleanTec to find out how you can create a more sustainable sewage system in your office. Look into B Corps (business-for-benefit) that are committed to being a force for good. In 2019, five hundred B Corp companies committed to net zero carbon by 2030.[3] Invite others to help find solutions to the problems that matter most to you.

Deepen Your Inner Game

Let's get a refresher on everything you've learned as you've journeyed through this book so that through your conscious leadership, you can influence your existing company or create a new one that spreads joy and fulfillment and makes the world a better place. We'll walk one more time through the six conscious inner-game qualities you've been learning and growing over the course of the book. As we have seen, these are all qualities that support your internal operating system and are important skills to have so you can create a strong outer game. This will empower you to engage in the brave exchanges that are needed to shift corporate work cultures to create belonging and remeasure success in ways that put people and planet first.

Increase Your Self-Awareness

We started with self-awareness in chapter 1 for a reason; it's the foundation of conscious leadership. We can't change what we can't see, so awareness is key. It supports all the other inner game skills, conversations, and intentions you develop. If you have not already done so, I invite you to begin a meditation practice or recommit to the one you already have. It's the quickest, most direct way to enhance and sustain the inner game of self-awareness.

Meditation will support you in innumerable ways. It allows you time to be, to pause, to shift your mindset, and to be more present. It allows you to become more compassionate, emotionally intelligent, resilient, courageous, and aligned with what really matters. Ten minutes a day is the minimum effective dose—and I highly encourage a daily practice—but you can start by meditating three days a week for a few weeks and then gradually increase your practice until you're doing it every day.

Once you get into the groove, you can reinforce your practice with longer meditation sessions. You might look for daylong meditation retreats at your local spiritual center or try a longer silent retreat (three, seven, ten days, or even longer). These long sessions will strengthen your foundation. As I mentioned earlier, I've been doing long silent meditation retreats for years as a way to reset and deepen my practice and bring mindfulness into everything that I do. This retreat time has been a very healing experience for me and a game changer in many ways. Creating space in your life is the key to changing old habits and patterns.

Develop Greater Emotional Intelligence

As you learned in chapter 2, emotional intelligence is one of the most important qualities leaders and managers can develop. Humans are emotional beings, and each feeling we experience has an underlying need and powerful wisdom to impart. Get to know your feelings, be with them, and name them to tame them, and be sure to tune in to the physical sensations in your body as you experience them. Welcome everything and allow feelings to arise and pass.

To move to the next step with this quality, you can incorporate a simple affirmation into your day, *What am I noticing? What am I feeling? What do I need?* Being able to respond to situations that arise with emotional intelligence instead of reacting to difficult feelings will be a huge gift to everyone you influence at work and in the world.

Reinforce Your Resilience

How do we navigate the constantly changing complexities of our world with grace and grit? By developing a strong inner game of resilience.

This quality is all about reinforcing a growth mindset, moving our bodies to find balance, and meeting challenges with compassion and empathy. By expanding this inner game of resilience, we can shift the mood of our teams, bounce back more easily, and create thriving organizational cultures.

Lead from Love

Love is not a word many use in the workplace, but together, let's make sure we change that. Without love, we lose sight of the bigger picture—the fact that we are all in this together. The more we can offer feelings of love, compassion, and appreciation to ourselves, the better able we'll be to offer generosity of spirit to our coworkers. Taken together, the inner and outer game of love helps create compassionate companies where all voices and groups collaborate and innovate.

Make Your Well-Being a Priority

Strong leaders and managers know that well-being—both their own and others'—should be a priority. You can bring your brightest gifts to support the well-being of your company and the highest good for the world by prioritizing self-care. Burnout leads to breakdown, while self-care leads to enrichment—it's not really a hard choice, is it? What does self-care look like? It's nourishing your body with healthy food and good rest, playing, making time each week to connect to nature, and fine-tuning your balance of give and take.

Use Your Whole Self to Lead the Way

Leading from your whole self means listening to your deeper truths, your *yes* and your *no*, embracing all parts of yourself, forgiving, and communicating authentically. This is where your power is. Your willingness to be courageous and vulnerable will also give permission to the people around you to have brave exchanges. As more and more of us show up and shine our unique torch, we will find the solutions our businesses and the world need to flourish.

Brave Exchanges Create Trust and Belonging

Developing a conscious inner game and bringing our wholeness (our struggles, our wounds, and our dreams) enables us to have the kinds of brave exchanges with our coworkers that create an inclusive workplace. Clear, open communication is one of the most important qualities for cultivating trust, optimism, innovation, and collaboration. Commit to listening, being mindful of your bias, and being an ally. Choose authenticity, and learn to give and receive feedback with courage and kindness.

A brave exchange is a dialogue in which all perspectives, experiences, and differences are invited, acknowledged, seen, and heard. Creative solutions to the world's problems require that we all come together as human beings, drop the stories we have created that separate us, and collaborate toward one united mission. The role of male allyship in sponsoring women, people of color, LGBTQIA+ people, and nonbinary genders into positions of influence and power will ensure a workplace that works for everyone. Diversity, inclusivity, and belonging are not simply moral imperatives—they're business imperatives.

For a quick visual refresher on how to have brave exchanges, see the illustrations in appendix B.

Remeasure Success with People and Planet First

Remeasuring success invites all stakeholders in the activities of a business into the process of making decisions. As a conscious leader, you can advocate for policies that level the playing field, particularly for local businesses and our natural world. I invite you to dig deep and see to it that new systems are put in place in your business operations that mitigate climate change and advance sustainable development. If you need help in creating a more sustainable workplace, you can host a Climate Corps fellow.[4] These are people who work with companies in the US and China to help them accelerate and accomplish their sustainability goals. Since 2008, they've helped 450 organizations that, together, have achieved an energy savings of $1.6 billion.

Honor the Mother: Waking Up the World Together

We have but one planet, our magnificent Mother Earth. Protecting her means we need to collaborate with one another, share information and resources, and create partnerships for the well-being of all people and all life. We have the opportunity now, given our complex challenges, to live more meaningful lives than any generation that has come before. Far from being a burden, this is an enormous privilege, and it all comes down to each of us having a wise mindset, being willing to sit with discomfort, being authentic, finding our allies, being brave, and, of course, shining our unique light.

Make a Commitment

Now is the time to make a commitment. With consistent practice of the new skills you have been exploring, you can create new and transformative patterns in your life. To begin, I suggest you commit to practicing and growing in two of the areas we have discussed in this book—the ones that speak to you most—for a period of one month and then reassess what areas you want to continue to deepen and grow. Carve out time on your calendar and set the intention to follow through.

I'll do it with you. The thing about cultivating the inner game is that you never stop growing. There are always deeper layers and new applications for your outer game. As I write this, I have recommitted to focusing on the inner game of authenticity over the next month. I will pay attention to knowing what is true on the inside with my words, heart, and feelings so I can align that with my behaviors on the outside. Having spent time cultivating this inner game quality before, I already know some of the things I need to watch out for in this regard. One is that I need to watch out for saying yes. I like to help and to be of service, but I don't want to feel overextended, and if I say yes when I really mean no, that is being inauthentic.

What are you willing to commit to? What would serve you in the coming month? There is a wealth of practices to choose from in this book, but if you don't have a strong sense of where to start, here are some choices from previous chapters:

- Choosing to have brave exchanges

- Leading from love

- Making well-being a priority

- Turning emotional upset into emotional intelligence and agility

- Growing your mindset and resilience

Inner Game Practice

RAISING YOUR TORCH

Now it's time for one final inner game exercise to support you in making your commitment to being a conscious leader from the inside out.

First, read the following brief guided meditation. Then bring your awareness inside; close your eyes or shift your gaze downward. Bring your awareness to your belly and do a minute of the breath of fire exercise we learned earlier. Breathing in and out through your nose quickly can connect you to your fire, your passion. Then, answer these questions. Your answers will help you know where to put your focus and energy this month.

- What are three qualities that make you unique? Allow the answers to drop into your awareness.

- How do you want to bring these unique qualities forward in a new or more dedicated way in your life?

- What are you willing to let go of that is not serving you to be your best? For example, stories, stuff, busyness, resentments, self-protection, and/or control.

- What kind of support do you need to share more of your light and gifts with the world?

Once your answers arise, spread your arms and take up space. Say, "I have a voice. I own my yes and no. I have a say in how I show up and how this goes. I have a say in the kind of life I create for myself. I am powerful, and my actions will now create my future."

Now let's go further. Ask yourself:

What is the outcome I would like to generate?

Ask this question three times.

Listen to the answers. Be aware of where you are going. What does this look like in your actions now? You are a leader and you have the ability to create the outcome you want to manifest.

Now, ask yourself:

What qualities do I need to show up with to make this outcome happen? For example, grace, strength, confidence, courage, and joy.

See it and feel it now. You have permission to do this. You have the power to influence and create what you want. You have the ability to shape and catalyze the greatest good in this situation and in your relationships. *May it be so. Aho!*

. . .

Now open your eyes. Write down the action steps that emerged, the commitment you made to yourself, and then share it out loud with three people you trust. This is all about intention and surrender. When you are in alignment with your sacred intention, things flow.

Your New Beginning

I feel grateful you've allowed me to guide you and join you on this journey. And when one journey ends, another one begins. Now you're ready to take the reins and become the conscious leader that your community, business, and the world needs. I feel excited that you've chosen to shine your unique light as a force for good at work and in the world. *I know you can do this!*

I know, because I've seen it. When leaders spend time raising their consciousness by growing and deepening their inner game, they can shift their thinking from scarcity to generosity, from aversion to love, and from delusion to wisdom. When we all do this together, we will start to demand something more from our colleagues, our neighbors, and ourselves—on behalf of this sacred planet.

When we appreciate the distinctions between responsible and irresponsible uses of power—and the importance of practicing responsible, socially intelligent, and just forms of it—we take a vital step toward promoting healthy workplaces, peaceful playgrounds, flourishing ecosystems, and societies built on cooperation, trust, and belonging.

Honor the Mother Recipe

The world is my body.

The mountains are my bones.

The forests are my skin;

The rivers are my blood;

The air is my breath;

The sun is my sight.

I stand up in love for the Earth and life.

I commit.

I shine.

Acknowledgments

I would like to thank my family and my chosen family who encouraged me to shine, stand up, and show up: my incredible sister, Jessica McCoy; my uncle, Glenn Livingston; and my parents, Penni and Charlie Hauck, as well as my soul family James Baraz, Fred Luskin, Maite Acedo, Ananda Bhavani, Kimberly Karuna, Nancy Fraser, Bob Hoffman, Aaron Rabideau, and Sasha Idunno.

I share deep gratitude to my book midwives Laura Elliott, Jaime Schwalb, Anjali Alban, and Caroline Pincus. Thank you to Tami Simon and the amazing Sounds True family for believing in me and the message of this book.

Thank you, Lynne Twist, for the light and wisdom that you share with the world. You are truly an inspiration and I feel grateful for your support and presence in my life.

Thank you to all the leaders who contributed their stories, heart, and time during the process of writing this book. I feel inspired by all of you and wholeheartedly believe in you and your missions. My motivation for writing this book is to bring your wisdom to others so they can blaze their own trails of conscious leadership and support a thriving and sustainable world.

Thanks to Victoria Ayres, who gave me a beautiful space to write the proposal and foundation for this book and offering.

Fred Luskin, you have been chosen family since we first met, and I am immensely grateful for your mentorship, support, and friendship—you always see my light and support me to *shine*. Thank you for the early opportunities to collaborate and teach with you at Stanford University, where we created workshops and trainings together. You have always pushed me to grow with your no-nonsense but loving feedback on life, love, and the world.

I want to thank James Baraz for being my dharma dad, friend, mentor, and advocate. I can't imagine my life and path without you. I will always remember our first in-person meeting more than fourteen years ago during one of my first silent meditation retreats at Spirit Rock Meditation Center. Your unconditional love, handholding, and support through all my light and dark have been a true gift. You've influenced me more than you might ever know, and you have my utmost respect and love. Thank you to Spirit Rock Meditation Center, its staff and teachers. This space has been a true refuge for me to deepen my practice and learn and grow for many years.

Thank you to Barry Boyce and the Mindful.org staff for inviting me to contribute to and support your amazing publication many years ago. I'd also like to thank Dacher Keltner and the Greater Good Science Center and the amazing work that you do. Thank you to all the wonderful staff at Conscious Company Media. I feel so aligned with your mission to inspire conscious leaders and businesses to thrive. It is a joy and privilege to be an author and support your community. Thank you to Chip Conley, Jennifer Brown, and Mike Robbins. Your support, friendship, and allyship have been beautiful gifts in my life.

Lastly, I am sending gratitude and respect to the leaders, managers, teams, and organizations I have been able to serve these last several years. I appreciate Stanford University and University of California, Berkeley's Haas School of Business for the continual opportunity to serve students, faculty, and staff. It is one of the great joys in my life.

Thank you to everyone who reads this book. I feel honored by your interest and attention.

Appendix A
Feelings List

This is a list of feelings that will enable you to have a greater toolbox of feelings to identify and communicate with. I have categorized them in alphabetical order. In the first column are the expansive feelings, and in the second column are the contracted feelings. I encourage you to keep this list in view so you can familiarize yourself with these expansive and contracted feelings and state them aloud. You might identify one to two feelings a day that you want to use in conversation as a way to develop more comfort with them. Notice how you feel in your body as you label these and say them aloud, expansive or contracted? We experience many feelings throughout the day, and each feeling corresponds to different needs and parts of ourselves. The more we can name, claim, and embrace all our feelings, the more we can lead from our wholeness and invite others to join us.

	EXPANSIVE	CONTRACTED
A	Acceptance, Accommodating, Affectionate, Amazement, Appreciation, Appreciated, Assertive, Attuned, Accomplished, Acknowledged, Adaptable, Admiration, Adoration, Adoring, Agreeable	Angry, Abandoned, Afraid, Aggravated, Aggressive, Alarmed, Ambivalent, Anxious, Agitated, Ashamed, Awkward, Apprehensive

	EXPANSIVE	CONTRACTED
B	Balance, Beautiful, Beauty, Being, Belonging, Beloved, Benevolent, Blissful, Blooming, Blossoming, Bold, Brave, Brilliant, Brotherhood	Betrayed, Bitter, Bored, Bothered, Broken, Burdened
C	Calm, Capable, Care, Cared For, Carefree, Caring, Celebrated, Centered, Certain, Cheerful, Cherished, Collaborative, Comfort, Compassion, Compassionate, Complete, Confidence, Confident, Connected, Connection, Content, Courage, Courageous, Cozy, Creating, Creative, Creativity, Curious	Cautious, Cold, Complacent, Compulsive, Contracted, Closed, Concerned, Conflicted, Confused, Contempt, Contrite, Controlling, Cranky, Critical, Cruel, Crushed
D	Decisive, Declare, Dedicated, Deliberate, Delicious, Delight, Delighted, Deserving, Desire, Determination, Determined, Devoted, Devotion, Diligence, Disciplined	Defensive, Defeated, Defiant, Dejected, Depressed, Detached, Devastated, Devious, Disappointed, Disconnected, Discouraged, Disdainful, Disenchanted, Disengaged, Disgusted, Disillusioned, Disinterested, Dismayed, Dismissive, Distant, Distracted
E	Eager, Earnest, Earth, Earthy, Ease, Easy, Ebullient, Eccentric, Ecstasy, Ecstatic, Effervescent, Elated, Elation, Elegance, Elegant, Elevated, Eloquent, Embodied, Embrace, Embracing, Emergent, Empowered, Empowering, Enamored, Enchanted, Encouraged, Encouragement, Encouraging, Enthusiasm, Enthusiastic, Excited, Excitement, Exciting, Expansive, Exuberance	Embarrassed, Empty, Enraged, Envious, Exhausted
F	Fabulous, Faithful, Fantastic, Fascinated, Fascinating, Fascination, Fearless, Fervent, Fervor, Festive, Fierce, Flamboyant, Flexible, Flirtatious, Flourish, Flourishing, Flow, Focus, Focused, Forgiven, Forgiving, Fortunate, Free, Freedom, Fresh, Friendliness, Friendly, Fulfilled, Full	Fatigued, Fearful, Flawed, Flustered, Foolish, Frightened, Frozen, Frustrated, Furious

	EXPANSIVE	CONTRACTED
G	Generous, Gentle, Gentleness, Genuine, Giddy, Giving, Glad, Glamorous, Glee, Glorious, Goodwill, Gorgeous, Grace, Gracious, Grateful, Gratified, Gratitude, Grit, Grounded, Growth, Guided, Gumption, Gutsy	Gloomy, Greedy, Grief-Stricken, Grouchy, Grumpy, Guarded, Guilty
H	Happy, Harmonious, Harmony, Healing, Healthy, Held, Helpful, Homey, Honest, Honored, Hope, Hopeful, Hot, Humility, Humble, Hunger	Heartbroken, Helpless, Hesitant, Hopeless, Horrified, Humiliated, Hurt
I	Important, Included, Inclusive, Incredible, Independence, Indulgence, Indulgent, Ineffable, Infinite, Influencing, Influential, Innovating, Innovation, Innovative, Inquisitive, Insightful, Inspiration, Inspirational, Inspired, Inspiring, Instinctive, Integrity, Intent, Intentional, Irresistible, In-Service, Invited	Ignorant, Impatient, Impractical, Inadequate, Indifferent, Insecure, Irrational, Irritable, Irritated, Isolated
J	Joy, Joyful, Joyous, Jubilant, Jubilation, Juicy, Jazzed	Jaded, Jealous, Judged, Judgmental
K	Keen, Kind, Kindness, Kindred, Kinship, Knowledgeable	
L	Liberated, Liberation, Light, Lighthearted, Lightness, Limitless, Lively, Loose, Lovable, Love, Loved, Lovely, Loving, Loyal, Lucid, Lucky, Luminous, Lush, Luxurious	Lazy, Leery, Lethargic, Listless, Lonely, Lost
M	Magnetic, Magic, Magnificent, Manifesting, Mesmerized, Mighty, Mindful, Miraculous, Momentum, Mothering, Motivated, Motivational, Moved, Moxie, Mysterious, Mystical	Manipulate, Meddle, Mistrust
N	Natural, New, Nimble, Noble, Nourish, Nourished, Nurtured, Nurturing	Nasty, Needy, Neglected, Neglectful, Nervous, Numb

	EXPANSIVE	CONTRACTED
O	Open, Open-Minded, Optimistic, Opulent, Organic, Organized, Orgasmic, Outrageous, Outspoken, Overflowing, Overjoyed	Offended, Outraged, Overpowered, Overstimulated, Overwhelmed, Overworked
P	Passion, Passionate, Patient, Peace, Peaceful, Perseverance, Playful, Pleased, Pleasure, Positive, Potent, Power, Precious, Presence, Present, Pride, Primal, Productive, Professional, Profound, Prolific, Prosperous, Protected, Protection, Proud, Pumped, Purpose, Purposeful	Panicked, Paranoid, Passive, Peeved, Perturbed, Pessimistic, Petrified, Petulant, Powerless, Preoccupied, Pressured, Prickly
Q	Quiet, Quandary	Quarrelsome
R	Radiant, Rapture, Rapturous, Real, Realized, Receptive, Recognition, Recognized, Refreshed, Relaxed, Relaxing, Released, Reliable, Relief, Relieved, Remarkable, Renewal, Renewed, Replenished, Resilience, Resilient, Resolute, Resonance, Resonating, Respect, Respected, Resplendent, Rested, Restored, Revealed, Reverence, Righteous	Rage, Rattled, Reluctant, Remorseful, Repressed, Repulsed, Resentful, Restless, Rigid
S	Safe, Satiated, Satisfied, Secure, Seductive, Seen, Self-Sufficient, Sensual, Sensuous, Serene, Serenity, Sexual, Sexy, Shining, Significant, Silly, Simplicity, Sisterhood, Smart, Soft, Softness	Sad, Sarcastic, Scared, Scornful, Selfish, Serious, Self-Righteous, Shocked, Shy, Sick, Skeptical, Sorrowful, Spiteful, Startled, Stressed, Stubborn, Stuck, Suffocated, Suspicious
T	Temperance, Tenacious, Tenacity, Tender, Tethered, Thankful, Thoughtful, Thrilled, Touched, Tranquil, Tranquility, Transcendent, Transformed, Triumphant, True, Trust, Trustworthy, Truth, Truthful	Temperamental, Tense, Terrified, Threatened, Timid, Tired, Tiresome, Torn, Trapped, Triggered, Troubled

	EXPANSIVE	CONTRACTED
U	Understanding, Understood, Union, Unique, United, Unity, Unleashed, Unwrapped, Upbeat, Uplifted, Useful	Ugly, Unappreciated, Uncertain, Uncomfortable, Undecided, Uneasy, Ungrateful, Unhappy, Unheard, Unimpressed, Unseen, Unsettled, Unsteady, Unsure, Uptight, Used, Useless
V	Validated, Valor, Valuable, Valued, Vast, Versatile, Vibrancy, Vibrant, Victorious, Vigor, Visceral, Visionary, Vital, Vitality, Vivacious, Voluptuous, Vulnerable	Vain, Vexed, Victimized, Violent, Volatile
W	Warm, Warmth, Welcome, Well, Well-Being, Whimsy, Whole, Wholehearted, Wholesome, Wild, Willing, Wisdom, Wise, Witty, Wonder, Wonderful, Worldly, Worthy	Wary, Wasted, Weak, Weary, Weepy, Whiny, Wired, Withdrawn, Worthless, Wronged, Worried

Appendix B
Visual Guides
to Brave Exchanges

CREATE CONNECTION IN 6 STEPS

1

Invite a
conversation
to repair quickly

3

Lead with
personal responsibility
and authenticity

5

Make
requests and
agreements

Acknowledge
your
feelings first

2

Create
context for
the conversation

4

Find
your shared
reality

6

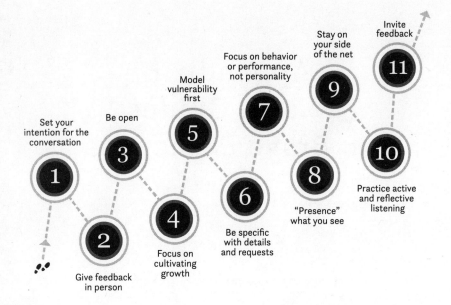

Set your intention for the conversation — 1

Give feedback in person — 2

Be open — 3

Focus on cultivating growth — 4

Model vulnerability first — 5

Be specific with details and requests — 6

Focus on behavior or performance, not personality — 7

"Presence" what you see — 8

Stay on your side of the net — 9

Practice active and reflective listening — 10

Invite feedback — 11

Notes

Foreword

1. Google Sustainability, "Once Is Never Enough," Google, sustainability
   .google/progress/projects/circular-economy.

Introduction

1. Andrew Ross Sorkin, "BlackRock's Message: Contribute to Society, or Risk
   Losing Our Support," *The New York Times,* January 15, 2015, nytimes.com
   /2018/01/15/business/dealbook/blackrock-laurence-fink-letter.html.
2. Erica Volini, et al. "Leadership for the 21st Century: The Intersection of
   the Traditional and the New," Deloitte, April 11, 2019, deloitte.com/us
   /en/insights/focus/human-capital-trends/2019/21st-century-leadership
   -challenges-and-development.html.
3. Andrew Winston, "The Scale of the Climate Catastrophe Will Depend
   on What Businesses Do Over the Next Decade," *Harvard Business Review,*
   October 9, 2018, hbr.org/2018/10/the-scale-of-the-climate-catastrophe
   -will-depend-on-what-businesses-do-over-the-next-decade.
4. Coral Davenport, "Major Climate Report Describes a Strong Risk of
   Crisis as Early as 2040," *The New York Times*, October 7, 2018, nytimes
   .com/2018/10/07/climate/ipcc-climate-report-2040.html.
5. Peter Lacy, "UNGC—Accenture Strategy CEO Study on Sustainability,"
   Accenture, September 24, 2019, accenture.com/us-en/insights/strategy
   /ungcceostudy.
6. Meir Shemla, "Why Workplace Diversity Is So Important, and Why
   It's So Hard to Achieve," *Forbes,* August 22, 2018, forbes.com/sites
   /rsmdiscovery/2018/08/22/why-workplace-diversity-is-so-important-and
   -why-its-so-hard-to-achieve.

7. Adele Peters, "Most Millennials Would Take a Pay Cut to Work at an Environmentally Responsible Company," *Fast Company*, February 14, 2019, fastcompany.com/90306556/most-millennials-would-take-a-pay-cut-to-work -at-a-sustainable-company.

8. "2016 Cone Communications Millennial Employee Engagement Study," Cone Communications, LLC, conecomm.com/research-blog/2016 -millennial-employee-engagement-study.

9. "The Deloitte Global Millennial Survey 2020," Deloitte, deloitte.com/global /en/pages/about-deloitte/articles/millennialsurvey.html.

10. Shemla, "Why Workplace Diversity Is So Important."

11. Lacy, "UNGC—Accenture Strategy CEO Study on Sustainability."

Chapter 1: Cultivating Self-Awareness

1. Lauren A. Keating, et al., "Good Leaders Are Good Learners," *Harvard Business Review*, August 10, 2017, hbr.org/2017/08/good-leaders -are-good-learners.

2. American Mindfulness Research Association, goamra.org/resources.

3. D. Smith, "Multitasking Undermines Our Efficiency, Study Suggests," American Psychological Association, October, 2001, apa.org/monitor /oct01/multitask.

4. Julia Gifford, "The Secret of the 10% Most Productive People? Breaking!" *DeskTime*, May 14, 2018, desktime.com/blog/17-52-ratio-most-productive -people.

5. Travis Bradberry, "Multitasking Damages Your Brain and Career, New Studies Suggest," *Forbes*, October 8, 2014, forbes.com/sites/travisbradberry /2014/10/08/multitasking-damages-your-brain-and-career-new-studies -suggest/.

6. David Mizne, "Multitasking: Does It Fit into the Future of Work?" *The Economist*, August 2, 2018, execed.economist.com/blog/industry-trends/ multitasking-does-it-fit-future-work.

7. Eyal Ophir, et al., "Cognitive Control in Media Multitaskers," Proceedings of the National Academy of Sciences of the United States of America, September 15, 2009, pnas.org/content/106/37/15583.abstract.

Chapter 2: Learning What Our Feelings Can Teach Us

1. "Putting Some Emotion into Your Design—Plutchik's Wheel of Emotions," Interaction Design Foundation, interaction-design.org/literature/article /putting-some-emotion-into-your-design-plutchik-s-wheel-of-emotions.

2. Peter Salovey and John D. Mayer, "Emotional Intelligence," *Imagination, Cognition and Personality*, March 1, 1990, 185–211, doi.org/10.2190 /DUGG-P24E-52WK-6CDG.

3. Adrienne A. Taren et al., "Dispositional Mindfulness Co-Varies with Smaller Amygdala and Caudate Volumes in Community Adults," *PLOS One,* May 22, 2013, doi.org/10.1371/journal.pone.0064574.

4. Jill Bolte Taylor, *My Stroke of Insight: A Brain Scientist's Personal Journey* (New York: Penguin, 2009); Alain Morin, "Self-Awareness Deficits Following Loss of Inner Speech: Dr. Jill Bolte Taylor's Case Study," *Consciousness and Cognition* 18, no. 2 (June 2009): 524–29, doi.org/10.1016/j.concog.2008.09.008.

5. T. A. Ito et al., "Negative Information Weighs More Heavily on the Brain: The Negativity Bias in Evaluative Categorizations," *Journal of Personal and Social Psychology* 75, no. 4 (October 1998): 887–900, pubmed.ncbi.nlm.nih .gov/9825526.

6. Carley Hauck, carleyhauck.com/resources.

7. "bell hooks Tells the Story of the First Time She Met Thich Nhat Hanh," *Lion's Roar*, December 21, 2017, lionsroar.com/bell-hooks-on-meeting-thich -nhat-hanh.

8. Jenna Goudreau, "Crying at Work, a Woman's Burden," *Forbes,* January 11, 2011, forbes.com/sites/jennagoudreau/2011/01/11/crying-at-work -a-womans-burden-study-men-sex-testosterone-tears-arousal.

9. Hauck, carleyhauck.com/resources.

10. "Is Empathy Boss? The Science Behind Soft Skills—What Really Drives Performance?" Development Dimensions International, Inc., slideshare.net /ddiworld/high-resolution-leadership-study.

11. Justin Bariso, "There Are Actually 3 Types of Empathy. Here's How They Differ—and How You Can Develop Them All," *Inc.,* September 19, 2018, inc.com/justin-bariso/there-are-actually-3-types-of-empathy-heres-how -they-differ-and-how-you-can-develop-them-all.html.

Chapter 3: Flourishing in Uncertain Times

1. "Gallup 2018 Global Emotions Report," Gallup, gallup.com/analytics /241961/gallup-global-emotions-report-2018.aspx.

2. Abiola Keller et al., "Does the Perception That Stress Affects Health Matter? The Association with Health and Mortality," *Health Psychology* 31, no. 5 (September 2012): 677–84, doi.org10.1037/a0026743.

3. "Decades of Scientific Research That Started a Growth Mindset Revolution: Dr. Dweck's Research into Growth Mindset Changed Education Forever," Mindset Works, Inc., 2017, mindsetworks.com/science.

4. SWNS, "Americans Check Their Phones 80 Times a Day: Study," *New York Post*, November 8, 2017, nypost.com/2017/11/08/americans-check-their -phones-80-times-a-day-study.

5. Carley Hauck, "A 5-Step Process for Befriending Your Inner Critic to Become a Better Leader," *Conscious Company,* November 23, 2019, consciouscompanymedia.com/personal-development/a-5-step-process -for-befriending-your-inner-critic-to-become-a-better-leader.

6. Jaruwan Sakulku and James Alexander, "The Impostor Phenomenon," *International Journal of Behavioral Science* 6, no. 1 (June 2011): 75–97, doi.org/10.14456/ijbs.2011.6.

7. William A. Kahn, "Psychological Conditions of Personal Engagement and Disengagement at Work," *Academy of Management Journal*, November 30, 2017, doi.org/10.5465/256287.

Chapter 4: Leading with Love

1. Bob Chapman and Rajendra Sisodia, *Everybody Matters: The Extraordinary Power of Caring for Your People Like Family* (New York: Penguin Random House, 2015).

2. Margarita Tartakovsky, "Why Ruminating Is Unhealthy and How to Stop," Psych Central, July 20, 2011, psychcentral.com/blog/why-ruminating-is -unhealthy-and-how-to-stop.

3. B. L. Fredrickson et al., "Open Hearts Build Lives: Positive Emotions, Induced Through Loving-Kindness Meditation, Build Consequential Personal Resources," *Journal of Personal and Social Psychology* 95, no. 5 (November 2008): 1045–62, doi.org/10.1037/a0013262.

4. S. G. Hofmann et al., "Loving-Kindness and Compassion Meditation: Potential for Psychological Interventions," *Clinical Psychology Review* 31, no. 7 (November 2011): 1126–32, doi.org/10.1016/j.cpr.2011.07.003.

5. Wendy Rose Gould "Go Ahead, Talk to Yourself. It's Normal—and Good for You," NBC News, October 9, 2018, nbcnews.com/better/health/talking-yourself-normal-here-s-how-master-it-ncna918091.

6. Shelley E. Taylor "Tend and Befriend: Biobehavioral Bases of Affiliation Under Stress," *Current Directions in Psychological Science* 15, no. 6 (December 2006): 273–77, doi.org/10.1111/j.1467-8721.2006.00451.x.

7. Kristin Neff *Self-Compassion: The Proven Power of Being Kind to Yourself* (New York: William Morrow, 2011; reprint edition 2015).

8. Sigal G. Barsade and Olivia A. O'Neill, "What's Love Got to Do with It?: A Longitudinal Study of the Culture of Companionate Love and Employee and Client Outcomes in a Long-term Care Setting" *Administrative Science Quarterly*, May 29, 2014, doi.org/10.1177/0001839214538636.

9. Barsade and O'Neill, "What's Love Got to Do with It?"

10. Sigal G. Barsade, "The Ripple Effect: Emotional Contagion and Its Influence on Group Behavior," *Administrative Science Quarterly*, December 1, 2002, doi.org/10.2307/3094912.

11. Austin Carr and Dina Bass, "The Most Valuable Company (for Now) Is Having a Nadellaissance," *Forbes*, May 2, 2019, medium.com/bloomberg-businessweek/the-most-valuable-company-for-now-is-having-a-nadellaissance-be9fa358e21f.

12. Kim Cameron et al., "Effects of Positive Practices on Organizational Effectiveness," *Journal of Applied Behavioral Sciences*, January 26, 2011, doi.org/10.1177/0021886310395514.

13. Cameron et al., "Effects of Positive Practices on Organizational Effectiveness."

14. Natural Resources Defense Council, The Global Climate Action Summit, nrdc.org/global-climate-action-summit.

15. "2020 World Changing Ideas," *Fast Company*, fastcompany.com/apply/world-changing-ideas.

16. Jane E. Dutton et al., "Compassion at Work," *Annual Review of Organizational Psychology and Organizational Behavior* 1 (March 2014): 277–304, doi.org/10.1146/annurev-orgpsych-031413-091221.

17. Jeffrey R. Spence et al., "Helpful Today, But Not Tomorrow? Feeling Grateful as a Predictor of Daily Organizational Citizenship Behaviors," *Personnel Psychology: The Study of People at Work*, June 18, 2013, doi.org/10.1111/peps.12051.

18. Robert Emmons, "Three Surprising Ways Gratitude Works at Work," *Greater Good Magazine*, October 11, 2017, greatergood.berkeley.edu/article/item/three_surprising_ways_that_gratitude_works_at_work.

19. Naz Beheshti, "10 Timely Statistics About the Connection Between Employee Engagement and Wellness," *Forbes*, January 16, 2019, forbes.com/sites/nazbeheshti/2019/01/16/10-timely-statistics-about-the-connection-between-employee-engagement-and-wellness.

Chapter 5: Creating Your Recipe for Well-Being

1. Clif Bar & Company, "The Five Aspirations," clifbar.com/stories/the-five-aspirations.

2. Shreeshan Venkatesh and Ishan Kukreti, "An Indian Consumes 11kg Plastic Every Year and an Average American 109kg," *DownToEarth,* June 6, 2018, downtoearth.org.in/news/waste/an-indian-consumes-11-kg-plastic-every-year-and-an-average-american-109-kg-60745.

3. Martin Stepanek et al., "Individual, Workplace, and Combined Effects Modeling of Employee Productivity Loss," *Journal of Occupational and Environmental Medicine* 61, no. 6 (June 2019): 469–78, doi.org/10.1097/JOM.0000000000001573.

4. Rhitu Chatterjee and Carmel Wroth, "WHO Redefines Burnout as a 'Syndrome' Linked to Chronic Stress at Work," NPR *Morning Edition*, May 28, 2019, npr.org/sections/health-shots/2019/05/28/727637944/who-redefines-burnout-as-a-syndrome-linked-to-chronic-stress-at-work.

5. Bob Chapman, "The Slow Burn of Poor Leadership," Bob Chapman's Truly Human Leadership, June 13, 2019, trulyhumanleadership.com/?p=4322.

6. Susan Cunningham, "The Hidden Stress of Cell Phones," UCHealth, February 6, 2018, uchealth.org/today/the-hidden-stress-of-cell-phones.

7. Chris Wilcox et al., "Threat of Plastic Pollution to Seabirds Is Global, Pervasive, and Increasing," *Proceedings of the National Academy of Sciences of the United States of America,* September 22, 2015, pnas.org/content/112/38/11899.

8. "Microplastics Detected in Humans for the First Time," Medical University of Vienna, October 23, 2018, meduniwien.ac.at/web/en/about-us/news /detailsite/2018/news-october-2018/microplastics-detected-in-humans-for -the-first-time.

9. Marc G. Berman et al, "The Cognitive Benefits of Interacting with Nature," *Psychological Science* 19, no. 12 (December 1, 2008), doi.org/10.1111 /j.1467-9280.2008.02225.x.

10. Jo Barton and Jules Pretty, "What Is the Best Dose of Nature and Green Exercise for Improving Mental Health? A Multi-Study Analysis," *Environmental Science and Technology* 44, no. 10 (May 15, 2010), ncbi.nlm .nih.gov./pubmed/20337470.

11. Neil E. Klepeis et al., "The National Human Activity Pattern Survey (NHAPS): A Resource for Assessing Exposure to Environmental Pollutants," *Journal of Exposure Science & Environmental Epidemiology* 11, no. 3 (July 26, 2001): 231–52, nature.com/articles/7500165.

12. "World Urbanization Prospects," United Nations Department of Economic & Social Affairs, 2014, revision, un.org/en/development/desa/publications /2014-revision-world-urbanization-prospects.html.

13. James Owen, "Farming Claims Almost Half Earth's Land, New Maps Show," *National Geographic*, December 9, 2005, nationalgeographic.com/news /2005/12/agriculture-food-crops-land.

14. Nadia Murray-Ragg, "60% of All Mammals on Earth Are Livestock, Says New Study," LiveKindly, May 28, 2018, livekindly.co/60-of-all-mammals -on-earth-are-livestock-says-new-study.

15. "Meat: The Future Series—Alternative Proteins," World Economic Forum, January 3, 2019, weforum.org/whitepapers/meat-the-future-series-alternative -proteins.

16. Philip Tuso et al., "National Update for Physicians: Plant-Based Diets," *The Permanente Journal* 17, no. 2 (Spring 2013): 61–66. ncbi.nlm.nih.gov/pmc /articles/PMC3662288.

17. Nadia Murray-Ragg, "30% of Swedish Millennials Eating Vegan Food for Health and Sustainability," LiveKindly, July 16, 2018, livekindly.co/30-of -swedish-millennials-eating-vegan-food-health-sustainability.

18. The Monday Campaigns, "Meatless Monday—The Global Movement," mondaycampaigns.org/meatless-Monday/the-global-movement.

19. Nadia Murray-Ragg, "Harvard Conference Emphasises Pressing Need for End to Animal Agriculture," LiveKindly, October 16, 2017, livekindly.com /conference-harvard-animal-agriculture.

20. "Salesforce Continues Commitment to the Sustainable Development Goals at Dreamforce 2019, Commits $17 Million and One Million Volunteer Hours to Address the World's Most Pressing Problems," Salesforce press release, November 18, 2019, investor.salesforce.com/press-releases/press -release-details/2019/Salesforce-Continues-Commitment-to-the-Sustainable -Development-Goals-at-Dreamforce-2019-Commits-17-Million-and-One -Million-Volunteer-Hours-to-Address-the-Worlds-Most-Pressing-Problems /default.aspx.

21. United Nations, Sustainable Development Goals, un.org /sustainabledevelopment/sustainable-development-goals.

22. Sonali Kohli, "You Really Can Work Longer Hours Without Killing Your Productivity," Quartz, December 16, 2014, qz.com/313397/you-really -can-work-longer-hours-without-killing-your-productivity.

23. Lisa Eadicicco, "Microsoft Experimented with a 4-Day Workweek, and Productivity Jumped by 40%," *Business Insider*, November 4, 2019, businessinsider.com/microsoft-4-day-work-week-boosts-productivity-2019-11.

Chapter 6: Shining Your Authentic Light

1. Michael Schneider, "Google Spent 2 Years Studying 180 Teams. The Most Successful Ones Shared These 5 Traits," *Inc.*, July 19, 2017, inc.com /michael-schneider/google-thought-they-knew-how-to-create-the-perfect.html.

2. Carley Hauck, carleyhauck.com/resources.

3. Michael McCullough, "Forgiveness: Who Does It and How Do They Do It?" *Current Directions in Psychological Science* 10, no. 6 (December 2001): 194–97, doi.org/10.1111/1467-8721.00147.

4. Frederic Luskin, *Forgive for Good: A Proven Prescription for Health and Happiness* (New York: HarperCollins, 2002).

5. Kyle Benson, "The Magic Relationship Ratio, According to Science," The Gottman Institute, October 4, 2017, gottman.com/blog/the-magic -relationship-ratio-according-science.

Chapter 7: Encouraging Brave Exchanges

1. Amy C. Edmondson and Zhike Lei, "Psychological Safety: The History, Renaissance, and Future of an Interpersonal Construct," *Annual Review of Organizational Psychology and Organizational Behavior* 1(January 10, 2014): 23–43, doi.org/10.1146/annurev-orgpsych-031413-091305.

2. Naomi I. Eisenberger et al., "Does Rejection Hurt? An fMRI Study of Social Exclusion," *Science* 302, no. 5643 (October 10, 2003): 290–92, doi.org/10.1126/science.1089134.

3. "Building a Movement of Corporate Philanthropy," Pledge 1%, 2020, pledge1percent.org.

4. Julie Bort, "Salesforce CEO Marc Benioff Makes Good on a Threat to Indiana over Controversial 'Anti-Gay' Legislation," *Business Insider*, March 26, 2015, businessinsider.com/benioff-makes-good-on-threat-to-indiana-2015-3.

5. Cindy Robbins, "2019 Salesforce Equal Pay Assessment Update," Salesforce blog, April 2019, salesforce.com/blog/2019/04/equal-pay -update-2019.html.

6. "Top CEOs 2019: Employees' Choice," Glassdoor, May 2019, glassdoor.com /Award/Top-CEOs-LST_KQ0,8.htm.

7. Jordan Novet, "Marc Benioff to Tech Industry: 'Your Employees and Executives Are Going to Walk Out' If They Don't Trust You," CNBC, September 25, 2018, cnbc.com/2018/09/25/marc-benioff-says-trust-should -be-the-top-value-for-tech-companies.html.

8. "Millennial Careers: 2020 Vision," ManpowerGroup, manpowergroup .com/wps/wcm/connect/660ebf65-144c-489e-975c-9f838294c237 /MillennialsPaper1_2020Vision_lo.pdf?MOD=AJPERES.

9. Alison Beard and Tomas Chamorro-Premuzic, "Why Are We Still Promoting Incompetent Men?" *Harvard Business Review*, March 12, 2019, hbr.org /podcast/2019/03/why-are-we-still-promoting-incompetent-men.

10. Adam Lueke and Bryan Gibson, "Mindfulness Meditation Reduces Implicit Age and Race Bias: The Role of Reduced Automaticity of Responding," *Social Psychological and Personality Science*, November 24, 2014, doi.org/abs/10.1177 /1948550614559651.

11. "Project Implicit," 2011, implicit.harvard.edu/implicit.

12. Anna Powers, "A Study Finds That Diverse Companies Produce 19% More Revenue," *Forbes*, June 27, 2018, forbes.com/sites/annapowers/2018/06/27/a-study-finds-that-diverse-companies-produce-19-more-revenue.

13. Carley Hauck, "The Role of Male Allyship in Conscious Leadership and Business with Vince Guglielmetti," January 10, 2020, carleyhauck.com/2020/01/29/the-role-of-male-allyship-in-conscious-leadership-and-business-with-vince-guglielmetti.

14. Hauck, "The Role of Male Allyship in Conscious Leadership and Business with Vince Guglielmetti."

15. "Drive Change: SPDR SSGA Gender Diversity Index ETF," State Street Global Advisors, March 2018, ssga.com/investment-topics/general-investing/2018/04/drive_change_gender_diversity.pdf.

16. Jack Zenger and Joseph Folkman, "Research: Women Score Higher Than Men in Most Leadership Skills," *Harvard Business Review*, June 25, 2019, hbr.org/2019/06/research-women-score-higher-than-men-in-most-leadership-skills.

17. Kellie A. McElhaney and Sanaz Mobasseri, "Women Create a Sustainable Future," UC Berkeley Haas School of Business, October 2012, eticanews.it/wp-content/uploads/2012/11/Report-Women_Create_Sustainable_Value.pdf.

18. "Drive Change: SPDR SSGA Gender Diversity Index ETF."

19. Thomas Pettigrew and Linda Tropp, "A Meta-Analytic Test of Intergroup Contact Theory," *Journal of Personality and Social Psychology* 90, no. 5 (2006): 751–83, doi.org/10.1037/0022-3514.90.5.751.

20. Jeanine Prime and Corinne A. Moss-Racusin, "Report: Engaging Men in Gender Initiatives: What Change Agents Need to Know," Catalyst, May 4, 2009, catalyst.org/knowledge/engaging-men-gender-initiatives-what-change-agents-need-know.

21. David Grossman, "The Cost of Poor Communications," PRovoke, July 16, 2011, provokemedia.com/latest/article/the-cost-of-poor-communications.

22. Debra Hamilton, "Top Ten Email Blunders That Cost Companies Money," Creative Communications & Training, 2010, pr.com/press-release/164492.

23. Craig Chappelow and Cindy McCauley, "What Good Feedback Really Looks Like," *Harvard Business Review*, May 13, 2019, hbr.org/2019/05/what-good-feedback-really-looks-like.

24. Brené Brown, "Finding Our Way to True Belonging," Ideas.TED.com, ideas.ted.com/finding-our-way-to-true-belonging.

Chapter 8: Remeasuring Success

1. Charlotte Alter et al., "*Time* 2019 Person of the Year: Greta Thunberg." *Time*, December 4, 2019, time.com/person-of-the-year-2019-greta-thunberg.

2. Business Roundtable website, businessroundtable.org.

3. Marc Benioff, *Trailblazer: The Power of Business as the Greatest Platform for Change*, (New York: Currency, 2019).

4. "Project ROI: Defining the Competitive and Financial Advantages of Corporate Responsibility and Sustainability," IO Sustainability, 2015, babson.edu/media/babson/site-assets/content-assets/academics/centers-and -institutes/the-lewis-institute/project-roi/Project-ROI-Report.pdf.

5. "Project ROI."

6. "Three-Quarters of Millennials Would Take a Pay Cut to Work for a Socially Responsible Company, According to Research from Cone Communications," PR Newswire, November 2, 2016, prnewswire.com/news-releases/three-quarters -of-millennials-would-take-a-pay-cut-to-work-for-a-socially-responsible -company-according-to-research-from-cone-communications-300355311.html.

7. "2015 Workforce Purpose Index," Imperative and New York University, cdn.imperative.com/media/public/Purpose_Index_2015.

8. Valérie Masson-Delmotte, et al., ed., "Global Warming of 1.5°C," Intergovernmental Panel on Climate Change, 2019, ipcc.ch/site/assets /uploads/sites/2/2019/06/SR15_Full_Report_High_Res.pdf.

9. "United Nations Climate Action: Climate Reports," un.org/en/climatechange /reports.

10. Rebecca Lindsey and LuAnn Dahlman, "Climate Change: Global Temperature," NOAA Climate.gov, January 16, 2020, climate.gov/news-features /understanding-climate/climate-change-global-temperature.

11. "Billion-Dollar Weather and Climate Disasters: Overview," NOAA–National Centers for Environmental Information, July 2020, ncdc.noaa.gov/billions.

12. "Fast Facts: Hurricane Costs," NOAA–Office for Coastal Management, coast.noaa.gov/states/fast-facts/hurricane-costs.html.

13. Kelsey Bartz, "Record Wildfires Push 2018 Disaster Costs to $91 Billion," Center for Climate and Energy Solutions, February 27, 2019, c2es.org /2019/02/record-wildfires-push-2018-disaster-costs-to-91-billion.

14. "The 2018 Report of the Global Commission on the Economy and Climate," The New Climate Economy: Global Commission on the Economy and Climate, newclimateeconomy.report.

15. Stéphanie Thomson, "What Are the Sustainable Development Goals?" World Economic Forum, September 16, 2015, weforum.org/agenda/2015/09/what-are-the-sustainable-development-goals.

16. Mahmoud Mohieldin, "Five Years into Implementing the 2030 Agenda for Sustainable Development: A Mixed Bag of Achievements and Remaining Challenges," World Bank Blogs, January 17, 2020, blogs.worldbank.org/voices/5-years-implementing-2030-Agenda-Sustainable-Development-mixed-bag-achievements-remaining-challenges.

17. Fourth Sector Mapping Initiative, mapping.fourthsector.org.

18. Adrian Monck, "World Economic Forum Announces New Board of Trustees," World Economic Forum, January 23, 2016, weforum.org/press/2016/01/world-economic-forum-announces-new-board-of-trustees-3447f94a-fd22-406d-bfbc-ec2fefd833b6.

19. "1% Model," Salesforce, salesforce.org/pledge-1.

20. "Tech Philanthropists: Marc and Lynne Benioff," Inside Philanthropy, insidephilanthropy.com/guide-to-individual-donors/marc-benioff.html.

21. "Step Up Declaration," Salesforce, 2020, stepupdeclaration.org/salesforce.

22. "Learn How Businesses Can Make a Difference," Salesforce Trailhead, 2020, trailhead.salesforce.com/en/content/learn/modules/positive-environmental-impact/learn-how-businesses-can-make-a-difference.

23. Sergei Klebnikov, "Bezos Pledges $10 Billion—Nearly 10% of Net Worth—Toward Solving Climate Change," Forbes, February 17, 2020, forbes.com/sites/sergeiklebnikov/2020/02/17/jeff-bezos-pledges-to-fight-climate-change-with-10-billion-earth-fund.

24. "Awards: Social Entrepreneur," Schwab Foundation for Social Entrepreneurship, 2018, schwabfound.org/awardees/david-yeung.

25. "A Cause Looking for a Company," REBBL, rebbl.co/our-story.

26. "Best for the World 2019 Overall Honorees," Certified B Corporation, bcorporation.net/2019-best-for-the-world-overall.

27. "The Path Forward to Systemic Change," J.E.D.I. Collaborative, 2020, jedicollaborative.com.

28. Bank of the West, bankofthewest.com/campaigns/personal-banking/one-percent-checking-offer.html.

29. "UN Warns Globally Only 9 Percent of Plastic Waste Is Recycled," EFE, June 5, 2018, efe.com/efe/english/world/un-warns-globally-only-9-percent -of-plastic-waste-is-recycled/50000262-3638548.
30. Carley Hauck, "Heartfelt Leadership," carleyhauck.com/podcast.

Chapter 9: Honoring the Mother

1. Danielle LaPorte, "The Dalai Lama: Women Are the Leaders of the Future," *Lion's Roar*, June 6, 2019, lionsroar.com/women-are-the-leaders-of-the-future.
2. Kenny Ausubel, "The End of Prehistory" (speech), 2019 Bioneers Conference, bioneers.org/kenny-ausubel-the-end-of-prehistory-zmbz1910/.
3. "Net Zero 2030: The Largest Constituency of Businesses Leading on Climate Action," Certified B Corporation, December 11, 2019, bcorporation.net /news/500-b-corps-commit-net-zero-2030.
4. "Climate Corps: Accelerate & Accomplish Your Sustainability Goals," Environmental Defense Fund, 2020, edfclimatecorps.org.

About the Author

Carley Hauck is a torch lighter who helps leaders and businesses shine their gifts to create a workplace and a world that works for everyone—a world where we can truly flourish. Carley is learning architect, leadership development consultant, speaker, and culture builder. She is the creator of the Shine Leadership System, and host of the podcast *Shine: Lead Consciously at Work and in the World* (carleyhauck.com/podcast). The organizations and leaders Carley has supported often describe her energy and enthusiasm as radiant, as though she's beaming from the inside out.

Carley enthusiastically teaches as adjunct faculty at Stanford University; University of California, Berkeley's Haas School of Business; and Spirit Rock Meditation Center. She encourages her clients and students to align with what really matters to them and then let that shine in their work, their relationships, and the greater world. Carley's work has been featured on Mindful.org, Greater Good Science Center, Conscious Company, 15Five, and Emerging Women.

Carley considers herself a citizen of the world and loves all cultures and people but has yearnings to live and serve more in Europe, New Zealand, and Costa Rica. She loves living in more harmony with nature.

Carley is a joyful auntie and wrote this book in service of all future generations in hopes that they will have the opportunity to enjoy and find refuge in the bounty of the Earth and nature as she has. She is a climate activist and graduate of Al Gore's Climate Reality Project Leadership Training.

Visit her website, carleyhauck.com.

About Sounds True

Sounds True is a multimedia publisher whose mission is to inspire and support personal transformation and spiritual awakening. Founded in 1985 and located in Boulder, Colorado, we work with many of the leading spiritual teachers, thinkers, healers, and visionary artists of our time. We strive with every title to preserve the essential "living wisdom" of the author or artist. It is our goal to create products that not only provide information to a reader or listener but also embody the quality of a wisdom transmission.

For those seeking genuine transformation, Sounds True is your trusted partner. At SoundsTrue.com you will find a wealth of free resources to support your journey, including exclusive weekly audio interviews, free downloads, interactive learning tools, and other special savings on all our titles.

To learn more, please visit SoundsTrue.com/freegifts or call us toll-free at 800.333.9185.